**Published by Ronnie Sellers Productions, Inc.**
Copyright © 2004 Ronnie Sellers Productions, Inc., Artwork © Westland Giftware, Inc.
Illustrations by Mike Dowdall, Text by Pat Welch
All rights reserved.

Project Editor: Robin Haywood
Production Editor: Mary Baldwin
Design: Pat Welch

P.O. Box 818, Portland, Maine 04104
For ordering information:
Phone: (800) MAKE-FUN (625-3386) • Fax: (207) 772-6814
Visit our Web site: www.makefun.com • E-mail: rsp@rsvp.com

ISBN: 1-56906-576-4
Library of Congress Control Number: 2004104068

10  9  8  7  6  5  4  3  2  1

Printed and bound in China

# Coots™

**illustrations by Mike Dowdall**
**text by Pat Welch**

RONNIE
SELLERS
PRODUCTIONS
PORTLAND, MAINE

# CONTENTS

# Identifying the Coot

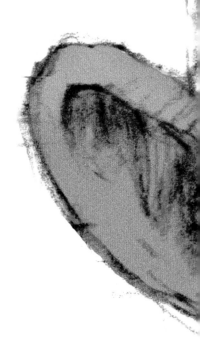

# COOTS: AN INTRODUCTION

The coot is a familiar figure to all of us. In fact, he seems to be everywhere: there, waiting patiently at a bus stop that has been off the route since 1987; over there, driving 40 mph in the fast lane of the freeway; and there, walking home from the parking lot of the Piggly-Wiggly because he forgot his shopping list — and then forgot that he drove to the store.

In these and other ways, hardly any of us has not had his life touched by a coot at one time or another. Most of us know one; many of us will someday become one. But what do we really know about him? What are his thoughts, his aspirations, his daily occupations? What are his reflections on life and the world around him? Where the hell did he leave his hat?

These, among many others, are the questions this book attempts to answer. And while this is a serious and objective scientific work, which must eschew sentimentality or flattery, we hope we have constructed it with the empathy and diffidence his venerated status deserves. Or, as the coot himself might say: *Hah?*

# CHRONOLOGY OF THE COOT

Since the observations in this book are intended to apply only to the true coot, it is important that we avoid confusion with his earlier stages of development — the duffer, codger, or geezer. Every coot passes through these stages, but simple chronology is not a reliable measure: some coots are barely 70; some late bloomers achieve coothood only well into their 90s. The guidelines below will assist the reader in separating the coots from the codgers.

## Duffer

Immediately following middle age, this is the first step of the transmutation to true coot. The duffer is generally more upright and robust than the coot, and it has been reliably reported that his clothes will sometimes coordinate. It is in this stage that he discovers the importance of having his socks match his tie.

## Codger

While the physical differences between the duffer and the codger are slight, the codger has crossed an invisible social line. He is now more or less expected to make inappropriate remarks to waiters, traffic cops, and doormen, and to repeatedly relate the story of how he once racked up 34 hours of overtime in a single week.

## Geezer

There are both both physical and behavioral differences in the geezer, but perhaps most significant is the difference in how others behave toward him. The codger is accustomed to hearing such phrases as "Daddy, please!" and "Oh, for God's sake, Herman." For the geezer, these diminish and soon cease entirely. Not that the phrases are no longer spoken; they are simply no longer addressed directly to him, but rather to the universe at large.

## Coot

The coot is no longer subject to such remonstrances, because everyone has clearly given up. However, he often gives the impression of consciously recalling the last time someone said "Oh, for God's sake, Herman" and taking great pleasure in the memory.

Duffer

Codger

Geezer

Coot

11

# COOTS ACROSS AMERICA

Marin County Coot

Dakota Coot

Plains Coot

Barrio Coot

Las Vegas Coot

El Paso Coot

Orthodox Coot

Manhattan Coot

Mountain Coot

Confederate Coot

Ft. Lauderdale Coot

# COOTS OF THE WORLD

Whatever his geographic location or cultural environment, a coot is pretty much a coot. However, while the coot's own attitudes, perceptions, and preoccupations may vary little, there are great differences in the various societies' attitudes toward him.

In Asia, for instance, the coot is venerated for the wisdom he is assumed to have amassed over the years, and his every utterance, however non-sensical, is written down in little books which his descendants carry with them everywhere. Conversely, among certain natives of the Arctic coastal regions — who have one word for "wisdom" but many words for "It is way too #!@*&?#! cold to hunt today" — he has a good chance of being set adrift on an ice floe at the first sign of true coothood.

African and Amerindian tribes have historically made the coot their chief, having determined that (a) he is too old to be of any other use, and (b) it doesn't make much difference who the chief is. There have been occasions when the modern North Americans have adopted this same policy.

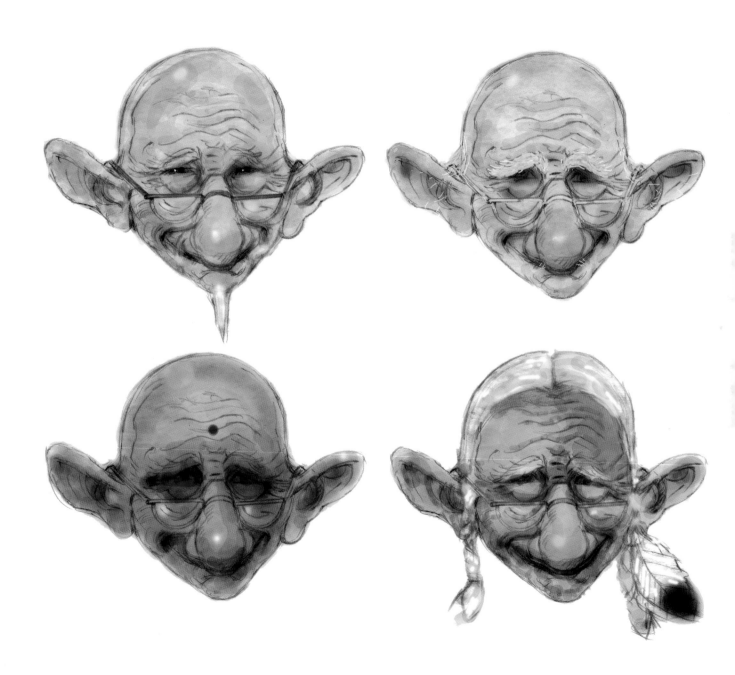

# INTERNATIONAL COOTS

While it is generally true that a coot is a coot wherever in the world you find him, naturally there are differences in dress, customs, language, and outlook on life. Unfortunately, a detailed examination of these is beyond the scope of this study. One thing we can tell you, however, is that it is obvious that the happiest coots are those from the beer-producing countries.

# Coots in History

To the modern population the coot may seem an inconsequential creature, but he has not always been considered so. Indeed, many of history's most noted characters have been just as effective and influential even in advanced coothood as in youth — if not more so.

This has led some scholars to speculate that the coots of the classical world may have had generally superior abilities to their modern counterparts. However, it should be noted that in most cases the ancient coot began his career at quite a young age and, the times being what they were, could not be discharged or retired by any external power.

So what the old coots had was not superior ability. It was superior job security.

Ramses I

Henry II

George III

# WHICH ONE IS NOT A COOT? (Answers found on page 128.)

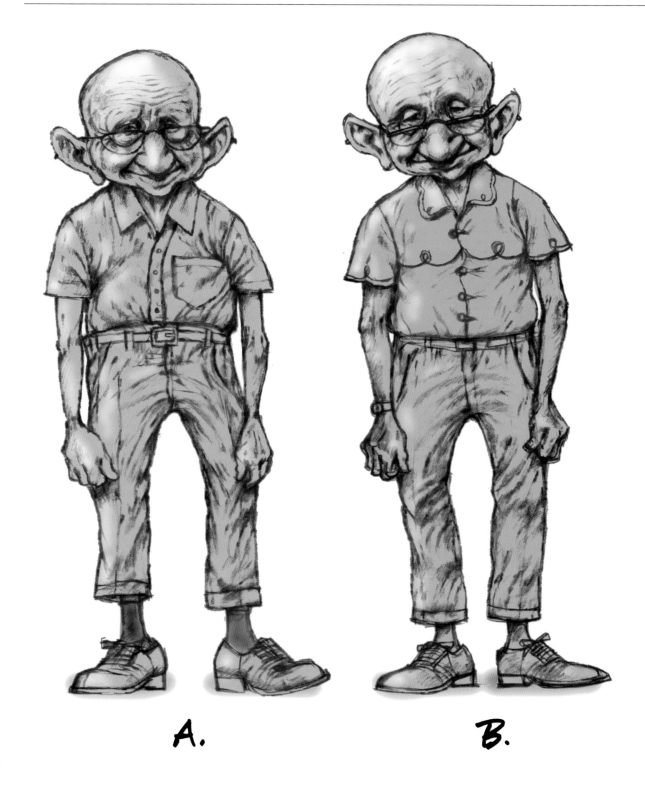

A.

B.

C.          D.

# THE COOT'S CROSSWORD  (*Answers found on page 128.*)

## ACROSS

1. Is incontinence a problem for the coot? That _____ .
7. I ain't a rabbit, so I'll have meat and potatoes and __ _____ .
14. Stuff they used to put on sailing ships from the South Seas. Nobody knows what the hell it is.
17. You can't fry bacon if you got __ ___ .
19. Almond ____ . Pretty good, but damn hard to chew.
20. She runs the house.
23. Either the first name of the guy who used to be on *Wagon Train*, or a part of a hospital.
24. What they use for money across the big pond.
25. Edgar Alan hardly ever got paid for what he wrote, so you could say he was a _____ .
27. Body of water. More than one. Spanish word for 'em.
29. Kind of fish. Or it might be the past tense of experiencing an odor.
30. Power units.
31. Kind of dance. They might do it in the places where they'd say 27 across.
33. Strong emotion. Or an old Plymouth.
34. Your first chance to get a share: Abbr.
35. Where bacon comes from.
36. Kind of wood. Make furniture out of it, or them little gods you hang around your neck.
37. If you get one, put tennis balls on it or you'll break a damn hip which is why you needed it in the first place.
43. The restaurant says it starts at 5:00 PM. I say that ain't soon enough.
49. Short for some kind of secret agent.
50. Makes the boat go.
51. You get it from the sun. If you don't get somethin' worse.
52. Lawyer who gets elected: Abbr.
58. Where it's __ .
59. If you're similar, then you're of the same ___ .
61. Time causes it. Nothin' cures it. Well, one thing.
63. What you'd call him if you knew Diddly.
64. Every damn street in the state is Peachtree Street: Abbr.
65. Latin. Could be the first word spoken in his presence that Lincoln didn't hear.
67. Corporate for BS: Abbr.
68. If you ain't at it, and you ain't comin' back from it, then you must be goin' __ it.
69. It's what you call a kid. Or it might be that Jack fella in the story you'd *tell* a kid.
71. More than one, but it ain't them and it ain't us.
72. If you show up for 43 across, it's what you came to do.
74. That damn stuff nobody wants at the luau.
76. What she does on the phone till all damn hours.
80. You pay the doctor to give it to you. Then you pay somebody else to take it away.
83. Egyptian sun god. This is a damn crossword puzzle, ain't it?
84. Turn it over in your mind.

87. One of what 80 across is prob'ly for.
89. Lot o'these in the umbrella stand at 43 across.
91. Fabricated.
93. Estivating amphibian.
95. How eggs are brought into the light.
97. Danced with Shirley Temple before he became a lawyer.
99. When you think you might be there.
101. One example of 27 across. Different language, though.
102. The other word for weasel __ _____ .
103. Make the ship go.

## DOWN

2. If ecru is a color, and one thing is that color but another thing is more so, then the other thing is _____ .
3. How you'd probably do if you're not good at something.
4. Place in Florida; kinda like a mall with mice.
5. Former "Moses," now a coot, speaks for them: Abbr.
6. Eighth note of the scale, as long as you're talkin'.
8. One of two possible conditions of clothes or the TV.
9. Could be plant/verb, could be pig/noun.
10. Not together.
11. Fancied-up rope. Got its uses.
12. Five ____ ____ make six.
13. If this were a map, this would be...
15. Easier than stairs.
16. Good deal on a car loan.
18. If this were a map, this would be...
20. Written reminder.
21. What your battery does if it's out of 30 across.
22. Where Simpson drinks.
24. Big damn bird. Only seen in zoos and crossword puzzles.
25. Cosh.
26. Is (Latin)
28. Sort of a union. Songwriters and screenwriters each got one.
29. Another city in 66 down: Abbr.
32. Corral where everything wasn't, at least this one day.
37. When the family plans an outing, you plan on this.
38. Printer's abbreviation for a paper container.
39. I putter, therefore I __ .
40. The way that Dempsey-Tunney thing ended (Abbr.).
41. Taken one at a time: Abbr.
42. Sign you see at some intersections: Abbr.
43. Latin conjunction. Or the past tense of 71 across.
44. If you want whiskey at this meeting, you gotta bring it: Abbr.
45. Say you get 56 down, you'll get to know at least one: Abbr.
46. Salutation in the hood, or half a toy.
47. Might be rocky, might be country: Abbr.
48. He's worse than an idiot, he's a ____ ____ .
53. A hot dog'll do it.
54. Your nose gets this as you get more of 61 across.
55. Your ears get this as you get more of 61 across.
56. Bad result of an uplifting experience.

57. Book you don't want to read in bed.
60. A city in 66 down, or a state west of 64 across: Abbr.
62. Medical jack of all trades: Abbr.
65. One of 42 down: Abbr.
66. State that contains 60 down: Abbr.
69. Part of an address, maybe: Abbr.
70. Part of a shopping list, maybe: Abbr.
73. A tool. This one ain't an abbreviation, so stop complainin'.
75. Conjunction implying a choice.
77. Got reporters, but got no newspaper: Abbr.
78. Could be dog/verb, could be bug/noun.
79. Recognize 'em by the gravy on their ties.
81. Kettle husband.
82. Pronoun, not the distaff.

84. Home to Portland. Not that one, t'other one.
85. Moo juice container.
86. Genuine French article.
88. First step of your shoes.
89. Firm abbreviation.
90. What the senorita said, at least the way you tell it.
91. Lindbergh carried it, sometimes.
92. If this were a map, this would be...
94. Name the Romans looked up to.
95. You don't have to eat 75 across to get one.
96. If this were a map, this would be...
98. Got nothin' to do with what we're talkin' about: Abbr.
100. Hall of Famer from 64 across.
101. __ it goes.

# Private Life of the Coot

# THE DAY OF THE COOT

Looking for car keys, finds them; heads for garage. Notices mail on hall table.

Decides to check mail first; puts keys down. Notices trash is full.

Decides to take trash out; takes mail to kitchen. Sees coffee he had been drinking.

Coffee is cold; puts mail on counter, moves toward microwave.

Notices vase of flowers that needs water. Puts coffee down by sink.

Finds his lost reading glasses by edge of sink.

Thinks he should put glasses in his room, but will water flowers first.

Puts glasses on kitchen table; spots TV remote left there by someone.

Must return remote to living room, but will water flowers first.

Attempts to water flowers, but spills most of it on floor.

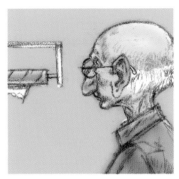

Discovers there are no paper towels. Decides to drive to the store.

Heads for his room for car keys; notices corner of hall runner is turned up.

Could be dangerous, but needs his cane to bend down and flip it over.

Continues toward his room to get cane; sees car keys on hall table.

Reaches for keys, discovers TV remote in his hand.

Realizes he must have been watching TV; heads for living room.

Can't find his glasses; falls asleep. Wakes up; remembers keys are on hall table and he was going to drive to the store.

Finds car keys; heads for garage. Wonders where the mail is.

27

# THE NIGHT OF THE COOT

Decides he's had enough TV; time to turn in.

Goes to kitchen to mix up his glass of fiber.

Makes sure glasses, cane, and teeth are in easy reach.

Settles in for a little reading before lights out.

Remembers he never finished organizing his sock drawer. Gets up again.

Decides he could do with a little more fiber; back to kitchen.

Settles back in; lost his place in book. Starts over.

Must have fallen asleep; wakes up to call of nature.

Call turns out to have been wrong number.

If a little fiber is good...

Lost his place in book again.

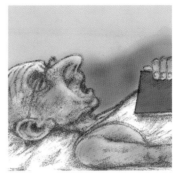

Sound asleep for about an hour.

Another call of nature...

Another wrong number.

Can't find book at all. Gets new book; settles in. Can't find reading glasses.

Realizes he must have left glasses in bathroom; gets up again.

Finds glasses; settles in; falls asleep for half an hour.

4:30 AM. Might as well get up and watch TV; can't sleep anyway.

# Puttering

While the non-coot does not usually consider puttering to be real work, for the coot, puttering has as many grades, permutations, and levels of difficulty as any full-time job. At least so it seems, since the coot who is interrupted during this activity may exhibit extreme agitation and annoyance, and will almost certainly have to start over at the beginning.

Interestingly, puttering does not necessarily bear any resemblance to the coot's former occupation. The retired insurance actuary is as likely to completely destroy the trash compactor as is the ex-mechanic, and it is impossible to persuade an old CPA that he should not try to re-upholster the couch in the family room.

It is no easy task to categorize the various forms of puttering, since there can be a great deal of shading and overlapping from one to another. In the end, we have had to satisfy ourselves with three general categories, based on the real or apparent effects of the puttering in question:

## 1. Destructive Effect Puttering
This includes re-wiring the table lamp by the phone, replacing washers in the bathroom or kitchen, and anything involving the VCR.

## 2. Constructive Effect Puttering
This category covers brushing stray tobacco from the kitchen table, sweeping up coffee grounds, flipping the corner of the hall runner down so that no one trips on it, and — that's about it.

## 3. Zero Effect Puttering
By far the largest category, this ranges from tightening screws which are not loose and organizing utensils which are not in disarray to making lists which will never be consulted and finding cigar boxes in which to store small items which, in all probability, will never be collected.

# DRESS THE IRASCIBLE COOT

There are times when the coot will wear anything. But there are just as many times when the coot will refuse to wear almost everything, and there is no hope of finding rhyme or reason in his objections. When he is being obstinate, getting the coot dressed at all is a chore; getting him dressed acceptably is more than most people aspire to. This section is for the reader whose life does not include an actual coot, so that you may test your ability to dress the coot at least well enough to be taken out of the house. We have provided the clothes and, of course, the coot.

Plaid flannel shirt.
Buttoned up to neck.

Cardigan sweater vest.
Buttoned wrong.

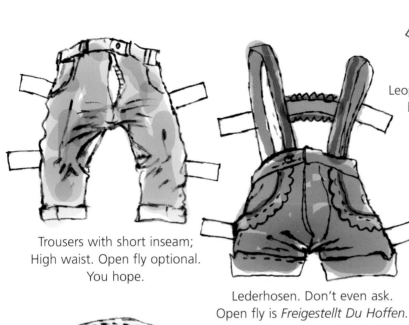

Trousers with short inseam;
High waist. Open fly optional.
You hope.

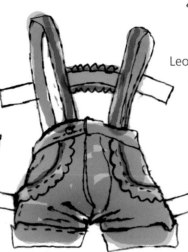

Lederhosen. Don't even ask.
Open fly is *Freigestellt Du Hoffen*.

Leopard print speedos. You were way
better off with the lederhosen.

Cowboy hat.
'cause I like it, *that's why*.

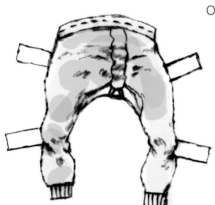

Long underwear. Not because he's
cold, just likes his shorts bunched.

Bolo tie, preferred by all
coots, especially with
plaid flannel shirt.

Bermuda shorts. So what if it's
a funeral? *It's hot out, and
I ain't dead.*

Those ain't my socks.
*Never seen 'em before.*

Any fool knows you can't wear slippers
except with red socks, and I don't have
any red socks.

Ordinary sensible shoes. Once in a while
you should get so lucky.

# SEX AND THE SINGLE COOT

Contrary to popular belief, it is not unusual for the coot to remain sexually active well into coothood, or even for his entire life. Of course, as in any sample population, there are wide variations in the ways in which sexuality is expressed. Among coots, these can be divided into three general categories.

### The Club Med Coot

These inveterate swingers of the geriatric jet set are rarely far from the beaches, casinos, and *moineau en avance* dinner seatings of the world's more exotic locales. They identify each other by their costumes (which are minimal) and their auras of desperation (which are unmistakable). Whether they actually engage in sex or not is far less important to them than that everyone *believes* they are doing it *à la les lapins* night and day. In this, at least, they differ little from their younger counterparts.

### The Rockwellian Coot

In contrast to the blatant displays of the foregoing, this coot is devoted to subtlety and decorum — and the picture he presents to the public at large may be as far as he ever goes. After all, having performed so much careful manipulation of form, color, light, and composition, it would be a shame to ruin it by actually getting up to go to his room with the object of his fancy.

The vast majority of coots belong to the third category of sexual behavior, a group which is It's called the Optimist's Club.

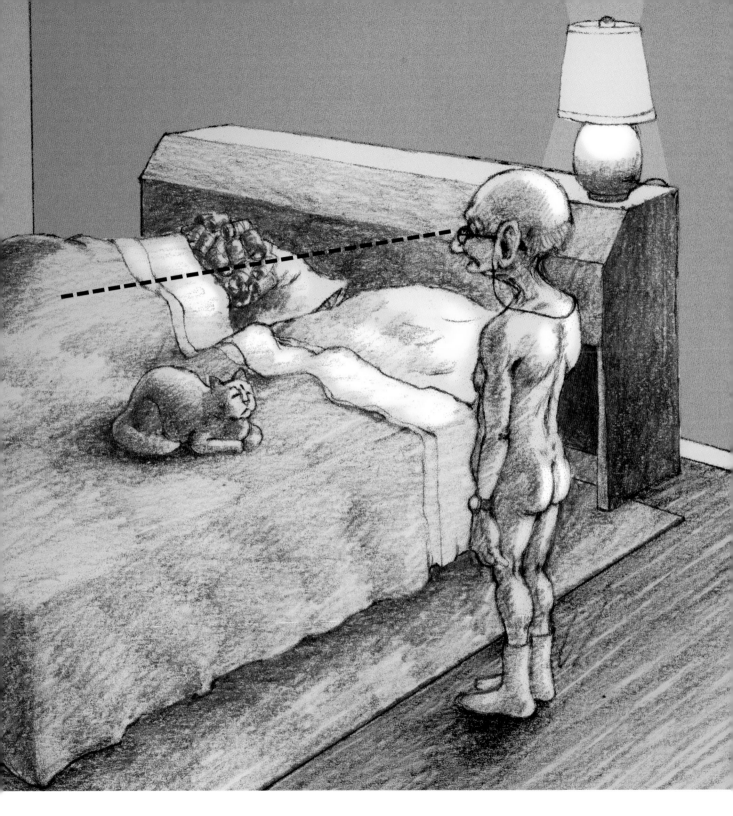

so large that they have formed their own international organization.

# The Coot in Public

# SATURDAY NIGHT COOT

Difficult as it is to dislodge the coot from his armchair or his musty room, many relatives of coots will occasionally take the trouble to try and do so in the belief that he "needs to get out more." Most often this is to their everlasting regret, because there is something about the proximity of a dance floor that can trans-

form an evening in the company of an ordinarily quiet and unassuming coot into an unforgettable experience.

It is unclear whether the coot has actually come to believe that his moves are something the rest of the world wants to see, or whether he has just ceased to care. But the real puzzle lies in the fact that by the time he has achieved coothood, he will have had occasion to dance in public many times. The difference is that in his pre-coot days he had to be forced; now no force on earth can hold him back, though the forces that try include his wife, his children, his pastor, the local police, the entire staff of the establishment, and people seated at nearby tables . . . and possibly even not-so-nearby tables.

A sense of competition remains strong well into coothood, and while the participants take

it seriously, the spirit is friendly. The winner above, for instance, has agreed to buy supper.

# WHICH HAT?

The coot has finally been persuaded to attend his grandson's graduation from seminary school. The ceremony is to take place at 2:00 in the afternoon, immediately followed by a reception at which families will be introduced to the school's dean, Bishop Patrick McFather. Which hat would the coot *not* wear?

*(Answer, in the coot's own words, on page 128.)*

**A.**
Bright plaid novelty cap with
crown as big as a peach basket

**B.**
Baseball cap with plastic dog
excrement and funny legend

**C.**
Canvas fisherman's hat fitted
with beer cans and straws

**D.**
Souvenir
renaissance faire
hat with sweeping
plume

**E.**
Novelty railroad engineer's hat
with funny legend

**F.**
Pearl gray snap-brim fedora
with satin band

# FASHION SENSE OF THE COOT

It is generally believed that the coot has lost all sense not only of fashion, but even of remotely appropriate models of dress. The many instances of coots appearing in sombreros at weddings, Christmas sweaters at funerals, and Speedos anywhere at all are no doubt the source of this widespread belief.

This, however, is not entirely correct. In some cases, what has actually happened is not that the coot has lost such judgment as he may ever have had in this area, but that he is applying the judgment of a bygone time, perfectly sound in its day. Determine the period of his life when the coot most likely considered himself to be a snappy dresser, and you will have found the source of his sartorial choices. Thus a coot wearing a nine-inch hand-painted tie is fashion-frozen in, say, 1943, whereas the one who favors four-button cinch-back tweed coats is likely hovering somewhere around 1919.

In other cases, the coot's fashion motivation is entirely different. We're referring to the coot who will, without hesitation, attend the General Assembly of the United Nations or his great-granddaughter's christening in an oversized bright yellow hat with rhinestone and rattlesnake band for one reason and one reason only.

He likes it, and he doesn't give a damn who doesn't.

# GROOMING OF THE COOT

Those coots who, in their youthful days, were known as "Dapper Dans" — always sharply turned out and carefully groomed — often retain such tendencies well into coothood. Of course, in the old days their purpose was to get themselves noticed by attractive members of the opposite sex, or "Sweet Patooties," as they were known. As coots, their purpose is much the same, except that now the Dans realize full well that the only Patooties they're likely to get next to are the ones actually doing the grooming.

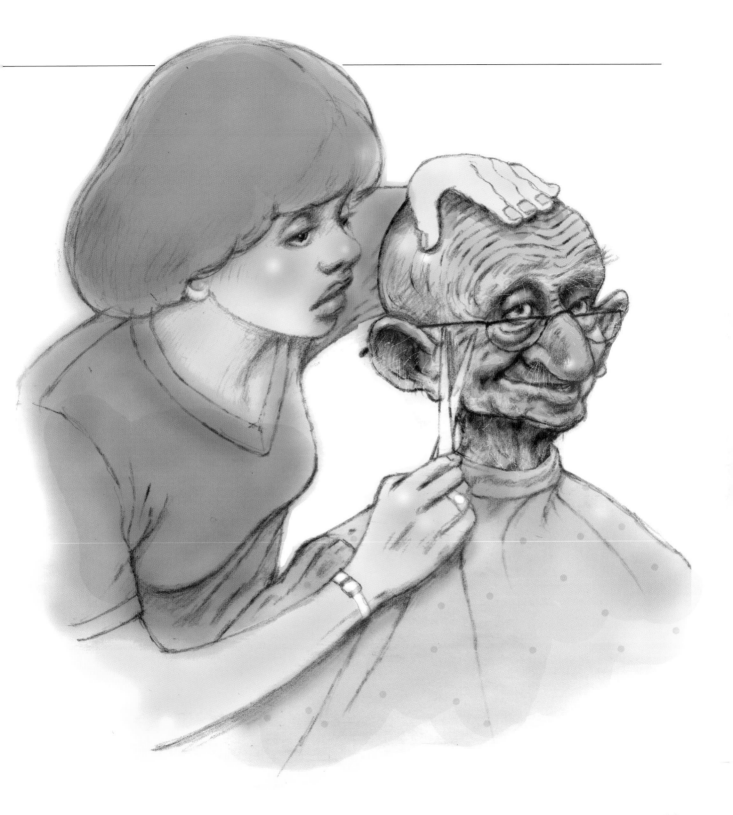

# THE HIRSUTE COOT

In approximately one coot out of three, baldness is one of the many physical manifestations of the onset of coothood. However, simple baldness is not quite the punchline of nature's little joke: for every hair that has long since packed its bags and moved from the coot's head, he finds that a new one has taken up residence on, or in — or on *and* in — his nose and ears.

Also, the coot cannot help but notice that the new hairs are invariably darker, coarser, and of a far less shy and retiring nature than any that may once have adorned his dome. What all this demonstrates is that the coots pictured below have not sprouted their facial adornments as compensation for their bald heads, as is widely believed. They are simply trying to distract attention from certain other extremities.

# THE COOT HAIR CLUB

Everyone "knows" that the coot reviles and will have no part of modern technology. But, as in so many other areas of coot lore, this is not entirely true. As has already been noted, not every coot is able to grow lush and elaborate facial shrubbery, many are denied the compensatory adornments of their hirsute contemporaries.

1938: HAIR: NO PROBLEM

1998: PROBLEM: NO HAIR

2001: NO-PROBLEM HAIR

For these coots, the yearning for the hair they once had is acute. So the non-hirsute coot, without a backward glance to his reputation, turns to technology to stay the hands of time — with varying degrees of success in the battle with vanity versus pragmatic reality.

1996: NO HAIR, NO PROBLEM          1998: NO HUMAN HAIR

2001: Keep the fifty bucks and use it for
a couple of early birds at IHOP

# COOTS ON WHEELS

There are times when the coot has places to go. He will probably forget how to get there, and once he arrives, there will be no apparent reason for his having gone. But he is going in any case, and most of us have learned that it's a good idea not to be in his way — in fact, mainly because the "P"(for park) and the "R" (for reverse) look much the same to the coot, it's a good idea not be be anywhere in his vicinity.

Ironically *(considering that the coot, by definition, is living on borrowed time)*, he is rarely in a hurry. On the freeway he is unlikely to approach, much less exceed, the speed limit. He is, however, certain to be in the fast lane. At city intersections, he will carefully weigh all options before proceeding. He may or may not decide to turn; he may or may not be in a turning lane; he may or may not be in any particular lane at all. The experienced observer knows that the coot's turn signal is not going to provide any clue to his intentions, because it has been on since he left his driveway.

The coot's preference for cars the size of battleships adds considerably to his

travel time, since it takes, on average, 4.7 minutes for the coot to get into the car, and at least three times as long to get out — not because it is more difficult to get out of the car, but rather because, about halfway through the process, he loses track of whether he is coming or going.

Over-cautious drivers have rest stops; slow big rigs have turnouts; occasional
But when you're behind a coot, you're beyond help.

fender-benders have the Highway Patrol; even stray ferrets have the SPCA.

# Reality and the Coot

# THE COOT'S REALITY

There are many outward signs of the arrival of coothood. These include (but are not necessarily limited to) shriveled and stringy muscles, legs as white and hairless as a school of smelt, ear and nose hair that sprouts like crabgrass after a heavy rain, jowls like a bulldog, and a neck that resembles a turkey. These may be accompanied by any number of miscellaneous bumps, blotches, and spots.

However, while these characteristics are obvious to even the most casual observer, they seem to be completely invisible to the coot himself. Indeed, the coot considers not that his skin has lost elasticity, but rather that it has gained character; not that his flesh has sagged, but that it has settled in a pleasing manner; and that if he has become somewhat wrinkled — and the tiniest bit spotted and blotched — this is more than compensated for by the superior *je ne sais quoi* he has developed over the years. In short, it seems that the coot's ability to rationalize his shortcomings and exaggerate his strengths has finally become total. But not without a lifetime of practice.

Another coot whose grasp of reality has left the building.

# Memory of the Coot

Any coot you encounter can remember his serial number from his military service 60 years ago, the name of the girl who sat three rows behind him in the third grade, the license plate of his father's '29 LaSalle, the entire menu of the Henny Penny Diner on the corner of 12th and Madison in Columbus, Ohio, which closed in 1937, the starting lineup of the 1951 New York Yankees, and the exact place on the radio dial to tune in Fibber McGee and Molly, The Shadow, Amos 'n' Andy, and Charlie McCarthy.

This same coot will be unable to recall his middle daughter's married name, the ages or the exact number of his grandchildren, and when the hell he put on that sweater, not to mention where the hell it came from in the first place, because one thing he knows for sure is it isn't his.

To the beginning student of coothood, the coot at right may give the impression of having forgotten where he parked his car, or perhaps what it was he came to the store to buy, or whether he has come to the right store. But the experienced cootologist will know that the coot is just trying to remember whether he drove to the store at all — or took the bus.

# THE GUARDFATHER

The coot believes, though it is rarely spoken aloud, that the entire community is aware of the enormous power and influence he exerts through his position as school crossing guard. Such is the awe with which he is regarded that he is never referred to by name, but by such appelations as "The Old Guard," "The Old Fart Who Yells at Us at the Corner," or sometimes simply "The Guardfather."

Someday he may require a favor in return. If he remembers.

# HUMOR AMONG COOTS

To the coot, anything having to do with body parts, sex, passing gas, passing foreign objects, passing anything, sex with anything, or any combination of these which take place in a rowboat, at the gates of heaven, or in the presence of a priest or rabbi is hysterically funny.

Especially passing gas.

In other words, the coot's sense of humor is the one thing he has that is exactly the same as when he was twenty.

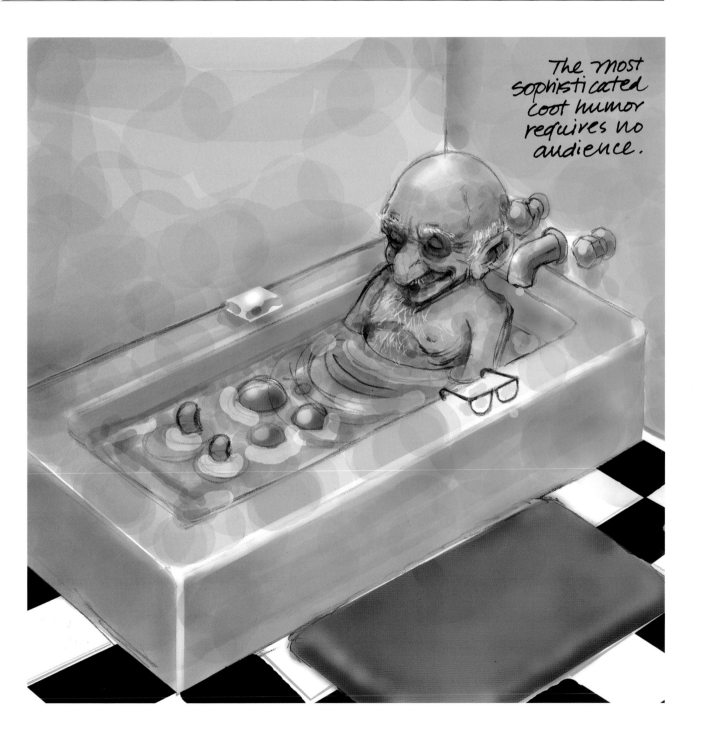

# COOT NOIR

She had the kind of voice that made you wish you'd trimmed your ear hair.

"Mr. Hardcastle?" she purred.

"That depends," I said. Technically, I was, but I knew I wasn't the Mr. Hardcastle she wanted. That would be my son. I could have told her I was just the old coot who lived in the spare room, but like I said, she had that kind of voice.

"Well, are you the head of the household?"

I looked around. Everyone was at the Miles Archer Elementary School Spring Pageant. Came within an ace of being stuck there myself, but the sudden onset of one of my "spells" had lessened the pressure. Nobody in the house but me.

"Looks like it, sweetheart."

"Well then, I'm happy to inform you that you have won a valuable free gift!"

"What did I do?"

"Excuse me?"

"How'd I win? Don't remember entering anything." That was true, but I knew it didn't mean much. I also didn't remember where my pants were.

"Your name was drawn at random. Now, all you have to do to claim your prize is answer a few questions."

"I'll ask the questions, cupcake," I growled, but the effect was more or less ruined by a coughing fit that lasted a while. I sort of lost the thread of our conversation.

"What did you want to ask?" she was saying.

She had me there. I decided to play a hunch.

"Does this valuable gift look anything like a black bird?"

"What? No, it's a —"

"Is there a little foreign guy who smells better than he ought to?"

"Do you mean my supervisor? He's —"

I kept pressing my advantage. "Where does the fat man figure in all this?"

"*What* fat man? I'm calling from Meteor Marketing, and I'm authorized to offer a valuable free gift to the head of the Hardcastle household. But I'm beginning to think that isn't you. Is there another, maybe a younger, Mr. Hardcastle?"

"That would be convenient for your little scheme, wouldn't it, brighteyes?"

"Sir, I have no idea what you're talking about."

They never do.

# COMMON COOTISMS

"You call that a car? That's no car. Your '26 Packard. *That* was a car."

"I remember when you could get a steak dinner in this town for 35 cents. Steak this thick. All the fixin's. Yes sir, 35 cents."

"Ballplayer? That ain't no ballplayer. You want a ballplayer, now your Satchel Paige. *That* was a ballplayer."

"What the hell is that?"

"You keep doin' that, you ain't gonna grow nothin' there. No sir."

"That's no train. You want a train, now you take your California Zephyr. *That* was a train."

"In my day, we did a day's work for a day's pay. 'Course back then you could get a steak dinner for 35 cents. Steak this thick...where you goin'?"

"Who the hell you gonna call on that thing?"

"You call that a fight? That wasn't no fight. Now your Dempsey — Tunney. *That* was a fight."

"You ain't gettin' me in one of those. No sir."

"You call that a dog?"

"Who the hell are you?"

# UNCOMMON COOTISMS

Not all coots' conversation is limited to the proper cultivation of pole beans or the days when you could have bought the Brill Building for $32. As in any group, there are those coots who stand out among their fellows by virtue of greater than normal insight and power of expression, and who invariably leave a legacy of observations and pronouncements that echo through the ages. Here are a few such quotes from some of history's more notable coots.

### ON LIFE
Life is like a box of chocolates. No matter how careful you are, you're gonna run across a few nuts.

### ON HEALTH
It's better to be healthy for a single day than sick for an entire year.

### ON THE CALL OF NATURE
If it weren't for the call of nature, how would you know when you've stayed on the bus all the way past the city limits again?

### ON THE COSMOS
It's pretty big. But it was bigger in my day.

### ON RELATIONSHIPS
Figure out how you want to be treated, then treat everybody else that way. It ain't gonna help, but it'll give 'em somethin' to say at your funeral.

### ON AGING
It's amazing how much pleasure you can get out of not going to a place you would have killed to go to 40 years ago.

### ON RELATIVITY
Life is full of heartbreak and bitter disappointment. But it's still better than wearing new shoes.

# The Coot at Large

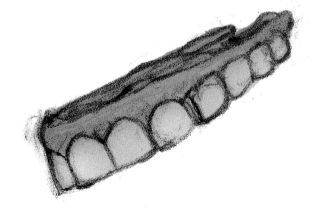

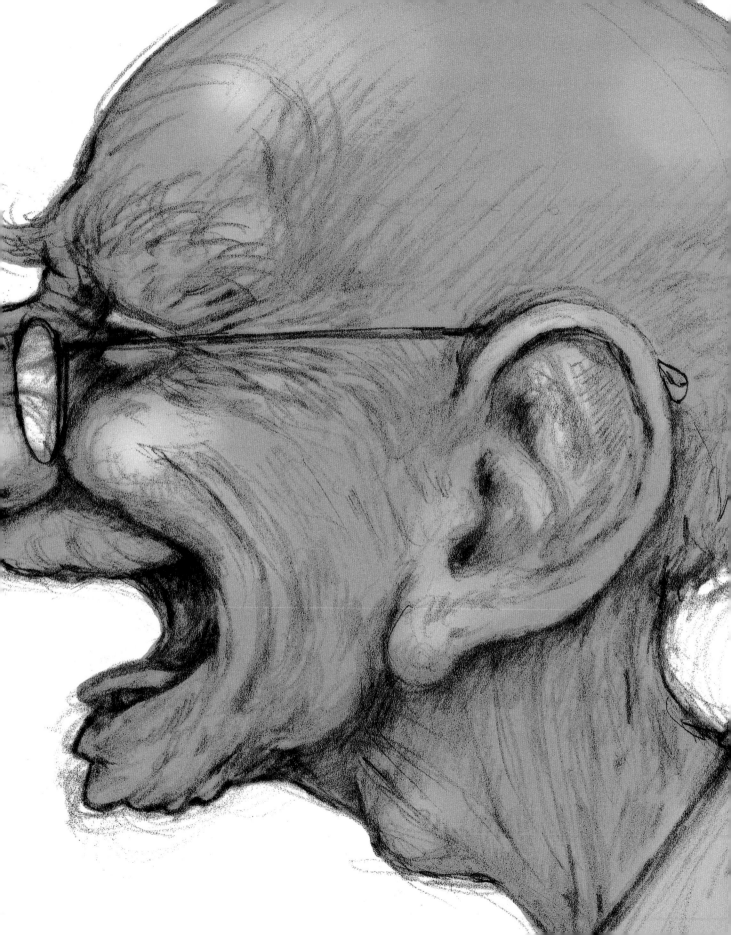

# COOTS IN THE WORKFORCE

Though the coot is most often associated with retirement, many actually remain in the workforce well into coothood, and many others re-enter the world of employment once their wives get a taste of the true meaning of retirement.

Often the coot's career is uninterrupted in spite of the fact that he has long since ceased to be useful or effective. Examples of this are the captain of industry (C) and the cowcoot (E). The former is the owner of the business, so there is no one to tell him that his constant bungling is driving the firm into insolvency. In the case of the latter, it may be that his coothood has gone unnoticed, since the business of riding the range through blistering summers and freezing winters soon gives even a 25-year-old a face like an antique catcher's mitt.

A.                    B.                    C.

Cab driver (B) and security guard (D) are, on the other hand, occupations usually taken up after a stint of retirement. It is a clear testimony to the esteem in which coots are held that a retired pipefitter or longshoreman who can't get his belt through all the loops is now entrusted with a ton and a half of hurtling steel or a loaded .357 Magnum.

The chef (A) and the foodserver (F), though seemingly identical, actually could not be more different. The chef who is a coot has always been a chef, and is now the undisputed master of the kitchen. The foodserver, conversely, is new to the job and without seniority, though he is three times the age of his manager.
This career's appeal to the coot is mysterious. It must be the uniform.

*D.*　　　　　*E.*　　　　　*F.*

# SUPREME COOTS

One other example of a coot career which need not be interrupted by retirement. To all private office, and many other perks; they only work a few hours a month, and spend the

appearances, this is practically the perfect job for any coot. Each is provided with a car, a rest of the time squabbling among themselves. Trouble is, there aren't that many openings.

# HOLY COOTS

Being a clergyman is an occupation that many coots prefer. Thankfully, many congregations prefer their men of the cloth to be coots.

The coot is preferred because:

- He probably doesn't remember how long it's been since the last time you showed up.

- When you do show up, he can't see far enough to tell whether you are awake.

The coot likes the job because:

- He gets to wear the same clothes every day.

- He gets to say the same things every day.

- The work involves a lot of muttering and talking to himself.

# NO COOTS NEED APPLY

We have seen that there are jobs the coot had when he was young but that he must give up in coothood; jobs that he may keep from youth to coothood, and jobs that he may acquire after coothood. But there are some positions you probably never want to see filled by a coot, no matter when he actually got the job.

## Cabbie

Only he stands between you and death. The coot, by his very nature, has come to terms with death as just another part of the circle of life, and he no longer regards it with fear or apprehension. This is not a quality one wants in a cab driver.

### Fireman

If you pass out from smoke inhalation, are you going to be carried to safety by a man who pulled a muscle this morning buttering his bagel?

### Internist

This coot has learned that age brings not only infirmity, but — perhaps more significantly — indignity. He sees no reason this should not be shared.

### Surgeon

If we have to explain this one, you should probably find an opportunity to observe a coot trying to get his key into his own front door.

### Rock Star

No one wants to see a wrinkled and stringy old man prancing and gyrating like an androgynous sex symbol — oh, wait. Maybe they do.

# IT TAKES A VILLAGE, PEOPLE

Maybe it could be said that Indian Chief is an occupation, but no one knows what the guy second

from the right does. The one thing that seems certain is that they all should have retired long ago.

Never shy about making his wishes known, the coot demands the Early Bird Special before its time.

from the right does. The one thing that seems certain is that they all should have retired long ago.

# THE EARLY BIRD SPECIAL

There are as many different personalities among coots as there are among humans of other ages. But whatever the differences between them, all coots have one interest in common: they all want dinner, and they all want it right around five o'clock. And they all want it to be easy to chew.

Many theories have been advanced to explain the tendency among coots to inch their dinner hour ever earlier, including age-related metabolic changes, age-related hyper-sensitivity to the passage of time, and age-related lack of anything else to do. As is the case with so many attempts to analyze coot behavior, these all miss the mark. The true reason is much simpler: if you got up at 4 A.M. every day, you'd probably be hungry around five yourself.

The Coot's Preferred Early Bird Order

Meatloaf-
Good choice;
easy to chew.

Gravy-and
Plenty of it.
Easy to chew.

Mashed Potatoes-
Lumps are kinda
like chewing.

Peas-
Take 'em or
leave 'em.

Parsley-
No damn good
for anything.

To hell with it- Plenty more
where that came from.

Never shy about making his wishes known, the coot demands the Early Bird Special before its time.

Unfortunately, for him, Bernice is not shy about letting him know he ain't gonna get his wish.

The Coot on His Own

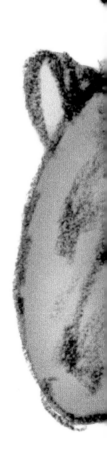

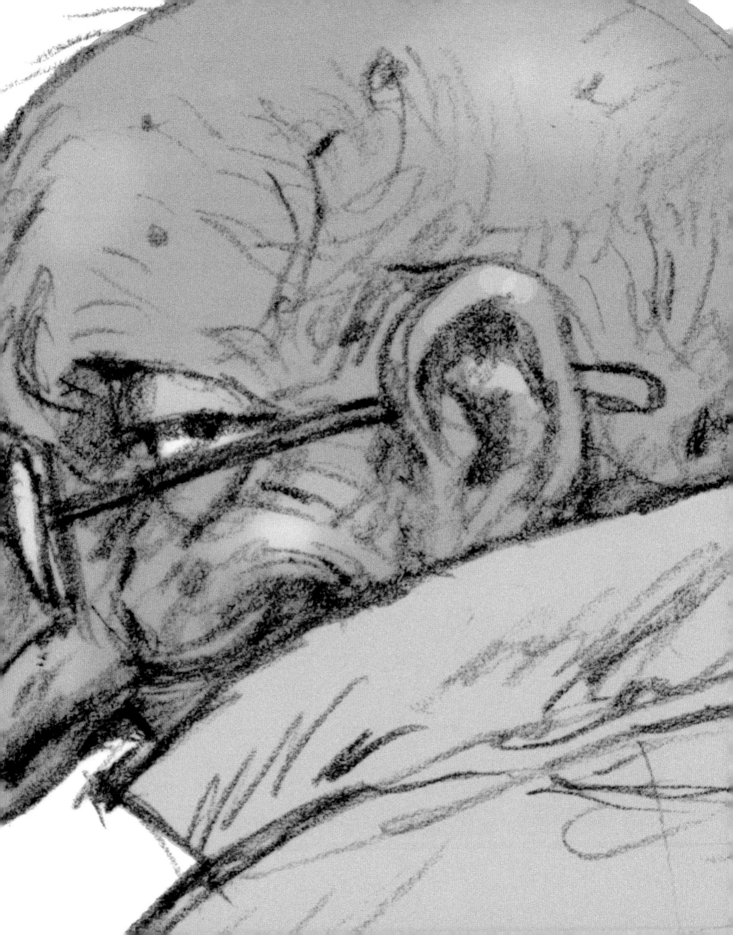

# New Coot Horizons

Occasionally, the coot who no longer benefits from a mate's helpful advice and counsel will make more sweeping changes in his life than merely taking up cooking or cigar smoking. He may hear the call of the open road, or feel the draw of the simple and self-sufficient life — or even both, in which case he is likely to trade the house for an RV or trailer, sell all the furniture (except for the La-Z-Boy and the TV), cash in the bonds, and take off for new horizons. These adventurers clearly contradict the common perception of the coot as a cautious and timid soul: it's obvious that they laugh at danger, since they now do all their cooking with propane but never stop smoking their cigars.

The majority of these coots who take to the open road eventually tire of the vagabond's life. They then sell the RV or Airstream, or contrive to lose it in a poker game, then return to their familiar routines of puttering, checking the locks on the doors and windows 17 times a day, and attempting to urinate.

But there is a small group who never return, preferring to live out their days in loosely organized societies of like-minded folk, being at one with nature and tending their small (and, for some reason, difficult to find) herb gardens.

Interestingly, almost all coots who join one of these societies stop smoking. At least, they stop smoking cigars.

# Coots in the Kitchen

While it is true that the female of the species usually has a longer life expectancy than the male, there are, of course, exceptions. The coot who thus finds himself alone in a world where he once had the benefit of his mate's constant watchful guidance must inevitably make a number of adjustments.

Often the coot will adopt one or more new hobbies to fill his empty hours, such as whittling in the living room, collecting worm-infested refuse from the streets to someday make a spice rack, or smoking big cigars one after the other with the thermostat at 78° and the windows sealed.

However, popular as these diversions are, by far the most common new coot undertaking is cooking.

The coot who is new to the kitchen will begin with such simple recipes as bacon and eggs, bacon and cheese, bacon and salami, bacon and mayonnaise, and so on. But he soon discovers the joy of experimentation, and it isn't long before he realizes that if you can cook with wine, well then, by howdy, you can damn well cook with whiskey.

**The Coot's Cookbook**

**Whiskey Bacon**
Take some bacon. Heat skillet up. Can't hurt to throw some butter in. Put bacon in. Pour some whiskey in. Little more, we ain't cookin' for the Ladies' Aid S'iety. Breathe fumes. *Whoo*, better sit down a minute. Turn off heat, put your face right over pan. *Whoo-ee*. Shut up and eat your bacon.

**Whiskey Pork Chops**
Pretty much same as the bacon, but a lot more damn trouble. Not worth it.

**Whiskey and Salami**
Take your salami in that white paper thing. Get your big knife. Get your whiskey and a little glass. Get your women's tennis or figure skating on the TV. Anybody comes to the door, tell 'em you got whiskey and a big knife. Don't need to mention the salami.

**Whiskey and Oatmeal**
Not as bad as it sounds. Easy to make. Breakfast or any damn time.

**Mashed Potatoes and Whiskey Gravy**
The potatoes is a hell of a chore, but the gravy comes in a little paper envelope, couldn't be easier. Heat it up, pour in the whiskey, heat it up some more. Worth the trouble.

**White Bread and Whiskey Gravy**
Easy version of above. Just as good. Don't need teeth for either one.

**Whiskey Sandwich**
Take two pieces of white bread. Put one either side of whiskey bottle, snap a rubber band around it. Tip 'er up and good night ladies.

# COOT DIVERSIONS

Those coots whose wives have not yet departed no doubt look forward to whiling away their golden years by attending flower arranging demonstrations, lectures entitled A Better World Through Feng Shui, cat shows, and the occasional ballet. The less fortunate coots without wives must, of course, find ways to fill this void.

By far, the two activities most popular among single coots are golf and fishing. It is sometimes thought that these pursuits are favored because they are relatively passive, being among the very few sports during which one either drives oneself from one play to the next or sits motionlessly from beginning to end. But the real reason for their popularity is that they remind the coot of the days when his wife was still around, because neither can be fully enjoyed without telling a few lies.

# THE CURSE OF GOLLUF

There is a place — though some say it is a state of mind — which every coot would do well to avoid, but which calls to him as irresistibly as the honey-cured ham on the Early Bird Special. Once he has succumbed to its siren song, he is compelled to return again and again. Ultimately, he is lost — though the process is so slow and insidious that neither he nor those who might protect him are aware it is happening. Despite having lived a blameless life, of having once had a generous character, the coot becomes covetous, conniving, obsessed with the possession and control of the seemingly insignificant object which controls his mind and his destiny. What begins as an innocent hobbit — that is, hobby — becomes something evil and all-consuming that cannot be understood by those who have not experienced it themselves: he is a hopeless slave to the dark spell of the Golluf Curse.

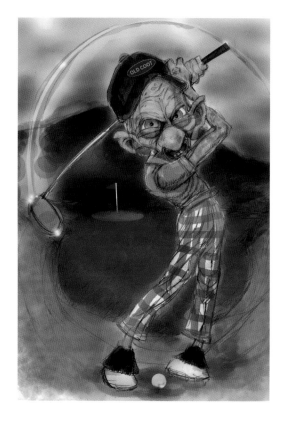

One of the coot's primary roles is
mentor to succeeding generations who benefit
greatly from his copious knowledge of the world —
especially of nature, and what to do if you're stuck in it.

# Coots Then and Now

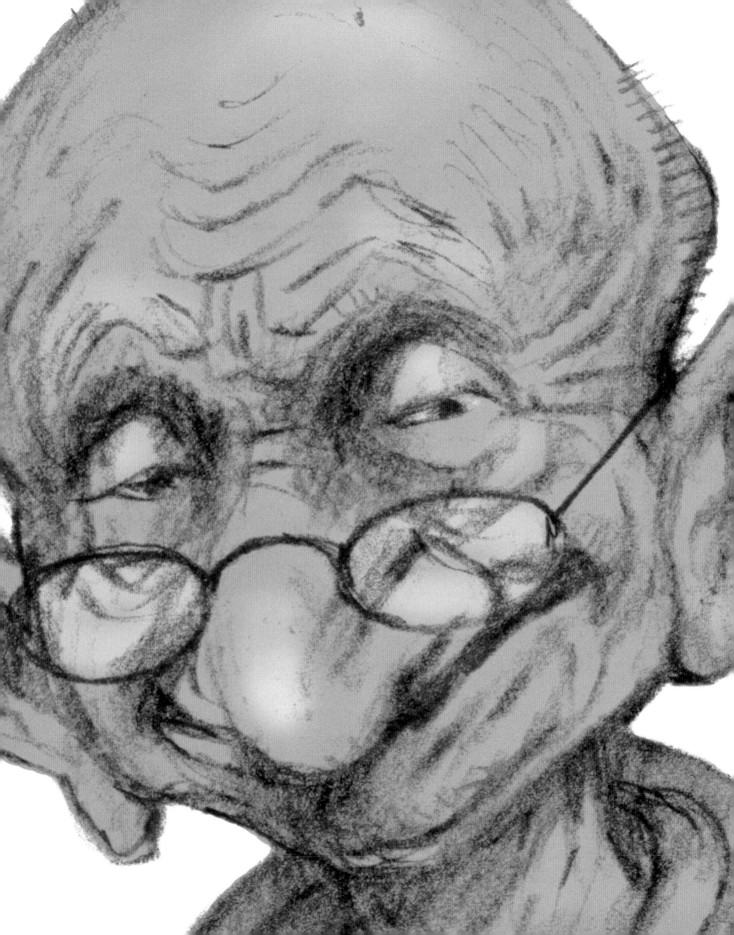

# GLORY DAYS

Every coot has a particular period in his past which he remembers, with pride and nostalgia, as being the best of times. When the veteran coot dons his old uniform, his eyes shine with the memories of digging slit trenches in Alabama, scrubbing huge pots in Texas, or typing company reports in New Jersey. This sentimental attachment to a bygone time may explain why coots, when they do seek employment, are drawn to positions that allow them to dress in attire that brings their glory days alive again.

In any case, it is an observable fact that the coot performing one of these jobs often seems to hark back to the call of a distant drum.

# Coots on the Rise

A congregation of coots who are, perhaps unconsciously, reliving some of the high points of their lives.

# CONVERSATIONS WITH A COOT

Oh, Bill, Grandpa has the most fascinating story. You *have* to hear it!

Oh — uh, is that the time? I really have to —

Nonsense, you sit right down here. Now Grandpa, tell Bill the story you told at dinner the other night.

*I don't know any Bill. Used to, but he's —*

I know, Grandpa, I mean my friend Bill right here. Tell him about the car.

*Don't have a car. Don't know any damn Bill.*

Grandpa. I just want you to tell Bill the *story* about the car.

*What the hell do I know I know about his car?*

No, Grandpa, *your* car. The day it wouldn't start, and then you —

*Wouldn't start?*

That's right.

*Prob'ly flooded it.*

What?

*Prob'ly flooded it.*
*Damn fools pump away on the gas.*
*Flood it every time.*

No, Grandpa, this was —

*Ever get it goin'?*

Excuse me?

*Ain't you this Bill I been hearin' about?*

Yes sir, I'm Bill, but —

*Well, ain't you the damn fool flooded your car t'other day?*

Uh, no...

*Well, what the hell we been talkin' about?*

Grandpa, it's not *Bill's* car. The story is about —

*Not your car, damned if I can see what business you got tryin' to start it anyhow.*

*Grandpa*. I'm trying to get you to tell Bill about the time your old La Salle wouldn't start.

*La Salle?*

Yes, your old —

*Why'nt you tell me it was a La Salle? You never flooded it. You prob'ly forgot to retard the spark.*

Grandpa, no one has a La Salle.

*I don't see what business these whippersnappers have settin' foot in a car like a La Salle. Waste o' good machinery is what I say.*

Grandpa. You're being impossible. I just want you to tell my friend Bill your story about you and Grandma and the 1939 World's Fair.

*World's Fair?*

That's right.

*Can't tell you nothin' about the 1939 World's Fair.*

Why on earth not?

*Never got there. Goddamn car wouldn't start. Got any more o' them cheese balls?*

# THE RENAISSANCE COOT

Even allowing for his long life, every coot seems to have racked up an amazing number of accomplishments. You will rarely find one who has not been, at one time or another, author, inventor, engineer, composer, statesman, and confidante and advisor to the rich and powerful. The world has seen few crises that he did not predict and even fewer periods of prosperity for which he was not at least partially responsible. He was present for, or was somewhere within a few miles of, every major event of his time — events which, of course, he saw coming long in advance. But the true measure of the coot's public spirit is in his willingness to share every detail of his experience and acquired wisdom.

With anyone who will listen.

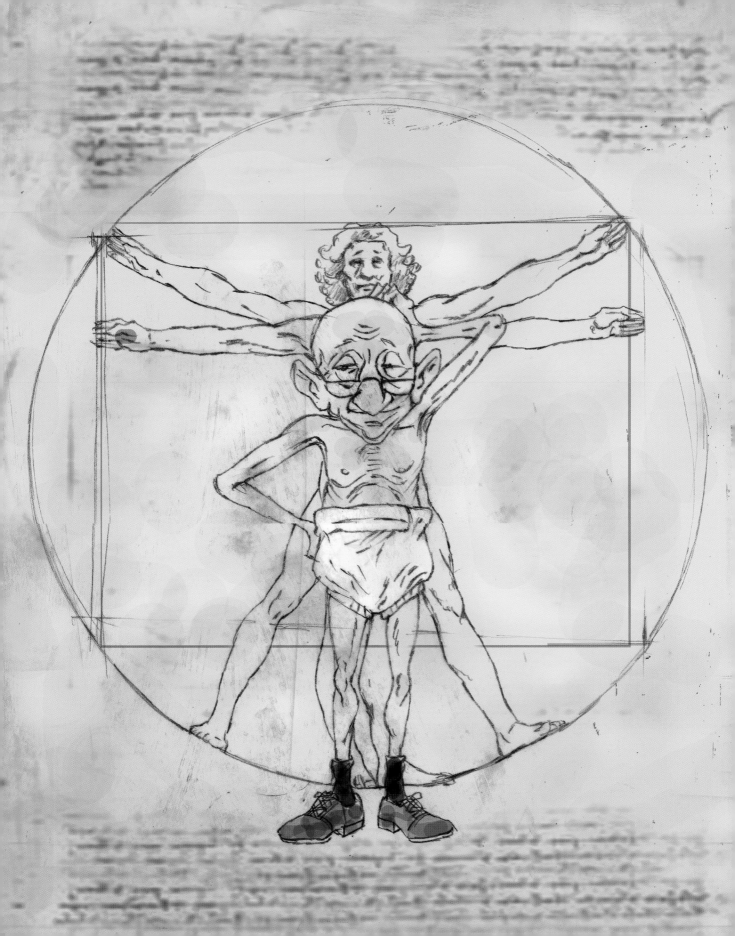

# Curing the Common Coot

# THE DOCTOR AND THE COOT

The coot is faced with a dilemma in his consideration of doctors and hospitals. On the one hand, he knows that any admission of infirmity on his part spells danger to his independence and his access to the liquor cabinet. On the other hand, the one thing the coot definitely does *not* resist is special attention, and no one knows better than he that he will get plenty of it in a medical institution or assisted care facility. So what does the coot do? He insists loudly and often that there isn't a thing wrong with him, that he'll lick any three men who try to say otherwise, that he knows damn well those young quacks make their money by supplying cadavers to medical schools and he by God ain't gonna be one of 'em, and so on. And on.

His beleaguered family believe he's covering up something that might be serious, so they check him into the hospital or home. After a week or so of being catered to, the doctors find nothing wrong and send him back.

Until the next time.

# Self-Medicated Coots

As mentioned in an earlier chapter, many things that were once easy for the coot have now become difficult or impossible. These include sleeping, urinating, digesting, taking a shirt out of the closet, putting a shirt in the closet, putting a shirt on, taking a shirt off, remembering whether he was putting it on or taking it off, and remembering whether it is, in fact, his shirt because the room suddenly doesn't look so familiar.

The coot realizes that many of these activities can be made much less troublesome by the prudent application of a little medication, and despite his general reputation for non-cooperation, he is surprisingly compliant when it comes to such things as his three daily glasses of fiber. This may be because he has also discovered that the medication itself can be made much more palatable by the prudent application of a little whiskey.

FIBER FLUSH PRUNE EXTRACT

A coot who is still experimenting with his dosage.

# HOME CARE OF THE COOT

Along with modern science, the coot believes that there can be no better remedy for what ails him than total rest, massive medication, and intensive round-the-clock care in the familiar surroundings of home.

No one can doubt this who has had the opportunity to compare the behavior of the coot under home care with that of the hospitalized coot. The coot at home is at least eight times as likely to call the nurse for a pill, some juice, or another attempt with the rectal thermometer.

He also takes more baths.

# THE CHURCH AND THE COOT

The coot's relationship with the church is likely to have undergone a number of changes during the course of his life. As a youngster, of course, he was taken to Sunday school by his parents and had no voice in the matter. As a young man, he probably recognized the advisability of making at least occasional appearances in the pew so that he would not be frowned upon by the mothers of the girls he wished to be acquainted with. Through middle age, there is little doubt that his wife made sure he heard, at a minimum, the Christmas and Easter sermons, and that he refrained from smoking, swearing, and improper conversational references when the pastor or priest was invited to dinner. In short, for all the coot's life, the church has encroached upon his leisure time, forced him at least twice a year to change from his slippers and robe into stiff clothes and tight shoes, and prevented him from speaking his mind or lighting his pipe at just those times he felt most inclined to do so.

So it is perhaps not surprising that, now that he has something the church wants, the coot can sum up his attitude in just seven words: "It's my soul, and I'm keepin' it."

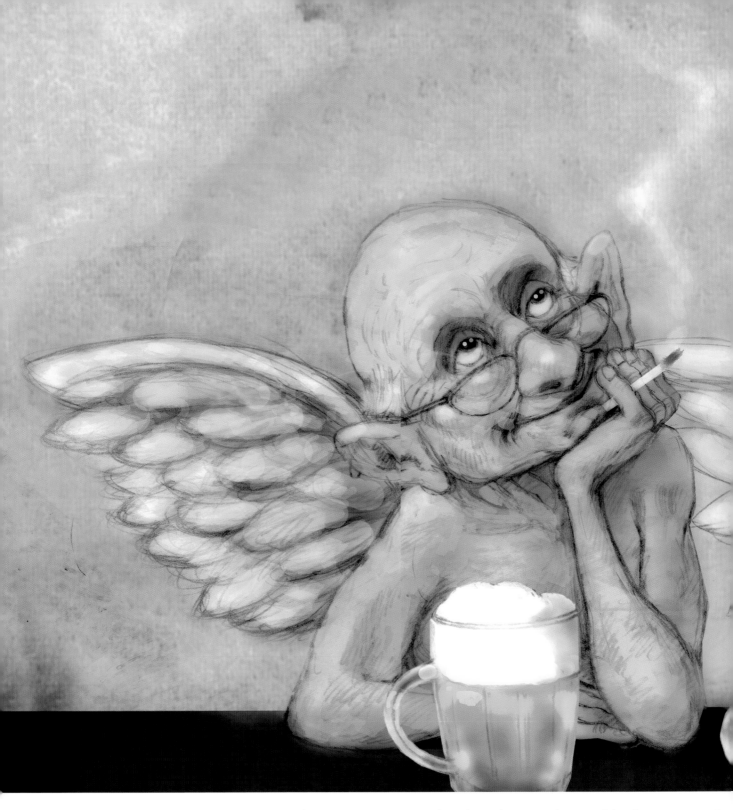

At the end of it all, perhaps the only relevant question is what has the coot learned in the course of

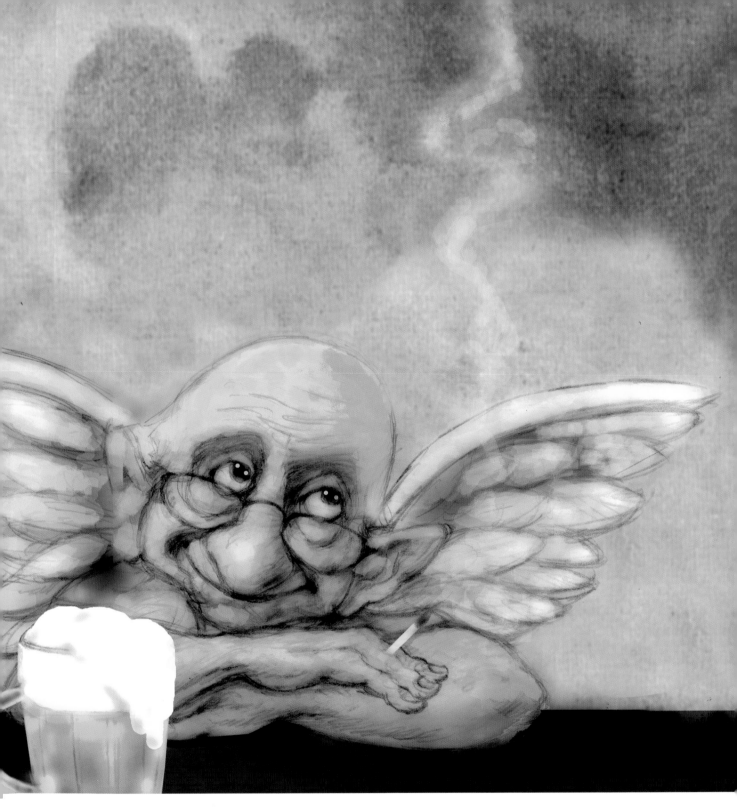

a long and eventful life? It may be this: If you want to learn to fly, you have to take yourself lightly.

# THE

# BALLAD

# OF

# DINAH

# CALDWELL

# THE

# BALLAD

# OF

# DINAH

# CALDWELL

## KATE BRAUNING

PAGE STREET
PUBLISHING CO.

## TO MY SIBLINGS:

*Tricia, Sean, Matt, Aimee, Rebekah, Sam, Lydia, Jake, Rebecca,
John, Hannah, and Mark, who are all so wonderful that they
have never once tried to cut me out of the family.
I wrote this book for them.*

T HE WHOLE COUNTY HELD ITS BREATH WHEN THE SILVER TRUCK
pulled away from that big, gabled house in the valley. The
wheel of Charlotte County spun around the axle of Gabriel
Gates, and when he moved, the county moved, too.

That silver truck hadn't pulled up the dirt driveway of Dinah
Caldwell's farm in four years—not since he'd called due the loan
on her father's garage in town. And since they hadn't been able to
pay it, Gates had taken the shop and the tools and the last shred of
her father's hope and said he could run the garage as an employee.

There wasn't much left for Gates to take, though, so Dinah
had no idea why he'd be parking his truck on the cracked dirt of
their driveway.

Her mother was home by herself. And no matter why that
man was here, she couldn't run to the little two-bedroom house
across the patchy grass of the yard. Because then her brother
would follow.

Warren slowly stood up from his seat on the old fallen tree. He was always putting his favorite stones and little figures he carved into the mossy, rotted-out end. "What do you think he wants?"

The door of that big, self-driving truck slammed.

"Nothing good." Dinah couldn't take her eyes off the man walking toward her house.

Warren picked up his gun. It was only a .243 bolt action, but it was still deadly.

Bright, late October sunlight spilled warmth over the dying grass, a lie about the cold in the air. But the sun couldn't reach them here, a few yards into the woods, and Gabriel Gates couldn't see them, either.

A gunshot ruptured the air.

"Damn it, Warren, if you can't be more careful with that, I'm taking it away."

"I am being careful. And you would not." Warren frowned, but he turned away from his target-shooting tree and held the gun more carefully.

She would so, and he knew it. Dinah watched him from the corner of her eye. Something about eleven-year-old boys must make them reckless.

Or maybe seeing that vehicle here made him a little sick, too.

Warren kicked a cluster of fallen maple leaves, flicking bright red sails into the air. Dust bloomed around them. In the drought of the last six years, half the lakes in the Ozarks had dried up. Too many people in the county had already caved to one of Gates's bad loans, sold to him for the money to start over, or straight-up given him their farm in return for a monthly paycheck to run it.

Her mother's deal to trade water from their well for food from the neighbors was the only reason any of them were still here.

"I bet I could hit his tires." Warren swung the gun around and took aim.

"Don't you dare." He wouldn't actually do it. Brian Shaw, the big white guy Gates had hired as a bodyguard from out in Kansas, sat in the back.

Besides, that truck was worth more than everything they owned—one of maybe three vehicles she'd ever seen in her life that had been made after the 2029 depression. The handful of other cars or trucks in the area were at least forty years old—most people rode little motorbikes, a lot of ancient Z125s and Honda Groms, since they were so cheap and easy to work on. People needed their vehicle to last through three or four rebuilds at least.

Warren didn't answer, but he lowered the gun and immediately coughed. The cold air and dust made his asthma worse. So did stress.

Every time, that sound made her desperate. He didn't use to wheeze like that when the temperature changed.

Warren reached into the end of the mossy log and brought out a little wooden bird, half-carved. Because he knew, too. They couldn't go home while that man was here. "We don't owe him anything," he said.

"We don't." Dinah rolled open her knife sheath and pulled out the middle blade.

Him taking the garage in town had settled their debt. Gabriel Gates wasn't a bank, just a local farmer whose family had been here for five generations, same as most.

But her mother had been crying some nights, for months, and she wouldn't say why.

Dinah stood, her favorite knife in her hand. Her lightest drop-point. All her knives were single-piece and double edged, but this one was her favorite for throwing. Good aim took constant practice, and if she imagined the tree was a man, a very specific man, her aim improved.

Usually she imagined this pin oak was her father, and she threw those blades until her arms ached. Today, she was picturing Gabriel Gates. But it didn't really matter. This tree was a skeleton man, and her knife would turn him from skin and blood into bones.

She was distracted enough for the blade to strike and bounce, instead of sink.

She shook her head once, hard, and pulled out a second knife. Her blades weren't true throwing knives, but she needed them for more than target practice. She balanced the blade and her body, and she whipped the knife into the air. It split tree bark and held.

Warren grinned. "There you go." His coat was too big, and he looked younger than eleven in it. It only belonged to him because it no longer belonged to their father. Warren's gaze strayed again through the trees to their house.

She yanked her knife out of the tree and sat beside him. He started working away on the little bird. She watched his knife tracing texture, so carefully, onto the individual feathers.

"Isn't it weird how birds have wings *and* legs?" he said. "Like, they can hop around on the ground, but they can also fly high up if they want. Which would you rather have? Wings or legs."

If she'd been born with either one, she'd be fine with it, but she didn't want to have to make the choice. "I dunno. Wings seem pretty risky."

"Legs are risky, too, though." Warren flipped the bird over and started working on the other wing.

A door banged. Gates strode out to his truck, but they could barely see him around the corner of the house. He was thin-faced and broad-shouldered, and in those suits he always wore, just a bit too long, he looked like a skeleton pretending to be human.

Warren pulled his gaze away from Gates back to her. Her brother's gray eyes were just like their mom's. Deep. Intelligent. Scared. Trying to figure out a world that didn't want him.

The driverless silver truck backed carelessly out of the yard.

"How about you go feed the chickens?" she said. "I should help Mom with dinner."

The rumble of the engine faded. Warren's shoulders relaxed. "Yeah. Okay."

Dinah headed for the house. Warren would mess around outside until she made him come in. Telling him to feed the chickens just gave him an excuse to avoid going inside. Because even as scared as he was, he didn't want to know. He wanted to do his carvings and take care of his chickens and climb around in the ravine. And she could at least give him that.

Dinah ran up the steps and left the door open. The house was too warm. "Mom?"

"I'm in here." The voice came from the kitchen. "Could you start the biscuits for dinner?"

Asking would only kill this spiraling, terrible hope that Gabriel Gates hadn't wanted anything bad. That everything was fine, and nothing would change. But she was helpless to stop herself. "What did he want?"

Ellen Caldwell came out of the kitchen, glanced around the living room. "Where's Warren? Kara's coming over after dinner,

I assume?" Her voice trembled a bit. Her hair hung down to her shoulders in long, brown waves.

Her mother's hair was never down. She always wore it up, out of the way. It had been up two hours ago, when Dinah had left the house.

"He'll be inside in a bit. And yeah, Kara will probably bring over her lesson planning." Dinah squinted. Her mother moved toward the window, and as her hair swung forward, Dinah saw the marks.

"Mom!" She touched her mother's shoulder, moved aside the hair. Red, oval bruises the size of fingerprints dotted her pale neck. Some ran together in a mess of darkening color on her shoulder.

"Don't, okay?" Her mother pushed her away, gently, letting her hair fall again. "I'm fine." She strode into the kitchen and pulled a mixing bowl from the cabinet.

Dinah had been right outside while that happened, fucking around in the woods. "He hurt you."

Her mother's shoulders dropped. She moved closer, put her flour-dusted palms on either side of Dinah's face. "I can see you taking on all this. I can see it on your face. That's the last thing I wanted."

Dinah moved her mother's hands and sat down at the table. The chair creaked. "So I have to be fine with him choking you?"

"He just grabbed my shoulder." Her mother scooped flour into the bowl. The metal measuring cup trembled. "He says fore-closing on the garage didn't pay the interest on the loan."

Bullshit. "He hasn't said anything for four years and suddenly he wants more money?"

Lines tightened around her mother's eyes. "Not suddenly. He's been sending notices. I pay a few dollars each time, I just can't pay it all."

Her mother was as threadbare as their dish cloths. One good tug might shred her to pieces.

"Why didn't you tell me?" She could have done something, at least tried.

Her mother's head snapped up. "Because you're barely seventeen, and there was nowhere to get the money anyway. It's not something I wanted you worrying about."

The bang of the henhouse door sounded outside.

"How much do we owe?" Dinah whispered.

"Five thousand dollars." Her mother set the measuring cup on the table. "He wants the well as payment."

And there it was. The punchline of a years-long setup. And they were just as helpless as if they'd been tied hands and feet, left in the road for his big silver truck to roll right over them.

Dinah stumbled to her feet and out the front door. She gripped the porch railing and sucked in cold air.

He could not have the well. She wouldn't let him take their water.

If her father had kept working as Gates's employee in the garage, they'd have been able to pay back the loan. Gates wouldn't have a reason to claim their well, to charge Kara's family and the Franklins and everyone else prices they could barely afford for water.

But no, her father had left with no explanation, with no good-bye, with no reason other than the fight she'd heard between her parents the night before he walked away. *I can't take watching it happen*, he'd said. *This is my fault*. Over and over.

She'd been asleep when he left, everyone had been, but her mind had still formed this memory of him walking down the driveway, a bag over his shoulder.

It hadn't been his fault before then. From that night on, it had been his fault.

A wasp crawled along the porch railing by her hands, then lifted its wings and flew to the pears. Three buckets from Kara's orchard, in exchange for water, filled until they were top-heavy with honey-yellow fruit for canning, for mashing into sauce, for preserving in syrup for pies.

Everything they'd done here didn't mean a thing if Gates decided to pull on the tentacles he'd wrapped around these mountains.

Dinah kicked one of the buckets over. Yellow spilled across the porch, tumbled down the steps. Pears spinning into the dirt, bumping into each other like billiard balls.

Shit.

Dinah dropped to her knees. She picked up one of the pears by her leg and placed it gently into the bucket. Most of these would be so bruised they'd have to mash them all.

She scrambled after the ones by her feet, and then scooted to the steps.

But when she looked up, there was Warren. Around the side of the porch, watching her through the railing. Eyes wide in shock.

Overhead, the sky was as flat and calm as a pale blue sea.

"Sorry," Dinah said quietly.

Warren crouched down and, holding up the hem of his coat, loaded the pears by his feet into the basket it made. He picked one up off their river rock in the flower bed.

Seven years ago, she'd pulled that gray rock out of the dried-up creek. Her handprint in green paint rested on the rock across from Warren's, their names and ages written below. Dinah, ten. Warren, four.

When you are ten, you're already a whole person, holding the weight of what it means to have your brother be four and have him looking at you like that. And when he gets older, the years between you mean less, but you still think of him like he's four because he needed more than he got, and you helped him learn to walk, and brother meant mine.

Dinah bent down and picked up the pears on the steps, but every one Warren touched was one she should have reached. She was supposed to be the one making things okay.

When every piece of fruit was placed gently back in the bucket, Warren went inside, and Dinah sank down on the steps.

She ought to stand up. She shouldn't just sit here like this, letting the dusk hide her burning face and the breeze dry out her eyes. Dinah dug her hands into her hair, pulled on the strands until her scalp hurt.

Even with five thousand dollars hanging over her head, she still had to worry about bruised pears rotting and then nothing to eat in February.

None of this was helping. Dinah stood up, brushed off her jeans, and went back inside. The scent of hot butter and browning biscuits permeated the living room.

Her mother was sitting on the couch, hands folded. "Come here for a second."

Dinah sat down in the old rocking chair. At least this wasn't pretending.

Ellen spoke quietly, so her voice wouldn't carry to Warren in his room. "I haven't signed anything over to Gates. He might say I have, but I haven't. This house is ours and so is the well and everything else. No, let me finish. The deed is under the kitchen sink. If something ever happens, take the deed, take Warren, and leave. Just go, okay? Maybe if you have it, you'd eventually be able to come back."

"What do you mean, 'if something happens'? And where the hell would we go?" If somewhere to go existed, they would have left a long time ago. If Little Rock and St. Louis weren't already choked with people who'd left their dustbowl farms and ghost towns; if every job in the cities hadn't already been taken. There wasn't anywhere to go.

Moving to the city took money. Hiring a truck to move your things. A deposit for renting an apartment. Money for food, rent, and utilities while everyone searched for jobs. Money for nice clothes for interviews so no one would think you were poor and desperate and therefore unqualified.

A tiny crease appeared between her mother's eyebrows. "You've already taken on so much. We couldn't have made it through the last four years if you hadn't. But if something does happen, you've got to take care of Warren."

Of course she'd take care of Warren. "What are you talking about?"

"Just in case. That's all. No matter what, don't try to talk to Gates, just leave. Go to Kara's. Ask her parents for help. Or go to the Franklins' or McCaffreys'" Ellen stood and headed for the kitchen.

Dinah had zero desire to talk to Gabriel Gates. Use him as target practice, maybe. Put one of her knives through his eye.

But Dinah wasn't done with this subject. She grabbed her mom's sleeve as she walked past. "We'll figure this out."

Her eyes might as well be Warren's. "Honey, we'll see."

"No, I mean it. I'll—" She couldn't say this to her mom, because her mother would panic and tell her not to do things that obviously had to be done.

She'd quit school and find an extra job. Maybe at the store

in town, or as a teacher's assistant like Kara had started doing in addition to working at the orchard.

That wouldn't pay off their debt, though. And it wouldn't be enough to replace what the water had given them. It might not even keep them from starving.

CHAPTER

KARA TEXTED HER ALL THROUGH DINNER. DINAH'S SCHOOL tablet buzzed on the counter every five minutes. Tablets had never been allowed at Caldwell dinners and never would be, so Dinah couldn't read the texts until after the dishes were done.

> Mom made pea soup again. What is it with her and peas? I'm dying

> She never remembers how much I hate peas. They're like tiny green brains. Is this all Germans or just my mother? Save me

> Matías and Hannah are the noisiest kids on the planet. Why does being a child equal constant screaming??

> Ok I've got my work stuff, headed over

Reception wasn't great and sometimes texts took a while to send, but at least they had service—when she was Warren's age, there hadn't been any. It wasn't until she was twelve that Amazon Internet had sent their high-altitude drones over rural areas, piecing together an aerial wireless network. She'd never thought of herself as poor before, but when the Department of Education had put an antenna for the drone network at school, her teachers had talked about why the government had given money for it. To "address the education crisis of the American rural poor," they'd said.

She'd biked home extra slow after school that day, thinking, *I am a crisis.*

Dinah toasted one of the leftover biscuits, and by the time she was spreading it with apple butter, Kara had dropped her backpack on the couch. Her black hair, pulled into a high ponytail, made a fountain of curls past her shoulders, like always, and like always, she wore a puffy sweater and those denim cutoffs she'd had since she was fourteen. They'd been too big then, but now they showed off her brown legs and fit so well that Dinah turned back toward the counter. Kara's German mother was as pale as Dinah herself, but Kara had inherited her Dominican father's warm, tawny brown skin.

When she handed the biscuit to Kara, the girl's eyes went wide. "For me? Thank God." She took it and talked around a bite. "This is exactly why you and I should just get married."

Dinah's whole body went hot. "What?"

Kara swallowed and licked her thumb. "I'm so hungry."

A joke. Like always. Dinah wanted to bang her own head against the wall. Something should only be called a joke if it was funny.

Kara leaned against the kitchen counter. "So, what did he want?" she asked quietly.

There was no other way to say it. "The well."

Kara stopped breathing.

"He's not going to get it," Dinah said.

Kara slowly breathed in. "Last night, my parents were talking about selling."

The Hernández family might as well be her own. Dinah turned off the faucet. "And do what?"

Kara shrugged, looked out the window at the dusk beyond it. "The city. Jobs."

But. Then Gates would charge money for the produce. And they wouldn't be able to buy even half of what they were using now.

And Kara would be gone.

"Are you really moving?" Dinah forced herself to look Kara in the eyes, because if she couldn't do that then she didn't deserve her.

Kara shrugged. "Papi kept saying 'Dominicans don't take bad deals; he's taking advantage,' and Mom said, 'Germans go somewhere they can eat.' But she knows what he does—the deal he offered us didn't even match what he gave the Walkers."

Because that was the other thing. There was always some business excuse for it, but there was the rate he'd just offered Kara's parents. And there were the Franklins, the Liberian family who had sold fifty acres to buy a truck—the price per acre had been fifty dollars lower than what he'd paid for similar land from the McCaffreys. And then there was the Kangs' store. They'd had to leave Dinah's freshman year.

If they lost the well to that man, her neighbors might have no choice but to sell, and what he'd offer most of them would be far from enough to start over.

"Girls." Her mom came into the kitchen, a notebook and the household folder in her hands. "I've got to do some things at the table. Would you mind working in the bedroom?"

They always went to Dinah's room. This was just her mom's

way of asking them to please go away and be quiet. Which was fair, because her mom was digging through every piece of the farm, every financial projection, every possible scenario to find a way to come up with five thousand dollars.

Kara spread out her notebooks on Dinah's bed and Dinah closed the door. Warren had caught her staring at Kara enough times to tease her about it mercilessly when they were alone, but he at least had the good sense to let them have some space when Kara came over. So he was carving another little hen to add to his collection in the living room, and they had the bedroom she shared with him to themselves.

"I just wish to God my parents would stop coddling me." Kara flopped cross-legged on the bed. "Every time I try to work at home, they're looking over my shoulder, asking about lesson objectives and if I'm grading Warren and Hannah and Matías fairly and all this stuff, like they think I'm not qualified." She picked at the bedspread. "And I'm just an assistant, you know? I'm *not* qualified. But Mr. Simmons lets me help with lesson planning, proctoring the tests, and a lot of the grading. I've read all the books and training materials he's given me, and I've got this massive list of educational psychology reading—"

Mr. Simmons was using her to do all his work so he could take the credit and the bigger paycheck and go home early. But Kara needed to learn the job, wanted to be ten times better than Mr. Simmons and Ms. Breyer, so what else was she supposed to do?

Dinah sat on the edge of the bed. "Your parents underestimate you. And Warren says you're a better teacher than Mr. Simmons already." Kara had always been simultaneously brimming with hope and plans, but so scared of failing that she never just went for it.

A hopeful smile crept over Kara's face. "Did he really say that?"

Dinah nodded. "And you were so scared of the semester starting." This girl was destined to leave Charlotte County. Kara, the girl who had lived across the ravine for Dinah's whole life, who wanted so much to matter to the world that she was burning to leave their mountains. Who somehow felt that right here, now, she did not matter.

Kara flopped onto her side and buried her face in the blanket. "It's terrifying, walking into a classroom of kids, knowing what they learn is up to me. Three of them got in a fight today over who poked someone first and it turned into a big meltdown and I froze while Mr. Simmons handled it. I wanted to leave and not come back; I was so embarrassed."

"But you did stay." Dinah shifted closer to her.

Kara didn't reply, just stayed facedown in the blanket.

"You've got this," Dinah said.

"Ugh." Kara sat up and reached for one of the notebooks.

The school printer had broken down, so Kara was supposed to be hand-making flashcards for the study session she was leading for the history test. Dinah helped her cut thick paper and marker the edges with a neat border while Kara wrote up the content.

When Dinah glanced over at Kara's notebook, she was sketching the Galaxy Girl logo in the corner. Flashcards be damned, apparently.

Dinah did not understand the fascination, but if graphic novels were Kara's obsession, hearing Kara talk about them was Dinah's.

"Explain it to me," she said. "Why do you love Galaxy Girl so much? What is it about a meteor giving people supernatural powers that keeps you up reading till three in the morning?"

Kara's pencil never stopped sketching. "They're soldiers of the revolution, Dinah. They fight the system."

Hearing Kara say those things fogged Dinah's common sense. Dinah dug her fingers into the bedspread. She could see it happening, every detail of it in her mind. Leaning forward, touching her lips to Kara's, the warmth and the electric fizz under her skin, the way Kara would realize this was what she wanted, too.

But that was about as real as superheroes, so she covered it up with something else. "Sure. But scientifically, there's nothing about a meteor that could give someone supernatural strength."

Kara rolled her eyes. "You have to use your imagination, girl, or you'll lose it."

If what was going on in her head was any indication, her imagination was just fine.

Once Warren was in bed asleep, Kara decided to stay the night like she did half the time on Fridays. Her mom had shut herself into her own bedroom with yet more paperwork and dark circles under her eyes.

Dinah should be helping, but her mom wouldn't let her.

Kara slid under the covers and rolled toward her, the light from the window falling on her face. "On top of everything else, Mr. Simmons and I got into a fight about Thanksgiving lesson plans," Kara said softly.

Dinah stayed quiet and listened.

"He said ridiculous stuff about colonists being the first Americans, and I wasn't going to say anything because, you know, he's my boss. But then I had to, and he said I had no right to change his curriculum."

Maybe Dinah could light his head on fire. Maybe that would help.

"It's just . . . being Dominican means my ancestry is European and African and Taíno. The Taíno were indigenous to Hispaniola. It was their home. But millions and *millions* of them were murdered by the diseases and labor conditions and slavery forced on them by the Europeans. The Taíno were wiped out of their own home." Her voice fractured. "Having to hear that man completely ignore the people who were here first—when this was their *home*—hear him claim that Europeans were the *first* Americans, when that implies indigenous people were not Americans at all . . . But he just said it wasn't relevant. Like I didn't matter and neither did they."

The two girls lay on their sides, face to face, while Kara whispered so quietly Dinah could barely hear her.

"This is my home, but is it? The rest of Papi's family is in St. Louis. We're the only Dominicans in this county, now that Tía Elena left. Even Galaxy Girl is Mexican. Which is great but it's not the same. Mom gets a little hurt, I think, that I connect so much to my dad's family, especially because her parents were German immigrants during the third war, you know? And they have this amazing story. But I'm brown like Papi, and I share that with him. He always says to make life work, we have to bring our whole selves. But do I have a whole self? I don't know."

Dinah reached over and touched Kara's hand with her fingertips. "Your whole self is my favorite thing."

Kara sighed. But she didn't move her hand, and Dinah couldn't move at all. She wanted to say all these words, but they just swarmed through her head and wouldn't come to her lips.

She would never be as brave or as strong as this girl. She couldn't even tell her *don't go, stay with me, I need you.*

By the time she worked up the courage to say literally anything else, Kara was asleep.

Whispers of dried leaves scuttling over the roof filtered down. The bed creaked as Dinah rolled over, tucking her pillow into a ball under her head.

Warren's asthmatic snoring lessened. She was waking him with her rustling around.

Kara was not leaving. No one else was leaving.

She sat up and touched her feet to the cold, creaking floorboards. She slid on the coarse wool socks on the table by her bed. Even with her flannel pajamas, the cold would seep through tonight.

Dinah tiptoed past Warren's bed, stepping over the creakiest floorboard by the doorway. She liked the house most at night. She could turn on a lamp and stare at the braided living room rug washed in yellow light, the windows dark, holding everything out.

Nighttime was when Dinah pretended.

Instead of turning on the lamp, she picked up the guitar case beside the couch. She opened the door and stepped onto the porch, careful not to let the flimsy screen door bang behind her.

It was one of those cloudless nights, where the sky looked like someone had taken the top off the world.

There had to be some way to help Kara and to keep her family from selling the orchard. To find the answer for her own farm.

Her mom's grandparents had cleared this land, her own grandparents had installed the wind turbine, her mother had kept it all together by connecting every local farm that needed an anchor.

It wasn't really even a farm—a few acres of woods climbing the side of the mountain for a trap line, a small clearing her great-grandparents had carved into the forest so they could plant a big enough garden.

Dinah sat on the porch, her feet on the step, and opened the guitar case. Her father's guitar. An old, worn one with bad strings, but it still made music. She rested it on her lap and curved her fingers around the neck.

The strings scraped cold on her fingers. Kara kept asking to hear her play, but Dinah hadn't played in front of her since her dad had left. It was too invasive, somehow. Her father had taught her.

He could be dead by now, for all she knew. All the possible reasons for why had curdled together, so she'd let it go. The *how* was the thing she couldn't leave behind. He had to have known what would happen, that this could happen, if he left.

She played for an hour while her mind turned over the water and five thousand dollars and those bruises on her mother's shoulder, and then finally her hands stilled on the strings.

If she talked to the neighbors, maybe together they could raise enough money to keep Gates from taking the well. It would be cheaper for them in the long run than paying cash for water anyway, and if she quit school and got a job somehow, she could slowly pay each of them back. Her mother would say no—she wouldn't want to ask. But Dinah would.

She shivered. The wind was colder now, leaking through her flannel pajamas.

Tomorrow everyone would be helping with canning at Kara's, so she could talk to them all together. Dinah pressed her cold palms to her eyes and took what felt like the first full breath of the whole day.

Her eyes still felt hot and swollen by morning. She'd tried so hard to sleep that she hadn't slept at all.

"Here, eat something before you go." Her mother set oatmeal in front of Dinah before she could protest. She didn't really have time for breakfast. Not today.

The bruises on her mother's neck had darkened. Even from here, she could see one of them under her chin.

Her mother sat down with her tea. "I hear you, you know. At night, when you play your guitar."

Dinah looked up from her bowl. "You do?"

"I love that you still play. That you're so musical."

She wasn't musical, not the way her mother meant. She was simply random notes, connected by nothing but air. Sound, maybe, but not music.

The whole way to the McCaffreys', Warren seemed to handle the biking just fine. But Dinah was so tired, Kara practically had to drag her up the blacktop for Saturday chores.

Laura McCaffrey took one look at her and brought a mug of strong, bitter tea. Dinah took a moment to drink it before milking the goats. The woman was a warm, motherly whirlwind of homemade bread, knitted scarves, fresh butter, and come in, shoes off, sit down, it's too cold out for skinny kids like you.

She, Kara, and Warren were helping with chores this morning so Laura and her husband could go repair a loose section of fence before they all went over to the orchard to help can produce for the Hernández family's winter pantry. The deal was at least one productive member from each household, rotating homes so everyone had enough hands for the work.

At Kara's, Warren and the younger Hernández kids carefully washed bucket after bucket of pears, bringing each one to Dinah and Kara at the sawhorse table outside. They cored and sliced while everyone else buzzed through the kitchen, Kara's mom supervising the men working the pressure canners and Laura McCaffrey directing the traffic of steaming jars.

Every time Warren came over with another bucket, he looked back and forth between Dinah and Kara until Dinah narrowed her eyes at him. He ran away, smirking.

Juice dripped everywhere, tracking down her arms, as she cored and sliced pear after pear. And then Dylan, Alex, and Chrissa Franklin set up more sawhorse tables, and they all switched to crushing garlic and chopping tomatoes, onions, green peppers, and cilantro for sofrito. Mr. Hernández used the aromatic cooking base all the time, but Mrs. Hernández used it also—the flavors went well with a lot of her family recipes, too.

The roasty smell of oil and garlic, three pots of mustard always on the table, crispy potato pancakes, windows always open to the outdoors even if it was cold out, a sunset peach–painted living room with a comfortable, sagging couch—these things meant the Hernández home. And she couldn't watch them disappear.

By noon, her shoulders ached. Tomorrow, it would be their turn to have everyone come help with canning. Their tomatoes and peppers were piling up, so they'd do sauce, salsa, and soup. And in another week, it would start over again to get the last of the produce before the frost did.

The worst of the drought was farther north in the plains, but it was so dry down here, even the trees were dying. Without their well, every farm in the area would be done.

Apparently there used to be a lot of small farms everywhere, all over the U.S. But they'd all been sold, leaving only the mountains behind. With the honey and crimson of the October trees, and little fairy worlds of burnt-red sumac hiding rabbit burrows, and the hills that made her feel like she was dying as she biked up one side and flying as she pulled her feet up to whoosh down the other, she couldn't imagine why no one had wanted her mountains.

But Amazon Agriculture and Tyson-Deere had deemed the Ozarks "not profitable." No good way to use the giant, remote-operated combines and planters in the mountains. So Charlotte County and the Arkansas counties surrounding it had been left behind.

Before she'd died, Dinah's grandma had loved to talk about the days before the depression. She'd even talk about the long and expensive war before it, and then the downturn from so much less government spending when the war ended. It triggered a problem with the banks, starting the economy-collapsing depression of 2029. But her grandma's stories always stopped there; 2029 she wouldn't talk about, even though it had been forty years since.

By the time Dinah was able to wash up, the Franklins and McCaffreys had already left. Today had gone long and everyone had their own work to do. Tomorrow. They were coming to her place tomorrow, and she'd get everyone's attention to talk about the well before they started work this time.

Warren rolled the bikes over from Kara's porch. Dinah held his handlebars while he climbed onto the seat; it would be too big for him for at least another year. "Wait." Kara pulled something out of her pocket and shoved it at Dinah.

Fifty-two dollars, in ones and fives. "What is this?" Dinah clutched the bills and met her brown eyes.

"It's for the well. If you give him a big payment, maybe he'll give you more time."

Dinah's lips parted. "But—where did you get it?"

"It's from teaching."

"Your savings?" For Kara to move. For her to study.

"I was just going to use it whenever I had to move out. Which isn't right now."

Warren's mouth had fallen open, too. He stared from Kara to Dinah.

She'd been going to ask everyone to help pay off Gates. But she hadn't meant Kara's savings. "You can't—"

Kara closed her hand around Dinah's arm. "Mi cielo, we can't screw around with this. If you lose the well, you'll have to move. And we'll all be worse off for it. Please don't argue. Just take it."

Dinah shoved the money into her pocket. Kara swung an arm over her shoulder and pulled her close for a second. "We got this," Kara whispered.

Dinah nodded into her hair, smelling pears and bar soap, and then she stepped back. Kara would understand how much she wanted to say more, and why she wouldn't.

She swung onto her bike and let it roll down the incline toward the highway, Warren following.

Fifty-two dollars. It wasn't enough, but it wasn't nothing.

Warren biked beside her, his feet stretching to push the pedal all the way down. The exertion was hard on him, but he was so self-conscious about his asthma that if he thought she was going slow for him, he'd get upset. She usually biked as slowly as she could without him noticing.

Today he wasn't coughing, but his chest heaved.

"Hey, my toe hurts from kicking those pears yesterday," she said. "Can we walk up this hill?"

"Sure," he huffed. "Don't want you to hurt yourself."

They slid off their bikes and walked them up the steep grade. Brambles and raspberry canes filled the ditches falling away on either side of the road. The trees were so huge, so old, their branches made a tunnel by threading together over the highway.

The afternoon had gotten oppressively humid and warm,

even though the sky was overcast. She was so warm by the time they reached the bridge over the ravine that she was unzipping her jacket when Warren stopped walking.

"Dinah. Look." His tone made her head jerk up.

That big silver truck sat in front of their house. Parked arrogantly sideways, the front tires off the driveway and into the grass.

"Roll the bikes into the ditch. Stay here. Don't move."

Dinah dropped her bike in the road.

"I'm not staying." Warren dropped his bike, too.

"You have to. I'll come get you if it's okay." She paused long enough to make sure he wasn't following, and then she ran.

Why would he be back again?

The house was still a quarter mile away, and she was coming up from behind it. She couldn't see anything but the reflection of the sun on the house windows and the gleaming silver of the truck. She gripped the hilt of the knife in her belt.

She had Kara's money. If he was here to force her mother to sell the well, she could give him that. Promise the rest in a week.

A few hundred yards left.

Twice now, she'd left her mother alone with that man.

Her feet hit her yard. Tore over the patchy grass.

Dinah slammed into the back door and almost tripped on

the steps. But it didn't open when she yanked on the doorknob. Locked. It was never locked.

A scream stuck in her lungs. She ran around the side of the house to the front door. But her feet involuntarily slowed, and then they stopped on the driveway all by themselves.

He stood on the porch. Gabriel Gates was leaning against the railing, smoking a cigarette. White skin tanned leathery, creases around his eyes from the sun. One boot crossed over the other, like he belonged there.

The door stood open, but she couldn't see through the screen door from here. She waited for her mother to look out the window. But nothing.

Dinah ran past him and into the house.

Her mother lay on the braided rug in the living room. Her arm was bent at an impossible angle. Dinah's knees hit the rug. "Mom. Mom, are you okay? Can you hear me?"

Everything in the house looked fine. Nothing was out of place. Nothing except the way her mother's head tilted, like something was wrong with her neck.

Dinah thought she'd been helpless yesterday. That yesterday had been the punchline.

She touched her mother's face. No response. She grabbed her hand, trying to feel a pulse. Anything to say this wasn't her whole world, gone.

Her mother's knuckles were scuffed, the skin on her hands creased from working in the garden, kneading dough, stitching up rips, chopping wood. Her hands looked a little like raisins, dried by the sun but with everything good still inside them.

The creak of the screen door had her turning around, pulling her knife out of the sheath.

Gates stood just inside the doorway. "Your mother got very upset."

His voice should have no power over her. She shouldn't freeze like he was her god and what he said next would determine her whole life.

"She hit her head when she fell."

Dinah touched her mother's face again. Her skin was cooling, but maybe that didn't mean anything. Her mother had to be alive. Dinah was just wrong. Because her fingers were turning numb and she couldn't feel anything correctly.

Her mother's eyes stared across the room. Maybe she'd blink. Dinah brushed the soft skin by her mother's eyelashes. Her eyelids felt stiff.

Gates shrugged, his thin lips moving into a flat line. "She was very emotional. Tried to make me leave when I told her I'd be foreclosing. It was a terrible accident."

Dinah's mind had left her body, gone somewhere safe, maybe just followed her mom to wherever she was now.

Gates was talking through thick clouds. He sounded miles away from where she sat on the braided rug of her living room floor.

She could feel the knife in her palm. She twisted the handle of her knife around and around in her hand. The blade flashed sunlight from the window. *Stand up. He's lying. Stand up. She didn't fall.*

His cigarette ashed onto the floor.

Dinah stood up. "Everyone is going to leave. All you're going to have is three empty counties of deserted forest."

He flicked his cigarette into the sink. "As long as people are desperate, there will be people who won't leave, and people who will come here to work for me. I'm creating jobs."

Dinah flung her knife at him. But he was already moving

toward her, and the blade buried itself in the doorframe where his chest had been.

He grabbed her braid, tilted her head up until she met his bloodshot eyes.

"You're right," she said. "We won't all leave."

His other hand gripped her jaw, and she couldn't have spoken then even if she'd wanted to. Looking into his eyes made her feel like she was leaving her own body. Rising out of his grip and out of the house until she could crush him inside it.

Something creaked. Then the metallic *pop-chink-thunk* of a shell hitting the chamber.

Warren stood in the doorway, looking down the sights of his rifle. His voice shook, but his hands were steady on the gun. "Get out of our house."

Warren, no.

Gates tightened his grip on her jaw, fingers pressing on her lips until they cut into her teeth. "You put that gun down, or I'll break your sister's neck right here."

Warren's shoulder steadied, went still. Dinah saw it. He squeezed the trigger. The bang was so loud in the small house. Gates ducked, and the shot hit the wall to his right. Dinah twisted her head and sank her teeth into Gates's hand.

He screamed and jerked back, but she kept digging her teeth in until they pierced flesh. He shoved her away. Her head snapped back. She bolted to her feet, reaching Warren in three steps.

Together, they moved away from the door, over to the table. Blood had spurted into her mouth. His blood, his iron and salt. She spit onto the floor.

Gates stepped toward Warren. "You really think you're going to kill me, kid?"

Warren kept his aim steady. "I've killed all kinds of things. Get out."

Gates went still. He watched them for a moment and tilted his head to the side. Then he walked out of the house and climbed into the truck. The bang of a truck door sounded, and a moment later the engine rumbled. The truck jerked as it turned onto the blacktop. Rubber screamed as the truck accelerated.

Warren lowered his gun. His pale gray eyes strayed to their mother's body.

Dinah had to do something. Even though her body was a husk. All her insides must have fallen out or blown away like smoke.

Dinah reached out and carefully took the gun from him.

"We have to call a doctor," he said.

Dinah shook her head.

"They have an ambulance in St. George. They'll take her to the hospital."

Dinah shook her head again. She wanted to scream, shake her mother's body just to see her move.

"I should've shot to kill him instead of threaten him. We could have taken her to the hospital in his truck."

"Warren, listen, honey." Dinah crouched down and set the gun aside. "You need to get some stuff together, okay? Get all your warm clothes. The potatoes, the cheese, all the meat. Fill the water jug, too."

His eyes finally met hers. "Why?"

A wet streak burned down her face and she wiped it away. "He's coming back, okay? Did you see how fast he drove off? He's coming back for us, and he'll have his bodyguard and other people with him. We have to be gone by then. Hurry, Warren. Go, go, okay?" She had to push him a little before he ran into his room.

Dinah picked up the quilt from the couch and draped it over her mother's body. She should do more than that. How could a quilt be all she could give her mother?

His blood was still in her mouth. She spit into the sink and rinsed, but the taste of iron wouldn't fade.

Warren's dresser drawers banged. If he was making noise, he was okay.

But he wouldn't be for long if she couldn't snap out of this. She ran to the kitchen, dug food out of the refrigerator. Hurried from room to room, piling things on the table.

Gates could be on his way back by now. She didn't know where he was going, who he'd be calling, how far away they'd be.

A tarp, a rope, the matches. Soap. The gun. Ammunition. Kara's money.

She couldn't even tell Kara or other neighbors. Because he'd go there to look for her and Warren first. If the neighbors knew anything, it would be trouble.

Tears still burned down her face. Hot and falling, no matter how many times she wiped them away.

Her knives. They didn't have a compass. No room for her guitar. She couldn't take her tablet or the school would be able to track her. She pried up the creaking floorboard in her room, shoved her tablet and her charger into the gap underneath it. Pounded the nail back in and to the side enough that it caught new wood and held.

They were taking too long.

Warren carried an armload of things to the kitchen and heaped them on the table. He ran out again and returned, carrying the backpacks—the heavy-duty waterproof ones their father had used for hunting trips.

"Warren." Words stuck in her throat and the sick feeling spread. She couldn't tell him he had to say good-bye.

He looked at the quilt-covered body, and his hands clenched on the straps of the bags.

She could not freeze like this.

Dinah took the backpacks from her brother and strapped the folded blankets to the bottoms. The water jug and the milk they could carry.

Warren glanced at the pile of things on the table. "You haven't packed anything."

Dinah looked up. Right. She needed her own clothing. "I'll hurry." She ran to the bedroom and grabbed socks, underwear, a tight shirt, a loose shirt, a sweater. Jeans. Softer, warmer pants. Hair ties. Antiseptic cream, toilet paper, tampons. Matches, the sewing kit. She paused by the kitchen sink. She bent and pulled out the plastic bag with the deed to the farm.

"Dinah?" Warren touched her hand. "I'll pack the bags. You said we have to hurry."

Warren was a natural organizer. She would have just crammed everything into a bag, but he'd put the things they wouldn't need right away at the bottom, roll the clothing tightly, and tuck tiny items into crannies.

Dinah knelt by her mother, pulled the quilt back, and touched her cheek. She'd told her she'd figure it out. Just last night, she'd promised that.

Rasping sounds. Warren dragged the backpacks across the living room. His own face was wet now, too. He wiped his red eyes on his sleeve.

Dinah reached for his hand and he gripped hers. They stood there, staring at the yellow quilt covering their mother, and all

Dinah could do was hold on to Warren's hand.

An engine growled on the highway. Two engines. Fear leaped into her throat. The rumble didn't slow; the cars barely braked for the turn onto the dirt. Dust surged up in a cloud. Seconds. They had only seconds.

Dinah sprinted for the bags and shrugged hers up on her shoulders, then held up Warren's for him. It was smaller, but not much. She grabbed the jugs of milk and water and stuffed them into the top of the packs.

They ran down the back steps and across the yard. The cars didn't stop on the driveway, tearing over the grass toward the trees.

The woods were only a dozen yards away. Dinah seized Warren's hand as they ran. Their feet pounded and sticks cracked under their shoes. They reached the edge of the trees. Voices yelled for them to stop. A shot fractured the air and a pine to their left shuddered. Then an elm and another pine.

The woods were sparse enough here for them to be seen. Dinah gripped Warren's hand both to keep him from falling and to keep them together. Leaves slipped on rocks. Wild raspberry canes caught their backpacks. Water sloshed in the jug.

She climbed up a mound of cracked boulders, hauling Warren behind her. Too wide to go around and it would block the gunfire. Warren jerked his hand free of hers to grab handholds. The soles of her shoes slammed into the ground as she landed on the forest floor.

The ravine cut through the steady slope upwards, decreasing the grade. Dinah grabbed a tree root and swung down, Warren scrambling after. The side of the gorge was rocky enough that finding footholds wasn't hard, but snakes sometimes hid in the pockmarked walls. Warren landed beside her.

The crunch of leaves and branches above grew louder. "Run, Warren, come on."

He scrambled ahead of her, his backpack bouncing. She'd be okay running like this, but he wouldn't be.

They raced up the ravine, dodging cracked boulders and nearly tripping every third stride. Warren stumbled and she grabbed him by the backpack to keep him from falling. The autumn leaf cover made running nearly impossible. Fortunately, the men crashing along behind them were having the same problem. Several men, it sounded like. Who? Gates had some farmhands who worked for him, some people who were friends of friends. Mrs. McCaffrey's nephew. But weren't they just—farmers? Not killers. Not people who'd chase kids down in the woods. Then this must be his body-guard, Brian Shaw, and at least two others.

Angry voices echoed down the ravine.

Her lungs heaved in air. Warren's must be burning. Think, Dinah, think. They couldn't outrun those men. The best they could hope for was to get far enough ahead so they could hide.

Warren looked back at her.

"Don't look back," she said. "You'll fall." The rock wall to her left erupted and fragments stung her cheek.

Shit. They had to get out of this ravine before one of them got shot. "Where's the gun?" she panted.

Warren stumbled and paused his scramble up the rocky trench. "We left it in the house," he whispered. "I forgot to pick it up."

No gun. Pebbles slid beneath her foot. "Come on. We can't stop." She reached for his backpack. "Let me take this so you can go faster."

Dinah swung the second bag over her shoulder. The incline

only grew steeper, but a few hundred yards and they'd be out of the ravine. She glanced back. The men rounded the curve of the trench, half-running as they navigated the rocks. She climbed faster, her shoulder aching under the added weight.

Warren reached the top. His face paled, and when he started coughing, he couldn't stop. He bent over and wheezed air in and out. Dinah scrambled out of the ravine and ran over to him. She touched his back. "Are you okay?"

He coughed once more and spit on the ground. "Yeah. But I don't think—" He coughed again.

Her hands turned into fists and she shifted the backpacks. She and Warren had explored all over back here. A hundred yards away, a shelf of the mountain rose into the air. Around the side, a split hid in the rocks, just big enough to hold a person. "Hurry, come on."

Warren followed her as she ran for the shelf. The wind had picked up, and the air was getting colder. She knew not to believe storms anymore—they sometimes gave the empty promise of dark clouds, lightning, thunder. But never any rain.

"Hide back in there and stay with the bags. I'll run the other direction and then double back to get you." She dumped the bags on the ground, and Warren crawled back into the split in the rocks. His breath still keened.

Shit. "Are you sure you're okay?"

Rocks tumbled and clattered into the ravine. The men were climbing out. Warren waved at her and pulled a bag in after him. "I'm fine. Run fast, sis."

She glanced away, then back to him. "Okay. Love you. Don't make a sound." She sprinted up the hill, sticking to rocks and moss and avoiding the leaf cover.

Without the weight of the bags, she leaped easily from foothold to foothold. At the top, she kicked down a small shower of
stones to draw their attention away from Warren's hiding place.
Shouts came from below. They headed in her direction, firing
wildly into the forest around her.

She grabbed a vine to steady her headlong sprint down the
slope. Up the next incline. The mountains were never downhill
for very long.

Gates himself wasn't with these men. He'd sent his farmhands after Dinah and Warren as if they were stray cattle.

A rabbit bolted past the bushy poison sumac she skirted,
nearly making her fall. Running through the forest was almost
impossible. She'd break her ankle and get caught.

The folds of the mountain were packed together, wrinkle
after wrinkle, pushed up against each other until their tops
cracked into knives. Scrubby undergrowth softened the edges,
but it was all dangerous.

She slowed down. Her options weren't much. Up a tree or
hiding in the rocks somewhere.

They couldn't sneak up on her if she was in a tree. She jumped
to grab a low-hanging branch of a black oak and braced her foot
against the furrowed bark. She'd taught Warren to climb trees
when he was six, and he'd been falling out of them since. The
narrow trunk made it easy to reach around for handholds; she
climbed twenty feet up before she heard them coming. If she could
get another seven to where that spruce leaned into the branches
of the oak, they wouldn't be able to see through the bushy cover.
They were headed her way, but slowing down, searching.

She grabbed the branch over her head, found leverage with
her foot, and hoisted herself up. One more and she'd be behind

the leaning cover of the spruce. She tested the branch above and to her left; it would pull her up behind the green cover.

Almost thirty feet down, three men and a woman strode around the forest floor, poking the clumps of sumac and sapling undergrowth, circling the piles of rock left from landslides. One was definitely Brian Shaw, his face lined and bitter, his bald head a sharp contrast with his heavy red beard.

The branch she'd have to brace her leg on wasn't quite sturdy enough. She could do it if she mostly pulled herself up with her arms and kept the weight off her legs.

The branch groaned but held. She cursed the fact she'd never had the kind of arm strength she wanted and pulled herself up, pushing off the limb below at the last moment to get high enough. A *pop-crack* sounded but she was already up and behind the cover of the spruce.

Nothing fell, thank God, so they probably wouldn't be able to place the sound. They fanned out, the one in flannel heading off west while Brian Shaw and the woman searched the rocks she'd been heading for. The fourth, a stocky white guy in a thermal vest, circled the trees a hundred feet to her right, peering up into the tops.

Cooler air trickled through the branches. Dinah looked up. The cloud cover had thickened, and the tops of the trees swayed, silhouetted against the sky. The breeze wasn't making it all the way down to the forest floor, but it was getting windy out there.

The woman shouted off in the distance, and the paunchy vested man hurried toward the yell. Whatever they'd found, it wasn't her or Warren. Dinah leaned back against the trunk.

She drew in a breath and held it, forcing her ragged breathing to stop. Warren needed her to keep it together.

She and Warren would go to Kara's. She'd climb down from this tree, go get him, and go to Kara's house. They'd figure it out.

Water splashed onto her hand. She looked up. The sky hung low and gray and the tops of the trees were blackened. Lightning crashed across the sky. Splatters struck her face.

Her gaze froze on the sky in shock.

Water. Rain.

The voices below rose. Yelling and crashing. Clearly these people didn't spend much time in the forest. And then all four of them climbed up the hill to her left, walking quickly and no longer glancing around. They walked right past her tree, barely fifteen feet away.

Rain in the mountains, after this much drought, that was flash flood territory. A splatter hit a leaf on the branch next to her, a shiver of fall color.

Shaw's voice carried. "They're kids. They'll die out here if they don't head to the neighbors. We'll watch for them there."

They strode out of earshot, heading for the ravine and their cars before they got caught in a flash flood or lightning took down a tree.

Run them off—had that been the assignment? Gates wouldn't care that Dinah didn't believe her mother's broken neck was an accident. He talked long and loud about how close he and the sheriff were. And if the sheriff believed that it was an accident, no one else would investigate.

Fifteen minutes had to be long enough to wait. If she did something reckless, she'd get them both caught right when they were almost okay.

Finally, she climbed down the tree. The woods were darker, but she could still see just fine.

Getting back to Warren took longer than it should have. No sign of Gates's people as she approached his hiding spot. She checked the treetops and looked into the ravine to make sure. If she had to, she could run again, and Warren would still be safe hidden in the rock.

Nothing. They'd actually left.

"Warren!" she whispered. "They're gone." She scrambled the dozen yards to the rocky shelf. One of the bags lays to the side. She closed her eyes for a moment and exhaled. He was still here. They hadn't found him. "Warren. I'm back."

The bags had tumbled a few feet away from the entrance to the tiny cave.

She froze. Warren lay sprawled next to one of the bags, half out of the cave. Asleep. He must be asleep. She ducked down and rock bit into her hands as she crawled into the space. Dinah shook his thin shoulders under his bulky coat; she dragged him out into the dimming light and kept shaking him.

Blue skin. No, no, no. She placed her palms on the center of his chest and pushed. Again. Again. Endlessly. She couldn't stop.

Tears soaked her face and dripped onto his body. His skin couldn't be blue. His eyes couldn't be unfocused like that. He couldn't be lying here like this.

Dinah couldn't even scream.

#

WATER COLLECTED IN RIVULETS AND HOVERED ON THE DIRT before soaking into the earth. The clay clung to her shovel.

The cars had left, leaving bruised tracks on the grass.

For hours, Dinah dug in her backyard. She dug the grave deep, wide, for all of them. Rain, the first in months, soaked the bottom of the hole and the blanket she'd wrapped around his body.

She'd had no choice but to go home. To take care of them.

When she looked at his face, his closed eyes, resurrection seemed so possible. He'd open his eyes. He'd sit up. Human life couldn't be stopped by something like this. A person couldn't be there one moment and the next, just gone.

Please, God, let people be more than bodies and blood.

She'd pressed the heels of her palms into her eyes for so long they were swollen. Her hands shook on the shovel. The handle had scraped her palms raw, so she wound kitchen towels around them and kept going.

She couldn't think about anything beyond this hole in the ground. Couldn't look at the two figures wrapped in blankets behind her.

Couldn't think about what she had to do next.

It was too deep, now. She jumped down into the grave and stumbled when she landed. It was deep and uneven. She kept digging.

The whole world reduced to her shovel, her hands, and the gulf she tore in the earth.

Dinah pulled the figure in the checked blanket in the grass closer. She had to let gravity help her slide her brother's body into the grave with her. Her arms shook from digging, but she couldn't put him down. Instead, she let her knees buckle, sat down in the grave, and held his body to her chest.

She left him wearing their father's coat—she wanted to tear it off him and she wanted him to have it if he wanted it, so she didn't know what else to do.

Her father had failed them, and now so had she.

She sat with him like that for more than an hour, until her arms had stiffened so much the pain shocked her when she moved.

So what if Gates came back. There was nothing after this.

Dinah set Warren down. She brushed a hand through his sandy hair before covering his face with the blanket. And then she pulled her mother down into the grave, too, and laid her body next to Warren's.

She'd just stay here. All three of them buried in the earth like this. Her whole family together.

When she looked up, all she could see were the dirt walls around her and the gray of the raining sky like a blanket over the grave.

No god was in that sky.

It would be fine to stay here with them. Because she was dead, too.

Warren had been afraid to die. She'd seen it every time he had a coughing fit. He'd said the asthma attacks felt like trying to breathe through a tiny straw. Her mother had been afraid, too—afraid all the time.

Somewhere out there, Gabriel Gates was breathing. He was dry. He was clean. His heart pumped iron and salt through his veins, and his eyes opened and closed when he wanted them to. He would sleep in his bed tonight.

She was still alive enough to make Gabriel Gates afraid to die.

Dinah stood up.

Her shaking arms almost wouldn't hoist her out of the grave. Slick and wet with mud, she caught a knee on the edge and pulled herself a few feet up the dirt wall. A root scraped her knee bloody, but she barely paused. It had to happen right now, this death of one life and rebirth into another, or it wouldn't happen at all. Her fingernails digging into the clay, she scrambled up the last few inches, then collapsed on her stomach in the mud. She rolled over to face the sky and closed her eyes against the rain.

He had bought everything and paid for nothing, but he would pay for her family.

She'd stop his heart. She'd take his lungs. She'd break his neck for what he'd done.

Dinah rose to her feet. She pushed the first shovel of dirt

down into the grave. The muffled crush of dirt hitting the quilts sounded like summer, like hoeing in the garden and sifting through soil to pull out the rocks. Like planting tomatoes and melons, all four of them sweating in the early spring sun.

She picked a smooth gray stone out of the dirt and rubbed it between her fingers before shoving it in her pocket.

The mud cooled her palms. She held them up. Her skin was blistered and raw, bleeding, but all she felt was a distant heat.

Her clothing dripped rain. She'd left the bags back in the woods. She hadn't been able to carry them and Warren.

She couldn't live here anymore, but she could shower. If Gates came back before she left, that would just make things easier. Before she went inside, Dinah lifted the latch on the plank door to the henhouse. It swung open.

The chickens would probably be caught by feral dogs. But being hunted was better than dying in the henhouse, trapped and waiting on someone to save them. At least this way they'd have a chance.

Dinah climbed the steps to the house. The door still hung open. She pulled off her boots and crossed the living room in her wet socks.

She turned on the five-minute water conservation timer to get the shower to work. Cold water poured from the showerhead and struck her skin, but she'd been wet and numb for hours, so this didn't make a difference. Shivering, she rinsed the dirt from her hair and fingernails and focused on the mud-stained water swirling down the drain. The five minutes the shower timer allowed wouldn't cut it, so she had to sit shivering in the tub for another ten until it unlocked and she could reset it.

They'd stopped buying propane for the water heater when

she was six, so she barely remembered hot showers. In the winter, her mother had used the large woodstove to heat pans of water to warm up baths in the tub.

Dinah sat on her bed to pull on dry socks and then changed into clean pants and a long-sleeved shirt. She lifted her guitar case from behind the couch. She'd come back. After Gabriel Gates was dead, she'd come back home.

A small thing, flat and white, lay in the driveway. Dinah nudged it with her boot. A yellow strip of split peel showed underneath.

A pear. Flattened by a tire. After she'd kicked over the bucket yesterday, it must have rolled far enough away that she'd missed it.

The rain had slowed to a hesitant drizzle. She carried the flat, gray river rock with their handprints from beside the steps over to the grave. It wasn't much of a headstone, but it was something.

She walked across her yard and paused in the road. Kara's house lay just across the ravine. The yellow glow of the windows shone in the dusk. Maisy whinnied loudly, the sound carrying from the hilltop. Kara must be going out to feed her for the night.

Go to Kara's, her mother had said. She could curl up on Mrs. Hernández's couch and stare at the warm sunset walls until she fell asleep. Kara would clean and bandage Dinah's hands. They'd figure out what to do.

But then what. He'd sent men to chase them through the woods. Why had he bothered? He'd tell his story to Sheriff Anders and that would be it. So why try to kill them? Because she'd thrown a knife at him, bitten him? Because Warren had shot at him? Because they'd made him angry?

Left turn to Kara's, or right turn to town.

Shaw had said they'd be watching the neighbors. If she went to any of her neighbors' houses, they would defend her if Gates came looking. And that would mean more bodies.

She would have to look Kara in the eyes and say my life is gone. And she'd have to say why.

When her family had needed her most, she'd failed them. She hadn't filled the gap her father had left, like her mom had said, or righted his wrongs, or done anything but abandoned them, too.

The guitar fell out of her hands as she bent over and puked.

Dinah wiped her mouth. Picked up her guitar.

Right turn. One foot in front of the other, into the woods beside the road to town.

Dinah reached the bags as the light filtering through the trees began to dim. She pulled out Warren's boots and his sweaters, repacked everything into one backpack. The bag, her guitar case, and the water.

The load was almost too heavy to carry, but struggling with it gave her something to focus on. Without the weight to lift, she might sit down and never get back up.

She left Warren's boots resting on top of his folded sweaters in the split in the rocks.

A mile with the backpack was exhausting, but she finally hit the rise of rocks that had framed her backyard for her entire childhood. A depression in the rock wall meant she had cover at her back and over her head. A fire in front of her would keep the animals away.

Town was fifteen miles to the east. Less than fifteen, now.

She scraped the ground bare in a wide circle. Found some dry leaves and sticks under the rock ledge. Building a fire was easy. While the sticks crackled, she cleaned the gun. It had sat in the dirt by the grave, in the rain, while she dug. She slid out the bolt and the magazine, cleaned the action and the barrel before oiling and reassembling it. After loading it and checking the safety, she set the gun under the rock ledge where it wouldn't get wet if it rained again.

Not until she shook out the tarp on the ground and rolled up in the blanket did Dinah pull out the stone she'd taken from the grave.

Somewhere today, a hole had torn open in the universe and she'd stepped through it into a void where things like this could happen.

A dog howled, the baying sound of a hound mix. She touched her knife, making sure it was still right by her hand.

The fire burned brightly. Orange and gold flames, crackling and popping, trails of smoke. Dinah pulled the blanket tighter and closed her eyes, and the heat warmed her eyelids and cheekbones. Eyes still closed, she watched the light of the fire play against the forest in front of her, and when she fell asleep, she saw gray eyes and blue lips, and tasted blood in her mouth.

DINAH SAT BOLT UPRIGHT, HER SKIN PRICKLING. NOTHING MOVED, no strange noises nearby.

The sun was high in the sky, and the fire was down to coals again. She'd have to tease it back to life. She shifted the ash and tossed on a few handfuls of pine needles. They smoked but still burned. Because her legs were falling asleep, she stood up and found the hatchet. Part of her knew getting wood was important, but the rest of her was angry that wood could matter right now or ever again.

Beyond the giant fallen limb lay two broken branches, crossed over each other in a dead, drying X. A few well-placed strikes, and she'd have her firewood. She climbed over the fallen tree and kicked the logs to make sure snakes weren't hiding under it. A centipede and a dozen ants scurried away, but nothing larger.

The wood gave way under a few strokes. The logs weren't big enough to last very long, but she didn't care.

An armload should be enough. It would have to be.

Dinah trudged back to her spot. As she stepped over the limb, she froze. Something moved through the trees. From here she couldn't see what. She waited a moment but didn't see anything else, so she kept walking.

A few yards from her bag, she stopped. A feral hound was dragging her backpack away. He dropped it by the fire, which was now dead again, and dug at the top of the heavy bag.

Shit. Dinah crouched and quietly set down her armload of wood. She pulled the knife from her belt and stood back up.

He was huge. Powerful tawny shoulders, a long whip tail, saggy-jowled muzzle.

That backpack had everything she owned in it.

She stepped closer. His ears pricked up and his dark eyes focused on her. His black lips lifted in a snarl around the fabric of her bag. He'd found food, and he wasn't going to give it up.

"Go away!" She grabbed a log from the pile she'd set down

and threw it at him. It fell with a thud by the backpack. He jumped but didn't leave. The second one she threw struck him in the ribs. He barked and dropped the bag. Instead of running away, he lowered his head and growled.

She gripped her knife. She could throw it and hit him from here, but it might not kill, and then she'd have nothing. Her other knives were still by the fire.

If she stepped back, he'd chase her. Nowhere to go but forward. Make noise. She waved her arms and yelled. He crouched just a little, and Dinah knew he was going to run for her before he did it.

She had her knife up when he hit her. His weight knocked her down, but she stabbed him in the shoulder. He yelped and his giant slobbery jaws snapped. Dinah kicked his stomach and rolled over, struggling to get up, but he was on top of her in a fury of paws and teeth.

Maybe she should let him. At least then she'd be done.

His teeth pierced her left bicep and dug in. She screamed and pain scorched her whole arm. He wasn't letting go. His neck was exposed. She gripped her knife and swung.

His breathing gurgled and blood sprayed out from the wound. His jaws released. She'd punctured his throat.

Dinah scrambled to her feet. He stumbled back, swayed, and fell. She couldn't watch that.

Her shoulder burned and just the weight of her arm was too much. She stumbled around the dying dog and back to her bags.

Why this, too?

She grabbed the backpack and hauled it with her good arm back to the blanket. A first aid kit was in there, shoved to the side. She pulled up her sleeve and grimaced. Her upper arm was mangled meat.

Her head swam and her vision blurred, so she held still for a moment and inhaled slowly.

Okay. Iodine. She could do this. So she didn't have to use both hands, she braced the bottle between her knees and unscrewed the cap. Her eyes watered as she tried to flush out the wound.

Flush, seal, wrap. She had to do it. Wincing every time her fingers touched the inflamed flesh, she spread a thin layer of antibiotic salve over her arm, and then wrapped it in strips of cloth from the kit.

Now she had to go back near the dog to get the wood. Her whole body was crawling with chills.

One armload of wood turned into three when she could only use one arm. Fiddling with the dying coals was too painful, so she used one of her matches to start a pile of twigs and sat there to feed the tiny flames.

She had to get rid of that carcass if she didn't want big cats or wolves coming for it. Though, maybe that was the answer. If she stayed here and a cougar came for the carcass and killed her, that was just nature. She'd be like a deer or a rabbit, there as food. Part of the cycle for something with bigger teeth and claws.

Maybe that was the case, regardless.

But she didn't want to look at it anymore, so she trudged over to the dead dog and grabbed a hind leg with her right hand. The dog's coarse fur rubbed her already raw palm. The ravine wasn't far, but dragging an animal through the forest with a torn-up arm and bloody hands took her twice as long as it should have. She pushed the body over the edge of the ravine with her foot and didn't watch it fall.

The fire was burning steadily when she returned. Dinah sank to the ground and wrapped up in her blanket.

She needed to get up. She needed to find Gates. But all she could do was lie there, feeling her bones turn numb as they pressed into the earth.

She felt like she'd stopped breathing without even knowing it. Like the gray fog inside her had suffocated the impulses that said lungs, breathe. Heart, beat. And it had taken her a while to notice that disconnected parts of her body hadn't been talking to each other.

But it was a good thing. It kept her close to them. If they weren't breathing and she wasn't either, then at least they still shared that.

By the time she woke up, the blisters on her palms had burst and her knuckles were sticky with seeping blood. When she sat up, the stiffness in her muscles made her groan. Moving her left arm was ridiculously painful. She dug the water jug out of the backpack and poured a little on her hands to wash off the blood.

It must be early afternoon already, and somehow she had to clean her arm again. She pulled her knees up to her chest and rested her forehead on them for a moment.

Procrastinating wouldn't make it hurt any less. She unwrapped the cloth strips. It didn't look too bad. A little inflamed, maybe. Flushing it out with iodine was hard one-handed and from the side, and she wasn't doing a thorough job of it. She applied salve and wrapped it in a clean bandage. Maybe it didn't look great, but she couldn't bother with getting help for it right now.

She kicked dirt over the smoldering coals and shouldered the backpack on her good side.

Gates lived on the other side of St. George, and that meant she was heading toward town.

A little over fifteen miles away. She wouldn't make it there today, but maybe by tomorrow morning. Her best bet was to find the road and stick inside the woods a few yards. She'd have taken her bike and used the road if she wasn't certain he had people watching for her. And he couldn't know where she was yet. Better for her to find him than for him to find her.

She touched the smooth pebble in her pocket and the knife on her belt, reminding herself they were still there.

She was the only person in these mountains who didn't owe Gates anything.

He owed her.

St. George used to be bigger. Abandoned houses and closed businesses skirted the ten busy streets that made up the town. Farms and small ranches spread out from it, but every year more fences came down between them—Gates's money spreading like a disease, infecting everyone until he owned their jobs and their homes and their heartbeats.

Dinah's own pulse felt weak, sick. Dizzy. The dog bite had gotten infected since yesterday, and now her whole arm was swollen. Her skin was stretched too tight, angry and red. And that meant she couldn't go around past the town and bang on the door of his ranch house. Not with yellow spots blooming in her vision.

She'd walked through St. George all afternoon, looking for the doctor's office. But it was empty, the schedule on the door showing he'd come around again in three days.

If she was going to live long enough to find Gates, she needed water and a doctor. And the sun was tipping toward the mountains, so she only had about an hour and a half until it was totally dark.

Her boots kicked up puffs of dust as she walked down Main Street. People moved around her, carrying grocery bags and dinging bicycle bells. A few motorcycles and lighter motorbikes buzzed up and down the street.

She'd been to St. George a lot when she was younger— sometimes she'd go with her dad to his garage to help him on Saturdays. She'd run errands and go to the package center to pick up orders for the garage, and he'd buy her an hour of time at the media den where she could use the computers for games she couldn't play on her school tablet. A few times he'd let her bring Kara and they'd play pinball together or watch shows on the wall screen. And once a year, her family and Kara's family and the McCaffreys all loaded up in the bed of the Franklins' truck and Mrs. Franklin drove all of them into town for the Christmas church service.

But otherwise, without a car and with no money to spend, there wasn't much reason to go to town. And since the school was farther north so it could reach Wright County too, she'd only been to St. George a handful of times in the past few years. And that at least meant no one was likely to recognize her.

She paused by the post office and sat down to lean against the empty flagpole, partially because her dad used to come here to get his deliveries for the garage and partially because she couldn't walk any farther. After the national mail service had collapsed, Gabriel Gates had set up his own package delivery service headquartered in the post office. He also owned the seed and feed company and the hotel above the bar, and he was on the school board. Mitch Harding, Judge Harding's son and Gates's buddy, was also on the school board, and she'd seen her teachers and now Kara struggle with funding cuts and new policies from the board so many times the dysfunction seemed like a normal part of school.

All she wanted was to sleep.

No, what she wanted was for her arm to be fine enough for her to have skirted town and kept going to the sprawling ranch in the valley. But she had to get her arm taken care of first. She had to figure out a way to do that, once she stood up.

A kid ran past her, carrying a bag, feet pounding on the sidewalk. All she saw of him were speeding legs and a flash of sandy-blond hair. He ducked behind the post office into the alley, just as a group of boys reached the cross street. One of them pointed to the alley, and all five of them ran behind the building.

Five boys on one kid. She sighed.

Dinah stood up and shouldered her bag again. She rounded the corner.

The boys, yelling and shoving, circled a heap of something in the alley. Dinah set her guitar down, grabbed one of them by the shoulder, and whirled him around. Her fist caught him on the nose and cheekbone, and it hurt her raw palm in a way that woke her up. The boy dropped to his knees, holding his nose and screaming.

Dinah shook her hand out. All the boys looked fourteen or fifteen. Young predators, smart enough to travel in a pack.

The boy with the broken nose wailed loudly enough that they all stopped kicking and taunting the heap on the ground and turned toward her. She backed up a step and pulled her knife from her belt.

The boy she'd seen running was the heap on the ground, lying pretty damn still.

His leg was twisted and his face so dirty she couldn't tell if he was really as young as he looked. His shirt hung in tatters and his bag had been flung across the alley. But he didn't have sandy-blond hair. His hair was brown.

Dinah set her feet. "You guys gonna leave, or are you gonna do something?"

One of the boys rushed at her, and the other three followed him. She kicked the first one in the groin, then bent and came up with a second knife from her boot. She kept her voice steady. If they could tell she was winded and her arm hurt, she wouldn't be able to handle all five of them. "I'm done punching. And the doctor won't be able to sew you up for another three days. So if you don't want to bleed until then, get out of here."

The three boys left standing shuffled back. "Let's go," one of the older kids muttered. "Not worth getting stabbed." The shortest one darted for the boy's bag.

"Don't touch that. You kids get out of this alley right now. All of you. Get up." She kicked the leg of the kid with the bleeding nose.

This was making her feel better. Her head was clearer right now than it had been for the last two days.

The two boys on the ground struggled to their feet and all five of them, grumbling and swearing at her, straggled out of the alley. She backed toward the boy and watched them leave.

The kid lying in the dirt groaned and tried to sit up. It was hard to tell how badly he was hurt.

"Hey," she said. "You okay?"

"Uh. I think so." But the boy was holding his wrist funny, and even though he was sitting up, he was kind of doubled over.

She knelt down by him. "Lemme see. What hurts?" Her brain must have filled in sandy hair, big gray eyes, because this kid didn't look at all like Warren.

"I'm fine. It's not bad." He was twelve, maybe thirteen. Older than she'd thought, but still. He seemed nervous, constantly looking toward the street, but he didn't move away from her.

She kept her voice quiet. "I'm Dinah. What's your name?"

"Cole." He let her check over his arm. She made him flex his wrist and track her finger with his eyes.

This should have been her helping someone who needed it, but it was only her rewinding time. Forcing the world back to four days ago, when she would have been cleaning Warren's cuts and checking his wrist after a fall from his bike or a tree.

"Just a second." She slid her backpack off her shoulders and dug around before pulling out her little medical case. Cole simply stared at her.

"What'd they want?" she asked.

He shrugged. "My deliveries, like always. Last time they got my bag, and my boss was so pissed I probably would have gotten fired if they'd gotten it away from me this time. My first job doesn't cover everything, so I really need the tips from this one."

"That's not right. I'm sorry."

Cole reached for his bag. "I can deal."

"Yeah, but you shouldn't have to." Cuts and blossoming bruises covered his pale face and arms. His peach-white skin was discolored from the dirt ground into it. She should be helping this boy just because of that, not because she wanted Warren to be here and alive.

"So you have a second job?" she asked.

He nodded. "This one is my second job. My main job is at the big ranch. Mr. Gates has me cleaning his barns."

Dinah slowly raised her head. He met her gaze straight on.

Everyone had to get by somehow. So he cleaned the man's barns.

No matter who he was, he deserved to have someone help him just because he'd been hurt.

She gave him water in some kind of failed atonement so he could rinse out his mouth and wash his face. She cleaned his cuts with iodine and applied some of her salve, made him stretch out his arm and wiggle his fingers. The whole time she chatted quietly with him about everything—his jobs, why she had a guitar with her, what he listened to on the radio. Everything except what had happened. The boy actually responded, even grinning a few times.

And then he picked at his shoe. "You said your name is Dinah—does your family have a well?"

She never should have told him her name. "Why?"

He looked up. "I don't think you should be in town. Mr. Gates was talking to the barn manager and his foreman about you. He thinks you ran off somewhere."

If he told Gates she was here, it would all be over. And she hadn't thought Gates even knew her first name. "What else did he say? Did he say anything about my home?"

Cole shrugged. "Just that he's got a guy running some kind of project there. I shouldn't tell you this—you can't be in town, and you shouldn't go back there, either."

Someone was working at her house? Someone else was there already?

Dinah eased back from Cole a little.

"Don't worry," he said quietly. "I won't say I saw you."

The packed dirt floor of the alley was seeping cold into her jeans. The night breeze gusted chills up her jacket sleeves and down the neck of her shirt. Cole looked toward the end of the alley, and so did she—this space with high walls and only two ways out felt like a trap.

Something rattled above them. On the roof of the building beside them stood a man. He was so backlit by the sun she could barely see him. Dinah leaped up and unsheathed her knife.

The man climbed down the side of the building, jumped the last few feet to the alley.

Not a man, really. Maybe eighteen, twenty. Tall, white and tanned by the sun, wiry under his bulky jacket.

Cole scrambled up. Lines settled on his forehead. "Hey."

The guy flipped his collar up against the breeze. "You okay?" he asked Cole.

"Just some kids trying to take his stuff. We handled it," Dinah said. "Who're you?" She turned the handle of her knife over and over in her hand.

Cole gathered up his things. "Johnny's my brother. He's okay." He glanced at her for barely a second. "I gotta go. Thanks. See you around, I guess."

"Wait," Johnny said. "I went home, saw Dad. Dropped off some stuff. He said he hadn't seen you in two days. You gotta check in more than that. Sleep at the house. Where you live."

Cole nodded. His lip and cheekbone still bled, his shirt was torn, and he moved like he was sore, but otherwise he looked alright. With one more glance at her, he jogged down the alley and disappeared around the corner.

Dinah shoved the water jug and her first aid kit into her

backpack. She winced as she shouldered the bag. "I need antibiotics. Is there anywhere in town I can get that tonight?"

But this Johnny guy took a moment to answer. He was obviously looking her over, she just couldn't tell if he was checking her out or if he recognized her somehow. Like maybe he knew Gates was looking for her. If Cole knew, his brother might.

"Is there?" she asked again.

He gestured to her hands, to the sores and blisters. "What happened? Are you okay?"

It took her a moment to find words. "That's not your business." She turned to leave.

He grabbed her good arm, but then instantly let her go. "Sorry. I wanted to say, thanks for helping Cole. Taking on those boys."

Dinah turned back around. "How did you know I did that?"

He nodded to the warehouse. "I was on the roof."

Cruel, that he would sit there and let that happen. "And you didn't help?"

Johnny snorted. "Cole would have been super pissed if he knew I saw him getting beat up. He gets angry and defensive when he so much as has a bruise. He'd hate knowing I saw someone rescue him." When she didn't change her expression, he shifted from one foot to the other and said quietly, "I would've jumped down if things got bad."

Things had gotten bad. Five teenagers had kicked his little brother until he couldn't get back up.

Dinah turned away. She was done with this guy.

"Painkillers," Johnny said. "Some over-the-counter stuff. You can get that at the general store, but they won't have antibiotics."

Dinah turned and left him in the alley.

She made it four blocks before she had to sit down again. Her arm had started throbbing, but all she could do was clean it out again. It was just a bite. It shouldn't keep her from what she had to do like this.

A straw. Like breathing through a tiny straw, Warren had said. It made her own chest hurt so much she couldn't breathe, either.

Three other travelers with bags had passed her since she sat down on the sidewalk. A lot of vagrants, a lot of homeless travelers. People walked by, either briefly glancing or ignoring her entirely. She wasn't unusual.

She looked up to the pale moon and the stars starting to show. Dusk was almost gone.

Something along one of the rooftops moved. A person— jumping from roof to roof. And then they disappeared.

Difficult way to travel. A good one, though, if someone didn't want to be seen.

Dinah rested her head on her knees for a full minute before taking a drink and standing up.

Back down the street.

Get medication, break into an empty house at the edge of town to sleep, find Gates in the morning. Cole was right that she shouldn't let Gates see her, and that was bound to happen if she stayed in town long. But she'd be delirious by morning if she didn't get the infection in her arm handled.

And she couldn't use Kara's money. Now that the well was gone, Kara would need it even more.

They would all know she was gone by now. Kara, her family, everyone. Kara would be messaging her tablet and not getting a response. They would have all come over to help with canning and found the house empty.

Or a stranger inside it.

The bell on the general store door jingled when she opened it. Small grocery items, basic household supplies, and a shelf of bottled beer and whiskey lined the back wall. A long counter separated customers from the small goods, medication included; only items too large to pocket were out on the floor.

She scanned the bottles behind the counter as she waited in the line of customers. "Do you have antibiotics or anything for infections?" she asked when she was next in line.

The boy backed up a step. "You got a disease?" Black hair buzzed short, dark brown skin with rosy undertones. Wide brown eyes full of questions. He looked maybe twelve, a little older than Warren.

People were looking at her. She shook her head. "Dog bite."

He stuffed a green glass bottle into a cloth bag for the man he was serving. "Nope. Some salve, but otherwise just painkillers or cold syrups."

"Will you take anything besides cash?" She could not spend Kara's savings on this ridiculous bite.

The kid snorted. "Nope."

"Where's the owner?" Dinah asked.

The kid dropped three cans of vegetables and a tin of tuna into the cloth bag. "In the back, but he'll say the same thing."

"I want to ask him myself."

The kid sighed and set the bag on the counter. "Twelve dollars and thirty-two cents," he said to the customer, then yelled over his shoulder, "Denton!"

"Twelve?" The customer checked the bag. "Why twelve?"

The boy shrugged. "The moonshine's gone up. Who's next? Next order?"

The customer grumbled and counted out change as a white man in a checked flannel shirt and jeans strode out of the doorway behind the counter.

Dinah shoved through the crowd to his end of the long counter.

"Denton Marlow." He spread his hands on the counter. "What do you want?"

"You guys are busy." She raised her voice over the chatter of people. Sweat and road dust hung heavy in the air, but she had to smell worse after two days in the woods.

"Not busier than we can handle. Me and the kid keep on top of it." He looked her up and down. "Sorry. Not hiring."

Dinah looked around the store. "When do you clean?" Dirt layered the floor and the merchandise on the shelves. Boot tracks marked a path through the aisles.

"When we got to." Denton stacked a pile of loose papers next to the cash register.

Dinah leaned forward on the counter. "I'll do it. Tonight. I'll clean everything if you let me shower and have some ibuprofen." It wouldn't kill the infection, but if it took down the swelling and her fever, that might be enough.

The man's eyebrows lowered. "You'll steal everything you can carry if I let you run around here at night. I'd have to stay up to watch you."

She tried to keep the panic out of her voice. "You don't even have to pay me. Just let me shower and have a few pills."

He paused his shuffling of papers to look at her closely. The lines around his eyes relaxed. "Fine. You shower immediately. And you can sleep in the woodshed, if you want."

She gripped the counter. "Really? Oh, thank you, you have no idea—"

"No stealing or I'll have Sheriff Anders run you out of town."

She bent to pick up her guitar case. "I swear. Won't bother anything."

"Bathroom's this way." He disappeared through the doorway behind the counter.

A tiny apartment hid beyond the doorway—a living room, kitchen, bedroom combo and a bathroom to the side. He flipped on the light in the bathroom. She stood in the doorway, holding her guitar case. Denton wasn't leaving.

He looked her up and down again. "You been digging in the dirt?"

"Um, the woods. I walked here." She set her guitar down.

Denton nodded. "I've jiggered the timer on the shower, so it works for ten minutes instead of five. Just get clean."

He finally stepped out of the bathroom and let her in. She didn't want to leave her guitar sitting out in the apartment like that, but he might think it was rude to take it into the bathroom with her. She couldn't offend this guy.

The bathroom door didn't have a lock. She looked at the door for a moment, but it wasn't like she could do anything about it. Dinah set her backpack against the door and stripped. Dirt and bits of leaves fell out of her clothing. Disgusting.

The shower was just a cement box with a plastic curtain, but it was clean. She turned on the conservation timer and stuck her hand into the water to test it. She yelped and jerked her hand back. Hot water. Actual hot water.

Simply rinsing the dirt off her body took the better part of ten minutes. The water and soap stung her palms and broke a few of the blisters on her fingers, but it was probably good for her hands.

She wasn't sure if it was good for her arm or not. Her pulse throbbed in the bite, and streaks of red were edging out from the marks. Cleaning it one-armed from the side was nearly impossible. She gritted her teeth and let the water rinse the whole area, but the streams were high pressure and it hurt so badly she saw fluorescent spots.

It didn't occur to her until after she stepped out of the shower that the only towel in the room was a frayed one already hanging on a hook.

Lice. Germs. Plus, disgusting. She used a t-shirt from her backpack to dry off and pulled on clean underwear, a clean shirt, and her other pair of pants.

Toweling her hair off with the damp shirt completely soaked the fabric. Her hair looked so dark when it was wet; she looked more like her mom like that.

Mirrors would be the only way she'd ever see her mother again.

Dinah slid her comb back into the bag and opened the door. Denton looked up. He was stirring a pan on top of a plug-in single stove burner. He nodded to the table. "You hungry?" A plate of scrambled eggs sat on the tiny kitchen table along with the bottle of ibuprofen.

"Um—yeah. Thanks." She sat down on the chair and looked around for her guitar. Still where she left it. Her shoulders relaxed a little.

"Coffee?"

She turned around. "You have coffee?"

He set a mug in front of her. "I got cream and sugar if you want it."

Dinah nodded. "Thank you." Her mom had collected odd change in a jar by the kitchen sink and was only able to buy coffee maybe twice a year. Once a year since her dad had left. Dinah had quit drinking it so her mom's supply would last longer.

He clunked a jar of cream and a bowl of sugar on the table and then sat down with his own plate of eggs.

Owning a store here must be a great job if you didn't have kids to take care of.

Maybe that was the reason her father had left. When she couldn't stop herself from thinking about him, she'd lie in bed at night and sort through it. Guilt over losing the garage. Regret from not having found another way out. Maybe just the constant erosion of not being able to do his share to feed them, get Warren medical care, pay off the debt. He'd always said they were too poor to be able to worry about what Gates and other people with money were doing. They had to handle their own business and let everyone else handle theirs. But now look what had happened.

St. George even had its own Economic Prosperity Commission, which was supposed to help with job creation and new construction and policies that would help the local businesses, but it hadn't done anything that she knew of, and when her father had gone to them before his garage closed, they hadn't helped him, either. Even though Mitch Harding sat on the commission and so did Gates's foreman. Her father had insisted that they would help because they were good businessmen who supported small businesses. But apparently there was a difference between their small businesses and his.

Maybe in the end, he'd just traded having a family for coffee and hot water and not having to wonder if the meat would last through the winter. She brushed the outline of Warren's stone in her pocket with her thumb.

She would have rather died than leave them.

Denton stabbed his eggs with his fork, so she took a sip of coffee. Not watery and gritty—rich and smooth and earthy. She tossed back three of the pills and when she put three in her pocket for later, Denton didn't stop her.

She'd be okay for tonight. One thing at a time, and she could do this.

Denton stood up. "The kid is running the counter by himself. You come out with me and start some cleaning."

Now that she'd gotten the chance to look at him, he was older than she'd thought. High forehead with fine lines there and around his eyes. Gray weaving from his temples into his brown ponytail.

Dinah pushed herself to her feet. He led her behind the counter and pulled a metal bucket and a rag from the lower shelves, then took a look at her palms and handed her a pair of rubber gloves.

Wiping shelves would be easy as long as she didn't use her bad arm. The boy behind the counter caught her eye. He raised his eyebrows when he saw her with the bucket, but he gave her a thumbs-up.

Cleaning the shelves, windows, counters, and stacks of canned food took her most of the evening, and her right arm wore out too fast from doing all the scrubbing one-handed.

Even with the door propped open, the air was musty from so many bodies. People bumped around her and nearly spilled her bucket as they hoisted sacks of fertilizer and animal feed, coils of rope, and buckets of brined pork ends. One in four asked for a bottle of the moonshine behind the counter—green glass bottles with corks.

Most of the items were secondhand: hammers with worn

handles, used clothing hanging on a rack. Even, way at the back of the store, a shelf of used books. Only a few, but still. With the books stood a plastic folder. Pausing for a moment to rest her arms, she pulled her gloves off, lifted it down, and flipped it open.

Sheet music. What she wouldn't do for something like this. No one she knew had sheet music—they'd have to pay for both computer time and printing in a media den. Mostly everyone played songs by ear or listened to whatever was on the radio.

But she knew there was better music out there than what she could play. Songs she didn't know. Kinds of music she hadn't heard before. These beautiful little notes on the page, each holding a piece of a mystery, of what they all would be played together.

If Denton caught her looking at this, he'd think she was stealing. Dinah tucked it back on the shelf.

By nine o'clock, the store had emptied. She'd just finished sweeping the dirt out into the street when a hand touched her shoulder. She whirled around.

Denton took the broom from her. "That's enough for now. Come have a drink."

A drink. This night just kept getting stranger. Dinah followed him behind the counter.

The kid, Victor, climbed down his ladder after restocking the shelves. "So how long are you working here for?"

Maybe younger boys would always remind her of Warren. Her throat tightened. "Just tonight."

Denton pulled a corked green glass bottle from under the cash register. He shuffled back to the apartment and returned with three glasses. He cracked the wax seal on the moonshine and pulled out the cork. "Ever had this?"

"No." And she shouldn't drink, not with her arm so bad, but

what did it matter? No one was left to stop her.

Denton poured three glasses. Victor picked up his, tensed like he was bracing himself for something, and took a swallow. He looked awfully young for that.

"What?" he demanded. "My dad says if I'm old enough to work, I'm old enough to drink." He took an even bigger swallow and coughed when he set his glass down.

It couldn't be that bad. She'd had whiskey once or twice before. Mrs. McCaffrey had let her try it when she'd made hot toddies at their Christmas party last year.

Denton pushed his stool closer to hers and handed her the drink before sitting down. She sniffed her glass—sharp, pungent—and took a sip.

She gagged. Rubbing alcohol. That's what this had to be. "What is this?"

Denton grinned. He pulled a cigar out from under the counter and lit it, then clenched it between his teeth. "That's moonshine."

It tasted about like she'd expect gasoline to taste, but she took another sip. Disgusting, and it burned.

Victor lifted his glass. "No, no. You've got to drink more than that at once. Really take a swallow. I'll do it with you."

Like breathing through a tiny straw. That's what he'd said. Every time she paused, she imagined it. "Okay, fine. Three, two, one." She swallowed almost half what was in her glass before common sense could stop her.

She was barely able to swallow before coughing. Her throat felt like it had been opened right up, and fumes scorched her stomach. But the burn from her lips down to her gut was cathartic. "Not too bad."

Victor laughed and Denton waved his cigar. "It's what people want around here. Undercuts the whiskey and beer Gates and Harding ship in. And it's better, too. Sometimes we get special batches made with strawberries."

The air hung heavy with Denton's cigar smoke. She took another swallow, almost finishing her glass. She shouldn't be sitting here drinking with strangers. She should be at home, playing guitar on the porch while Warren closed up the henhouse for the night.

But instead, some stranger, some ranch hand who worked for that man, was living in her house.

Dinah stared into her glass at the clear liquid. If it wasn't thicker than water, lazier swirling around in her glass, she might not know the difference.

Denton took her glass and refilled it before she could say she didn't want anymore.

She'd been feeling increasingly queasy for the last several hours, and the food had only helped a little.

It didn't matter how sick she was—she could have, eventually, made it to Gates's house tonight. Knocked on his door. Why had she done this instead?

Victor jumped down off his stool. "I gotta get home. Mom doesn't like me staying long after. See you around."

"Okay, kid." Denton waved him off.

"Does he live close?" Her gaze followed him out the back door. "It's dark."

He watched her over the rim of his drink. "Just down the block. This is my alley here. He's fine."

Dinah swirled the liquid in her glass and let it wash against the sides. She didn't want to sit here drinking with him with no one else around. "I should go to bed so I can get that floor scrubbed before customers come. What time do you open?"

Now he watched her glass. "Five. Aren't you going to drink that?"

She was dehydrated and exhausted. "I have to get up at four if I'm going to clean the floor. I should go to bed."

Denton watched her without moving, like he was thinking, and then he turned away and stared at the end of his cigar. "Well, here's the problem." He took her glass and downed the rest. "I happened to hear Gates wanted to know if a girl came to town, one with hair like yours and about your age. And if I bring you in, maybe he does me a favor sometime."

Dinah had her knife up before he stood. Why. Why had she hesitated like this? "You're not bringing me anywhere."

She lifted her backpack to her good shoulder, which meant she had to hold her knife with her left hand, and she wasn't at all sure she'd be able to stop him left-handed. The gun was strapped to her backpack. She'd never get it free in time.

Denton walked toward her.

She grabbed her guitar case and backed out the door to the alley. He followed her, and the door banged shut behind him. "Put the knife down, girl. You'll get hurt with it."

She headed down the alley. Killing Gates, standing on his doorstep with Warren's gun. She wanted that so badly she could taste it like she could still taste the dirty metal of his blood.

She'd hesitated, she'd let a minor injury stop her, and now look what it would cost.

Denton's words caught her. "You're supposed to have a little brother with you, aren't you? Where'd you leave the kid?"

Dinah kept walking. When he came up behind her, she

dropped the guitar case and whirled around, knife up. He lunged to the side and grabbed her infected arm, grinding his fingers into the inflamed tissue. The knife fell out of her hand and she screamed. Her knees buckled. But she forced herself up and slammed her knee into his groin. He stumbled backward and fell. Her guitar case snapped when he landed, the splintering song of the body crushing.

Pain vibrated through her arm so badly she bent over and braced her hands against her knees to keep from throwing up.

Denton staggered to his feet.

Someone leaped down from the roof across the alley. He grabbed her and flung her aside. She stumbled into the wall of the shed and slid down against it.

**S**HE HADN'T BEEN ABLE TO KEEP ONE SINGLE PROMISE. NOT *it will be okay*, not *I'll take care of it*, not *I'll save you*, not *I'll kill him*. Slumped against the woodshed behind the general store might well be where she'd die, and then what? She wouldn't even be buried at home.

Between her and Denton stood Cole's brother, Johnny. He'd thrown her against the shed. She couldn't quite get her feet under her. The cracked cement beneath her boots swam every time she moved her head.

Denton took a step forward, looming huge in the dark. "You."

A piece of pipe dangled from Johnny's hand. Dinah ducked purely from reflex when he swung it. The pipe slammed Denton's face. He drunk-stumbled backward and then went down.

No movement. Johnny walked toward him.

Dinah grabbed the corner of the shed to pull herself up. A slow breath once she was on her feet, and she followed Johnny.

Blood trickled down Denton's face from a split on his cheekbone.

Johnny crouched down and touched the man's wrist with a surprisingly gentle hand, considering he'd just knocked the man out. "His pulse is fine. I didn't hit him that hard. Pretty light pipe."

He still wasn't moving. "What if he dies?"

Johnny shrugged. "He shouldn't have attacked you. Hey, also, sorry. I had to get you out of the way quick so he couldn't grab you. Are you okay?" Still crouched by Denton, he squinted up at her.

No. She was not. "I'm fine. Thanks."

He nodded. Stood up. "It's Johnny, by the way. Johnny Buchanan."

She took a step back. "I remember. How did you—where were you?"

Johnny shifted his weight from one foot to the other. "I heard you scream."

Lie. "I screamed two seconds before you grabbed me."

"Well, fine. I was on the roof. I saw him come out." He gestured over his shoulder.

Her legs were shaking now, and she couldn't get them to stop. "My stuff is behind you. Can you—I can't—"

"I got it." He turned around, grabbed her smashed guitar and backpack. "This is pretty much done for." He opened the guitar case.

The neck had snapped, and the body was completely crushed. "Just leave it here."

Johnny slung her backpack over his own shoulder. "Sorry. That sucks. Come on. Inside."

Because she didn't know what else to do and couldn't stay

standing much longer, Dinah followed him.

"What does he owe you?" Johnny turned on the light in the store.

"Nothing. I cleaned in return for a shower and ibuprofen."

"But he didn't honor his deal and he broke your guitar. So, pick something you need."

She leaned against the wall to keep from falling over. Her arm was burning hot. Nausea washed through her in waves. Johnny moved, and she flinched before seeing he was just lowering the backpack.

He took a step back, moved slowly as he set the bag down. Like he'd seen her flinch. "He owes you. What do you want—canned meat? A blanket?"

No. Dinah pushed away from the wall and walked to the back of the store. Johnny followed her. "This." With her good arm, she pulled down the green folder of sheet music. Not that she'd ever get another guitar or have a chance to play these after tomorrow, but still.

Johnny took the folder from her gently and tucked it into her backpack, being careful with the paper edges.

He was being so careful with her stuff. Maybe she was okay with him. She shivered. Everything was cold instead of hot now, and those spots were showing up in her vision again.

Bracing his hands on his knees, Johnny bent a little to peer at her. "Geez, look at you." He hesitated, then touched her cheek with the back of his hand. "Why do you have a fever?"

This guy was pretty cute, actually. She liked his eyes. And his dark hair that stood up all over like that.

She really must have a fever, if she was thinking like this right now.

He looked her over carefully. "Are you sick?"

"No. I mean, it's my arm." She liked his shoulders, too. She didn't talk to cute people. Kara was the exception. Kara, who was so far away now. Kara, who called her cielo, sky, my sky, like Dinah was something wide open, full of possibility, some piece of the universe.

"Don't fall." He grabbed her arm when she stumbled. Not the hurt one. He seemed to know what she meant about her arm, somehow. "I'm just going to look at it, that's all."

Glancing at her like he thought she might yell at him, he rolled up the left sleeve of her t-shirt. "Shit. This is bleeding and really infected. No wonder you look so awful."

"It's not that bad."

He raised his eyebrows. "Right. Come on, we have to take care of this. I'm not letting you die in an alley somewhere."

She wouldn't die in an alley. The chills weren't so bad. Her body could beat the infection if she could just sleep and take the other dose of pills. She'd be okay enough in the morning to handle the walk to the ranch.

Dinah took a step forward so he could see she was fine. "I have a first aid kit. I can clean it." Except she had to steady herself with a hand on the shelf when she moved.

"Have you been cleaning it?"

"Not your business, but yes."

"Then clearly that's not working well enough." He crossed his arms. "Weren't you planning on staying here tonight? Where are you gonna go?"

She didn't answer, because she didn't know.

"That's what I thought. You can come with me." He swung her bag up over his shoulder.

"I'm not going anywhere with you." Johnny had saved her, but who knew why, and his brother worked for Gates. Denton had seemed like a decent person, too.

He looked annoyed, like she was being ridiculous. "You helped Cole. They could have broken his ribs or given him a concussion or worse. Now you need help. I promise I won't mug you."

Dinah crossed her arms to match him. No. No more strangers.

He huffed. "Look. We absolutely have to go before he wakes up and we have a huge problem. You helped my brother, so I'm just returning the favor."

Dinah said nothing. How long had he been on that roof, and why had he been right behind the one place she was staying?

Johnny sighed and unbuckled his belt. "Fine. Here." He slid off a gun in a holster and held it out to her.

His jacket had been covering it. He'd had a gun this whole time? She backed up into the shelf. "What's that for?"

"If I was going to attack you, I wouldn't give you my gun, would I?"

She was done trying to guess what other people would do. "I don't know."

"Well, I wouldn't. Geez. Just take it. Put it on your belt."

"I don't want your gun."

He waited, gun still held out to her, grip first.

She did need help. He was right that she had nowhere to go. She took the gun and slid the holster onto her own belt, awkwardly, with one hand.

"The safety is on, but it's loaded. Come on, we have to walk a few blocks. Seriously. I promise I won't hurt you." He turned toward the door.

She could at least take precautions. "Wait. Raise your hands in the air first. All the way up."

"What?"

Whether or not he resisted would at least tell her something. "If you want me to go with you, put your arms in the air."

Johnny did it, but slowly. His raised arms pulled his jacket away from his sides. He watched her, a bit suspiciously, as she felt the pockets of his jacket, but no knives, no second gun.

"Don't take my matches or my gloves," he said. "I really need them."

"I don't want your stuff." She went behind him, felt the shoulders of his jacket and down his back. "I'm just making sure. Can I—" Asking for permission to search someone probably missed the point, but it still felt weird to not ask.

Johnny shrugged, shifting his jacket. "Sure. Whatever helps."

She moved the back of his jacket and felt between his shoulders, down his spine. Ran her hands lightly down his ribs, felt the back of his belt. By the time she bent to check his low-top boots for a knife sheath, her face was flaming.

"If you'd wanted to feel me up, you could've just said so." He grinned, but she glared at him anyway.

He actually had given her his only weapon. At least she knew that.

He dragged Denton inside and then secured the back door while she gingerly pulled on her jacket. Whether something was better than nothing, she'd have to find out.

Johnny walked slowly down the alley, probably so she could keep up with him.

"How far is it?" She was so grateful he was carrying her bag. She wasn't even sure she could lift it right now.

"Just a few blocks." He watched her out the corner of his eye, like he thought she wouldn't notice. "Let me know if you want a break."

"I'm fine. It's just a fever."

"How'd you get hurt?"

"Dog bite. Why were you on the roof?"

He looked down a side street. "Safer for getting around town."

Apparently he thought she wasn't that bright. "No, why were you on the roof behind the place I was staying the night?"

He glanced up at the sky. "I heard what Cole said about Gates wanting to know if you came to town. I figured you'd hit trouble."

Dinah stopped walking. "You followed me? For how long?"

Silence.

She was tired, so tired. "You followed me all day."

He started walking again. "Not all day, really. And I didn't have anything else to do. Come on. We're almost there."

She still wasn't convinced this guy was a good idea, but he had given her his gun. "Why did you use a pipe on Denton when you had a gun?" The night breeze brushed her sweaty skin, flushing her with chills again.

"If I'd pulled out a gun, I would've had to use it." He nodded to a tiny shed behind a tiny house. "This is it. Just a second." They stood in a small backyard. A few patches of dry grass littered the space, but mostly dirt. Curtains blacked out the house windows.

He disappeared into the shed. An engine sputtered and rumbled. Johnny rolled out on a small motorcycle—a lime green and black Kawasaki KLR650, ancient but built for off-roading.

"Where are we going? You don't live here?"

One of the curtains swished in the window.

He held out the single helmet. "Nope. I'm not even supposed to be in town. I just hide my bike here when I visit. I live pretty close, though."

She had several questions about what he'd just said, but she was too tired to ask. And it wasn't like she had other options. She took the helmet and pushed the wisps of hair back from her face before trying to put it on, but she couldn't do it one-handed—Johnny had to help her, even though the helmet was a little big on her.

If she'd agreed to go home with some stranger who'd followed her around town all day, she might as well ride out of town with him on his motorcycle in the middle of the night.

She walked up behind the bike to climb on, but he held up a hand. "I don't want you holding on with that arm. You might fall off and die. Sit in front of me."

Dinah hesitated but didn't argue. She slipped onto the seat in front of him. The Kawasaki was older than both of them combined, but it looked well cared for.

He pulled on his gloves. "Scoot up some so I can still reach the bars."

She slid forward, and he moved up behind her. The buckle of his belt pressed into her lower back. If she relaxed, she'd be leaning on his chest.

He pointed to a strap on the seat right in front of her. "You can hang on to that if you want, but you should be fine." As she wrapped her hand around it, his arms reached around her to grab the handlebars. He kicked down to shift, and the bike rumbled out of the yard.

She tried to sit ramrod straight, but she tilted a little every time the bike took a corner.

Johnny kept the bike on back roads, and within a few minutes they hit the far side of town. He accelerated. The wind whipped around her helmet and played with her braid. The helmet muffled the sounds of the road and bike and wind, turning it all into white noise. Johnny said something.

She couldn't even hear him. "What?"

He leaned closer. "I said, you can lean back if you want."

Oh. She hesitated, then relaxed. His abs and chest muscles tightened to support her weight. She was so glad he couldn't see her face.

Johnny handled the bike like he'd been riding for years. Which he probably had been. They didn't talk for the rest of the trip—the wind made it almost impossible. The road turned into steeper hills the farther they went. They were heading farther and farther from her home. About ten miles outside St. George, Johnny turned the bike off the crumbling asphalt and onto a gravel road, then a dirt road that turned into hills rolling upward without coming down at all. The swooping s-curves made her feel like they would fly off onto the rocks below. Mountains climbed up either side of the narrow dirt track, closing around her and turning the road into a black tunnel with the night sky overhead.

"This part's bumpy."

They had slowed down enough that she could hear him now. A faint trail led off the road and through the darkened trees. It really was bumpy at first, low-hanging branches forcing her to duck and rocks and roots under the tires jarring her arm. Where the hell was he taking her? She could barely see anything. And no one lived up here.

Her dad used to tell her and Warren stories at night about the long-bearded trappers and hunters who lived high up in the mountains. Her mom would always say, "Oh, Neil, stop scaring them. Half of that isn't true."

But that meant half of it was true.

She didn't like this. She'd assumed he lived on a farm outside town. Either he lived with some of those isolationist weirdos in a mountain shack, or he was taking her way up in the mountains for some completely different reason.

A few hundred yards in, the trail widened a bit like someone had cleared it. Another half mile, and he slowed down and finally stopped. "Okay, we get off here." He reached into the bike's small saddlebags and pulled out a flashlight. He flicked the beam of light around the area.

"Here?" A tiny cave was the only thing she could see besides vines and moss and trees.

He grinned. "Yep. This is my garage." They slid off and he rolled the bike into the cave. A veil of vines hid half of the opening.

He couldn't live up here. Even though she had three knives and his gun, she was shaky enough that she didn't think she could fight him off or even run away. Of course, this would all end with her being killed way up in the mountains where no one would ever find her body. No one would ever know what Gates had done. Her whole family, all four of them, gone.

She should have just stuck it out in town. Walked until she found a church or tried some house that looked like kids lived there. Gone to her father's old garage and tried to break in through the creaky old window.

He left her standing outside for a moment while he slid a set of locks and a chain through the bike's tires.

Johnny had seemed like a nice guy. And Cole said he was okay.

The more she'd talked to Cole, the more he'd reminded her of Warren. Too old for his age, trying to be tough.

She'd failed her family worse than even her father had, and there'd been one way to make it right. Now she'd lost even that.

Maybe she was going to die up here—she couldn't drive his motorbike down the mountain feeling like this—but she could take him out, too. Dinah pulled the gun out of the holster, disengaged the safety, and waited. Keeping her arms up and level was hard. She could tell the muzzle of the pistol was moving too much even in the dark.

Johnny came out of the cave. He stopped when he saw the gun aimed at his chest. "Uh—what're you doing?"

"I'm sick, not naïve. I know you don't live up here."

Johnny raised his hands, palms out, holding the flashlight in one hand between his thumb and his index finger. "Okay, you're serious. Well, all I was going to do is give you some antibiotics and make you something to eat, so please don't shoot me."

"Stop being funny. I may die from this dog bite, but I'm not going to let you kill me. I'll kill you first."

"I live maybe four hundred yards that way. It's a short walk."

She'd never shot a person before, and before this week, she probably couldn't have. He even made a decent target, the only lit thing in the entire forest, but holding the gun steady was so hard with her arm like this.

Johnny threw the flashlight. Because it was light and everything else was dark, she looked. She heard feet but couldn't see anything. She had one second to know he was running before he grabbed her on her right side, her good arm. She kicked his shins hard, but he'd already grabbed the gun away and pinned her to him. He clamped her arms straight against her body and leaned his head against hers so his mouth was close to her ear. "Stop it. Stop fighting. That gun's gonna go off."

She couldn't stop fighting.

"This has to be weird and terrifying. But if I'd told you, you wouldn't have come with me. You're smart to be scared, but I'm not going to let you shoot me. If I can't convince you, all I can do is show you." His breath was hot on her clammy skin. "You really are going to die out here if you don't follow me. To prove I won't hurt you, I'm going to let you go, and you can either follow me or wander off and die. Your choice." He let go of her arms.

Dinah stumbled backward. She could barely see his outline, but she could tell he was watching her stare at him. He picked up the flashlight and then turned and walked away. He still had her bag slung over his shoulder, so she would actually die if she didn't follow him.

Maybe he really was just a stranger trying to help.

Dinah started down the path after him. "Can't you just tell me why we're all the way up here?"

He was a dozen yards ahead of her already, but when she spoke, he stopped and waited for her. "I've kind of been exiled."

"Kind of?" Stepping over the rocks and ruts and the downward tilt of the forest floor gave her vertigo. Just how sick was she?

"Gates doesn't want me in town. I'm not allowed inside St. George limits, which is why when I come, I hide my bike and use the roofs."

"You could have told me that." That at least explained a few things.

"People don't normally follow strangers up into the mountains, so I thought I should keep it to myself. And I had to make sure no one else found you."

This kid was so sure he was the only person who could help her. "Why do you still go into town if you aren't allowed?"

He shrugged. "Cole and my parents are there."

Too much walking. She wanted to sleep. Sitting down on the path right there and taking a nap might be a good idea.

No, it wasn't. Sleeping on the ground was how she'd got bit in the first place.

They didn't talk again until Johnny stopped in the middle of the path. It kept going, but he turned his flashlight toward a rock shelf. She nearly missed it because it was painted almost the same color as the rock, even flecked with dirt and moss.

The rock wall had a door. A small, oblong door, made to fit an opening that never expected to have one. Johnny opened the door and shone the flashlight inside. "After you."

Still nervous, Dinah glanced at him before ducking through the opening and then holding motionless in the total dark.

Johnny came in behind her and fiddled with an oil lamp on the rock wall. When it was lit, a narrow tunnel opened up in front of her, tilting steeply downward. She followed him down the tunnel. It was barely five feet high, so she had to bend several inches. When he carried the lamp to a curve in the tunnel, she stopped.

"You really do live in a cave." The tunnel opened into a wide room with a high ceiling. A warm room, with carpet. And shelves. A counter that held canisters and pans and a water jug with a spout.

Kara would love this place. Her sense of adventure would have her exploring immediately.

"Yep." Johnny took off his shoes at the edge of the carpet and lit a second oil lamp. He kept glancing at her then away, like he was nervous.

Her mom would like that he'd taken off his shoes. "Wow."

Johnny grinned. He shrugged out of his jacket, then opened a freestanding closet and dug around on one of the shelves. When he pulled out a pill bottle, he gestured to the table. "You can sit down if you want."

"How'd you get a table up here?" Or for that matter, the carpet. Or the mattress in the corner. She squinted at the walls. A light bluish gray. He'd painted the cave.

Now she almost liked him.

"Friends helped me."

"I like the paint."

He half-smiled. "Thanks. It helps reflect the light. And it seals the cracks, so I don't get dirt and bugs." He filled a water glass for her. "It's clean water. I sterilize it."

She took the glass and he handed her pills. "What are those?"

"Antibiotics. I'm not trying to drug you. Here's the bottle."

It was a prescription label, but no one just had antibiotics sitting around. "How did you get these?"

"I traded for them. And gauze, splints, a snakebite kit, etcetera. I know a doctor." He turned on a propane camping stove, and then slid a little tin panel high in the wall of the cave. A ventilation chimney of some kind, letting in cold air. "I normally cook outside and save this for blizzards, but it's like, after midnight. You should be flattered I'm using it for you."

"But why did you trade for antibiotics?" She was still suspicious. The cave was impressive; he'd put an intense amount of work into it. But this was all too weird. Books lined one of the shelves. Dishes were stacked neatly on the counter. The tunnel that bypassed this room had been boarded up, so it was completely secure, the wall painted the same soft blue-gray as the cave.

"I'm an outcast eighteen-year-old who lives by himself on the side of a mountain. I, of all people, need antibiotics." He set a pan on the single burner and turned to face her. "Is it okay if I make you, like, chicken on bread?"

He was asking? "You don't have to make me food."

"So, yes?"

"Sure." She rolled the pills back and forth in her hand. This guy might be trying to help, but she'd need to square up somehow. "What do you want for this?"

He looked up. "What?"

"The food. The pills. Staying the night."

Johnny stiffened and didn't look at her. He dropped two slices of wheat bread into the pan and spread them with butter. He opened a can of chicken, layered meat on the bread, and then sprinkled salt while she waited for an answer.

She crossed her arms. "Well?"

His words were clipped. "I don't want anything."

"Yes, you do." The pills waited in her hand. She didn't have many options, but she'd figure something out.

He turned around from the counter and faced her. "If you don't want help, that's fine. But helping is all I'm trying to do here."

Oh. Well, now she didn't know what to say. "It's just not what I was expecting."

He put a slice of the bread on each plate and set them on the table. "Eat, and then we can look at your arm."

"Sorry."

Johnny shrugged and sat down. "Not a big deal."

If she was going to do this, she might as well go all in. Waiting until he glanced her way, Dinah took a drink and swallowed the pills.

The crease between his eyebrows let up. He gestured to the bread. "I eat this a lot. Sometimes I add onions."

Dinah picked up the slice. She'd forgotten how good hot meat, even chicken from a can, could smell. "Thank you."

He looked up from his plate and met her eyes. "Sure."

Embarrassed but not really sure why, she went back to eating. The cave was quiet for a while, and then she asked, "Why aren't you allowed in town?"

"I used to have Cole's job, and then Gates decided he didn't like me."

"Cole's job?"

"Errand boy slash barn cleaner. Two years ago. Obviously, it didn't go well."

Dinah picked up a piece of chicken from her plate. "Why didn't it go well?"

Johnny wouldn't look at her. "I stay out of it now."

That seemed like what everyone was doing. Don't try to change anything, just wait for something that wasn't coming.

Johnny set down his glass. "Let's look at your arm." He reached for a giant bottle of hand sanitizer on the shelf and cleaned his hands.

Dinah gingerly rolled up her sleeve. "I've been cleaning it with iodine. It's hard to do one-handed."

Johnny knelt by her chair and unwrapped the cloth strips. "How did you get bitten?"

"On the way to St. George. Feral hound." His fingers touching her arm flushed little spikes of pain and chills through her.

He paused for a moment, just looking at the bite. "I need to soak this open." He stood up, got a clean pan, and started sterile water heating. "Let's move so we're not over the carpet."

That meant this would hurt. Whatever. It was already painful. Dinah stood up and he lifted her chair.

When the water was hot, Johnny carried the pan over. He crouched down beside her and shook his head. He soaked a rag, then held it to her arm. She flinched, but the heat felt good. Every minute or so, he soaked the rag again so it stayed hot.

He was using so much water on her.

"I hope I wasn't too . . . pushy. About you coming with me," he said. "It's just, your arm is so bad that another day and you might have gotten gangrene. This could kill you if it gets any worse."

He hadn't forced her. She hadn't liked not having more options, but at least he'd given her one. And she'd known how bad her arm was. She'd just hoped all she'd needed was one more day.

Her words were barely a whisper. "You weren't. Thanks."

He nodded, and silence fell again as he kept soaking her wound. The water turned cloudy.

"Okay, it's a little more open. I'm going to get clean water and add salt, so this time it will sting."

Whatever it took to get rid of feeling this weak. She'd do anything.

He came back with clean water and crouched down by her again. The knees of his jeans were almost worn through. "So are you glad you didn't shoot me now?"

She almost smiled. "I'm still deciding." He wrung the salted water into the bite. Dinah gasped and then bit down on her tongue.

He glanced up at her. "So tell me about yourself."

"I lived about six miles from here, on a small farm."

He wrung water over her arm again. The salt kept burning, and somehow the pain took up residence in her head. "Do you have any siblings?"

She almost whispered the words. "Warren. He's eleven." Her head pounded like someone was forcing a spike into it.

"What's he like?"

Dinah raised a hand, touched her fingers to her face. On her lower lip, she could feel it. The wet slip of blood in her mouth. "He's smart. Stubborn. He loves his chickens."

"You said 'lived on a farm.' You don't anymore?"

Dinah shook her head. The nausea was back, washing up from her stomach in waves.

What would he do with the graves? People would ask questions about them. Kara's family and the McCaffreys and the Franklins would all want to know why they'd disappeared. Gates might have his hand in basically everything, but he couldn't actually murder people and get away with it. Right?

"Ah. You guys sold to Gates and moved to the city, then? Why'd you come back?"

She'd answer one of those questions. "Loose ends."

"Loose ends . . . with Gates?"

Johnny's question sounded like idle curiosity, but it couldn't be. Dinah shifted to face him. His face swam a little.

He'd worked for that man, so he had to know things. Things she needed to know and had no other way to get.

She needed this guy, but he clearly wasn't going to say

something unless she did first. "You can't tell anyone. You have to promise not to interfere."

Johnny sat back on his heels. "There isn't much I wouldn't do to get my brother away from that man."

Dinah didn't look away from his eyes when she said it. She wasn't even sure she was the one saying it, really—the words appeared in her brain and they fell out of her. "I'm going to kill him."

The rag dropped out of Johnny's hand back into the pan of steaming water. Dinah waited, motionless, while she watched him.

His face gave away nothing. "Okay."

"You can't stop me."

"Wasn't gonna try."

"I have my reasons."

"Like I said. I don't get involved."

"Thank you."

"I'm gonna finish your arm."

She nodded, so he picked up the rag and continued wringing water into her wound. It did look a little better—still inflamed and red, but the puncture marks were open and clean. She rested her forehead on her palm, trying to keep from puking on his lap while he worked.

Johnny stood up and stretched his back. "Well, it looks better, but you're lucky I have antibiotics. We'll see how it looks in the morning."

"You don't think I can do it." Her tone was matter of fact, not accusatory. To him, it was probably a ridiculous idea. He, like every other man she'd dealt with recently, probably thought she posed no actual danger.

"What I think is you've tried to kill enough people for the night, and you should go to sleep so you can kick this fever." He wrapped her arm in a clean bandage.

Sleep. Here, apparently. Dinah stood and reached for the chair, but he grabbed it before she could and dragged it back to the table.

"I am tired." Her muscles were sliding off her bones.

Johnny closed the kitchen cupboards and dumped the wet rags in a pail, but he didn't seem to notice that she had no idea where she was supposed to sleep.

Well, she wasn't taking his bed, so anywhere would probably work. She unstrapped her blanket from her backpack and unrolled it.

Johnny glanced at her then pulled a sleeping bag out of the cabinet. "Um, you can sleep on the mattress. I'll take the floor."

Not fair at all. "I can't take your bed. The floor's fine."

He took the blanket from her, giving her that look again. "Like I'm going to let that happen. Seriously. You are incredibly ill. I have a sleeping bag. It's fine." She opened her mouth to argue, but he smiled and his voice turned pleading. "Come on. I never get the chance to have a pretty girl in my bed."

She narrowed her eyes. "Clever." She didn't know what else to say, so she grabbed her backpack and dragged it over to the mattress.

Johnny shook his sleeping bag out by the table, several feet away. "I don't have a second set of sheets but they're pretty clean," he said quietly. "I swear I wash them occasionally."

Dinah pulled the covers back. Forget sheets. She could melt into this mattress. Johnny went to turn down the oil lamps, and she started unbraiding her hair.

He wrapped up the loaf of bread and moved their dishes to the sink. But every few seconds his glance flicked over to her, watching her work through her hair. She caught his gaze, and he immediately turned away.

Johnny turned out the last lamp. The cave fell dark and quiet. Dinah waited until he climbed into his sleeping bag and stopped rustling around before she lay down. She rolled away, facing the cave wall. For the first moment since that violent silver truck had pulled up to her home, she felt safe enough to close her eyes.

# SEVEN

THE DIZZINESS WAS GONE BY THE TIME SHE WOKE UP. THE ODD floating sensation, the nausea. And in their place was a sinking horror. Everything she'd done yesterday had been so wrong. Telling people her name, trusting strangers, staying long past when her instincts had told her to go, telling Johnny her plan.

Wait. She stared at the empty water glass by the bed. Maybe it hadn't been yesterday.

She'd woken up twice, feeling sick to her stomach with her mouth dry, and he'd brought her water and another dose of antibiotics. "I'll leave the glass right here," she remembered him saying, before she'd fallen back asleep.

She was still in a stranger's bed, the cave utterly quiet. Johnny was gone. The room was neat and clean, though, like he'd somehow washed dishes and cleaned up the clutter quietly enough to not wake her.

If it even was morning still. It could be afternoon or evening.

No daylight in the cave, and her own internal clock must have crashed along with her body.

But she felt rested. Like someone had shut her off for thirty-six hours and let her reset.

She could probably get dressed if she was quick enough. Listening for the door to open down the tunnel, she yanked off her clothes and pulled on her cleanest jeans, a soft gray shirt, and her sturdy canvas jacket. Leaving her hair unbraided, she brushed her teeth and spit into his little sink with a bucket drain.

Johnny still hadn't come back by the time she'd made the bed and slid her knives into the sheaths in her worn, soft leather boots. She walked quietly down the tunnel to the door. It was hanging partially open, and through the gap she could see him moving around outside.

No better time to observe this guy a little.

He was just past the little clearing, a yard or two in the trees. Cleaning a catch of some kind, so he must have traps somewhere. In the clearing was a coal pit—a deep one, maybe to keep coals going overnight. Smart. A cast-iron skillet sat heating on a metal grate over the coals, next to a little kettle.

She pulled back from the door when he walked back to the clearing by the cave. He held his hand over the pan for a second, then threw in the meat.

Something splashed in a bucket beside the door. Two fish of some kind, on the small side. This must be how he kept them fresh until he wanted to cook them. She hadn't seen an icebox or anything like that yet. Probably no good way to keep one going up here. He must either make do with dried or canned meat, which was expensive, or eat what he caught that day.

So far, Johnny seemed to be exactly what he'd said.

And that meant it wasn't really fair to stand here spying like this. She nudged the door open with her boot. "Hey."

He turned around, smiling. "Hey. Want lunch? It's either rabbit or oatmeal."

She pulled her hair up into a ponytail and winced when she moved her left arm. She felt better, but her arm did not. "Whatever's fastest. How long was I asleep?"

Johnny stood up slowly. "A day and a half. It's Wednesday. Are you—leaving? Two doses of antibiotics won't kill that infection."

"Oh. I just meant don't go to a lot of trouble." Now that her head was clearer, she was done with the shoddy planning. But this guy probably hadn't counted on her doing more than staying the night. He might want her to eat and leave. "I'm not sure what my plan is right now. But I don't want to disrupt things for you."

Silence. Water bubbled in the kettle, so he took it off the coals. "Do you remember what you said the other night about Gates?"

Yet another bad idea. "Yeah."

He walked over with the skillet in one hand and the kettle in the other. She stepped aside and opened the door farther for him.

Johnny didn't say anything while they walked down the tunnel, but once he set the skillet and the kettle on the table, he sat down and faced her. "So, was your plan to just walk up to his house and, what, shoot him?"

Dinah sank down into the other chair. Rested her head in her hands. "Yep. That was my plan."

Johnny poured the boiling water into the small bowls of oatmeal that were waiting on the table. Shoved his chair back, stood up, returned with spoons, forks, and the sugar. He finally made eye contact with her. "So . . . how do you feel about that idea now?"

Dinah snorted. "How do you think? It was a shitty plan."

Johnny's face cracked into a smile. "Okay. Glad we both see that."

She narrowed her eyes.

He lifted his hands in a shrug. "It's just, he has five or six guys who live there in the bunkhouse. And he's got guard dogs, big noisy ones. His cronies like Mitch Harding and Sheriff Anders are always dropping by because he runs all his properties and stuff from the ranch. And there's no cover or anything nearby. You wouldn't even get up to his gate before someone stopped you."

She would have been dead, is what he was saying. Yesterday if she had gone right to his house, she would have been shot or overpowered at the gate before she even saw Gates, and she'd be dead by now.

Also. For someone who claimed to stay out of town business, this guy had that information pretty well thought through.

"Have some oatmeal." Johnny nudged the bowl toward her.

Oatmeal. Like there was a point to eating. Except she could smell the warm, sweet scent, and a wave of hunger usually reserved for Februaries surged through her.

Dinah took the bowl. Fine. She'd eat, she'd plan something that would work, then she'd kill Gates. If she didn't eat, she wouldn't be able to do that.

Johnny stabbed a piece of rabbit from the skillet with his fork.

"So how do I get past all those men?" Dinah chased a tiny lump of brown sugar through the bowl with her spoon.

Johnny shook his head, kept shaking it as he went for another piece of meat. "Nope, sorry. No way can I help you plan this. One, I'm done getting involved with other people's shit. Two, for all

Gates knows I'm dead, and I'd like to keep it that way."

Dinah waved her spoon at him. "Knocking out Denton, bringing me up here, helping with my arm, feeding me—all getting involved."

Johnny stopped with his fork in the air, a piece of meat hanging off the tines. "Huh. Okay, fine. From this point on, I cannot be more directly involved than feeding you food I was already going to cook anyway."

She'd never planned on doing this any other way than on her own, so whatever. And she barely knew this guy. He'd saved her in two separate ways already, but who knew at what point he'd decide it was better to turn her in for a favor from Gates.

If this guy was ever going to have a chance to live in town with his family again—she was it. That might get his exile lifted. And then maybe he could get a job again.

The more she thought about it, the more it seemed like yet another fatal flaw she'd overlooked. Johnny seemed okay, but that didn't mean he wouldn't use an opportunity when he saw one.

Johnny was quiet for a long time. Too long. And then he sighed. "Why is he looking for you?"

She couldn't tell him. She just couldn't.

Look up at him. Say something. But she couldn't even unclench her hands, much less say anything that would fool him.

Dinah didn't move for so long, Johnny shifted his chair closer to her, and since she wouldn't look up, he leaned down until he could see her eyes. "I won't get in your way. You're in trouble, obviously."

He'd pinned her with a question she hadn't been prepared to answer, so she could do it, too. "Are you going to turn me in?"

Johnny leaned back slowly. "Why would I do that?"

Why would Denton? "Gates has something you want, I'm sure."

"Dinah. I don't need his money, and anyway, it won't be much even if he was willing to pay. He wants to pin down loose ends, sure, but you're just not going to be that big a deal to him."

And that made it so much worse.

"Maybe you'd ask to live with your family again, instead of taking the money."

And he didn't have an answer ready for that. She lifted her eyes to his and watched him part his lips, then close them again. His eyes had the thinnest ring of light brown in the center.

"Look, whatever he wants you for, I guarantee it's not big enough to get me off the hook. And he can't give me what I want anyway. What I want is to get Cole out of those jobs and keep him in school instead of dropping out like I had to. He insists he's going to drop out to work full-time next year when he finishes eighth grade. And eventually Gates is going to have him doing the kind of stuff he made me do."

It made sense. It might not be true. "Like what?"

His shoulders went rigid. "I worked for him for four years, technically as an errand boy but then eventually a sort of business scout, looking for profit options anywhere he wanted me to. But that means more than it sounds like, and if he knew the stuff I shirked on, he would have thrown me out of town a lot faster than he did."

Well. If he wanted to turn her in, he could have done it last night instead of taking her all the way up here.

Okay.

"I don't need your help planning anything. I just need some place to stay tonight."

He gestured around the cave. "Not a soul will find you here."

"You don't mind?"

"The company is nice. It gets boring."

She had nothing but a rifle with a caliber too small to kill someone except at point-blank range, Kara's fifty-two dollars, and a place to stay for the night. That wouldn't put a man like Gates in the ground.

If she got a motorbike and followed him in that silver truck away from town, she could take out his tires and get a good shot at him when he got out of the truck. But he'd have a gun too, and she wasn't as good of a shot as Warren was. He'd kill her and walk away.

If she snuck onto his ranch at night, the dogs would find her. If she did it during the day, his ranch hands would. And probably the dogs, too.

If she found out places he regularly went and hid there until he showed up, other people would get killed.

The more she pulled up options and saw them fail, the further she sank into herself. Her hands gripped the bottom of the seat beneath her, but she stopped being able to feel it. Her chest felt so heavy. Lifting it to breathe took so much work that she quit doing it, until eventually her lungs forced her to.

The well. The whole time she'd been gone, Kara's family and the McCaffreys and the Franklins and everyone else wouldn't have been able to get water.

And the whole time she waited here, he was taking over her house, standing on the porch like he'd been the day she found her mother, letting someone else live there, putting his cigarettes in the sink. Walking across the yard where she'd buried them, not caring what was under the ground.

"You okay? Dinah. Hey." Johnny snapped his fingers.

She jerked back from him. "What?"

He paused with his hand in the air. Then he stood up slowly and scooted the chair back to its place under the table. "Maybe we should . . . you know what, usually I play for a while in the afternoon, since there's nothing else to do up here. Do you mind?" He reached for something on top of the cabinets.

Dinah went still, watching him unwrap the cloth covering. A dulcimer.

He sat down on the mattress and laid the hourglass-shaped instrument flat on his lap.

So, he was uncomfortable with her little panic moment and was trying to distract her. He must know she loved music too, since she'd had a guitar and she'd taken the sheet music from the store. But she didn't need to be distracted, she needed to keep her promise.

Johnny adjusted the tuning pegs. The wood had little carv-ings all over the surface, but she couldn't see what they were from the table. "Where did you get it?" It would have cost more money than she'd ever seen in one place in her life.

"I made it."

"You what?"

"I made it," he said. "A friend showed me how."

She hesitated for a moment, then came over and sat next to him. He glanced at her in surprise. "What?"

Johnny shook his head. "Just didn't expect you to be this interested." Or for her to sit next to him, maybe. But he'd made this beautiful thing, and it showed such care.

She leaned in a little to look at the leaf carvings. Warmth from her leaning toward him brushed her arm, and the only way she could explain the sudden ache it gave her was that she must be lonely. Maybe this kind of loneliness was a grief thing.

Stop it, Dinah. No more of this.

"One of my neighbors has a dulcimer," she said. Mr. Franklin. "They have such a cheerful sound, you know? Brighter than a guitar." She watched his hands as he played a few chords, studying his finger placement.

He smiled at her. "Do you want to play? I can show you. If you play guitar, you can pick up dulcimer no problem."

"It'll be nice to just listen. I never get to hear music unless I play it. Hey, can you play any of these?" She unzipped her backpack and pulled out the folder of music.

His hand paused on the fingerboard. He glanced at the sheets when she opened it and turned back to the instrument on his lap. "Sure. Which one do you want?"

She looked through the sheets. "Most of these I've never heard of."

"They're probably old."

"Here's 'Yesterday' by the Beatles. I've heard of them." She handed him the folder.

He looked at the paper. "This is for piano, but it's got the guitar chords." He studied the music for a moment and then began to play.

Dinah moved back on the bed and leaned against the wall. She tilted her head slightly as she listened, analyzing the music so she could play it later.

"Do you always do this?" he asked.

"Do what?"

"Take mental notes. Get so absorbed." He shifted sideways, one leg under him, so she could still watch him play.

She shrugged, which wasn't an answer, but she didn't really have one. There was Dinah before, and there was Dinah after, and she wasn't really sure which parts of her had lived through the break.

"Sorry about your guitar, by the way," he said.

She kept watching his hands. Long, slender fingers, large palms, working through the song on the strings for the first time. "It was old and not very good. I just can't replace it."

"You'll be able to someday."

No. "Maybe."

Johnny shook his head. "Don't think like that. You'll be able to get a fantastic guitar, and you'll have tons of new music to play. Say it. Say 'someday I'll get a new guitar.' "

She let out a soft breath that hurt. "Fine. Someday I'll get a new guitar."

"And?"

"And what?"

"Someday you'll get a new guitar, and what else? What else will you do?"

It was okay to say, because it didn't mean anything. "Someday, I'll get a new guitar, and hear professional musicians play in a concert hall, and go to college to study music."

He didn't smile, either. Nothing about it was funny. "You can totally do that." She didn't reply, and he started the song over.

Now that he was a little more familiar with it, he played it better. When he'd played all the way through it, she handed him another. Pink Floyd's "Wish You Were Here."

"I haven't played music for someone else in a long time," he said. "Cole used to ask me to when he was little, but that was years ago."

Halfway through the song, she smiled and he almost stopped playing. But he ducked his head and kept going.

"Your turn," she whispered. "What do you want?"

But what he said was clearly a fake answer, something about new projects for his cave and a refrigeration system.

He was so good at helping people. The way he'd taken care of everything she'd needed and asked for nothing in return, then played for her like this when he knew she couldn't handle her own thoughts anymore.

Yet, for some reason, this boy lived so far removed from anyone he could help. Even his own brother.

He played four songs before he got up to clean the trout he'd caught earlier, and she followed him outside. They ate in the clearing, sitting on stump seats he said he'd sanded down that summer, and he tossed the leftovers from cleaning the fish into the woods, maybe fifty feet away from where they sat. "Watch," he said. "She sometimes comes around at dusk."

"Who?" she asked.

He smiled. "This wolf. She's been coming around since last winter, after she found out I clean my kills right there."

They waited, but nothing stirred through the underbrush. Dusk filtered down, fogging the pines and dogwoods and blackhaw and turning the wild rose into shadows. Still, nothing moved. Dinah had nearly fallen asleep by the fire when Johnny nudged her arm. She jerked, but Johnny held up a hand. "Shh. There she is."

A shadow, lighter than the underbrush, moved toward them through the thinned-out fringe of trees. When the shadow was about thirty feet away, Dinah could make out pointed ears and a curve down a long back to a saber tail. Silver and black shading disrupted her gray coat, marking dark tracks down her long muzzle.

Dinah held her breath. The wolf stepped forward, stopped with one paw lifted slightly, and took the final step to the edge of the clearing. Her ears swiveled back and forth, filtering through the forest sounds as she lowered her head to hunt through the stubby grass and pine needles for the skins of the fish.

When she'd finished rooting around on the ground, she lifted her head, stared at them across the dying campfire. Tail still and ears pointed as far forward as they could go, she watched them. Black rings circled her eyes. Silver frosted her ears and down her chest and sprinkled her compact paws. The wolf's large round eyes met hers, questioning.

She was the colors of the forest at night—twilight shadowing the branches to black, the silver of poplar leaves glimmering in the dark, the foggy gray of the mist, and the moonlight hovering in the spaces open to the sky.

What are you here for? those eyes asked. What will you do to me, what should I do to you?

If only she was this wolf, able to melt into the forest because she was shades of twilight.

"I try not to scare her when she comes around." Johnny stood up slowly. "It's less disturbing to her, I think, if we leave rather than waiting till she runs off." The wolf slipped into the underbrush at the motion, but her bright eyes still showed through the dark.

Dinah eased to a stand, too, and backed up slowly, one foot at a time. "You're not supposed to feed wild animals, though. It alters their behavior and makes them more aggressive."

Johnny reached the door and held it open for her. "I wasn't

intending to, just cleaning my squirrels and stuff. I figured I'd rather let her have it than burn it. She was so skinny last winter."

Maybe it wasn't possible to be here without causing some kind of damage.

Inside, he tossed her the bottle of antibiotic pills. "You should probably go to bed early."

"I hate to make you sleep on the floor again."

He shook his head, dark hair spilling over his forehead. "I've slept worse places. Don't worry about it."

She brushed her teeth and unbraided her hair. When he wasn't looking, she pulled a five-dollar bill out of Kara's money and slipped it into the pocket of his jacket hanging on the wall hook. For the food, the gas, the antibiotics, the safe place to sleep. She climbed into the bed. "Are you going to sleep?"

He turned down the oil lamp by his bookshelf. "Yeah, soon." The cave went dark.

Oh. What was he doing, then? "Thanks for . . . all of this. Have a good night." She rolled over and faced the cave wall.

He left. The door closed behind him in the dark.

Where was he going?

The cave was quiet. So quiet. And she'd never been someplace so dark. Inside the mountain like this, there weren't even shades of black.

She had to reach out and feel the cabinet beside the mattress to make sure the room hadn't disappeared along with the light.

Dinah pulled the blanket up to her shoulder and stared at the wall she couldn't see until she fell asleep.

Scraping woke her up. A gritty slide, over and over again.

She sat up, listened. All she could hear was her heart. No scraping.

But she could taste the tang of iron, of that man's blood on her tongue.

Digging. She'd been dreaming about digging.

Dinah fell back against the pillow and her own tears blurred the darkness. She didn't even remember filling in the graves, but she kept dreaming about it. The crumble and fall of dirt, the muffled sound of it hitting quilts. The blanket shifting, showing her mother's hair, as dirt tugged it down. Had that really happened?

She rolled over and buried her face in the pillow so Johnny wouldn't hear her.

The graves.

Cole had said Gates had someone living there. That he was drilling down the well.

Dinah sat up, fumbled with the blankets until she found the flashlight. Flicked it on.

Empty. Johnny's sleeping bag was empty.

Where was he? What time was it?

If Gates didn't want questions, he'd dig up the graves so no one would find them. Lay sod over the dirt. And if he dug up the graves, he wouldn't bury her mother and Warren again. He'd have them dumped somewhere.

How could she have missed that? What if he'd already done it?

Enough of this. Her arm was a little better. She would not abandon her family again.

Dinah slid out of bed, lit an oil lamp. Packed up her bag, pulled on her boots, slid her knives into her boots and the sheath on her belt. Jacket, water.

Gun. There it was, sitting inside the cabinet where he kept it. Wherever he'd gone, he didn't need it, apparently. And no matter what he was doing in the middle of the night for hours, she couldn't risk it having something to do with her.

Dinah slid the holster and the pistol onto her belt.

She left a note on the table. *I'll return the gun somehow. You can have the rifle until I do.* Because no matter where he was now, he'd helped her.

And then she turned down the oil lamp, closed the door behind her, and waited to turn on the flashlight until she reached the road.

#  EIGHT

A TALL Lakȟóta woman in canvas overalls had given her a ride down the mountain. The bed of her truck was stacked full of tarped-over crates and sawdust. Dinah had been stunned to see someone else that far up the mountain, and with a vehicle, no less. An old truck, the manual-driving kind, not self-driving like Gates and Sheriff Anders and Mitch Harding had. The woman had looked at her strangely, but neither of them asked questions. The woman didn't give Dinah her name, but had driven her five of the six miles to her farm and had let Dinah out in the woods where she'd asked.

Through the trees, the peeling paint on the east side of her house glowed in the early-morning sun.

A giant truck guarded the well, hitched to a rig with cables and what must be the drill. The henhouse had been torn down, nothing left but a stack of lumber. Mud had been tracked all over the yard, suffocating the dried grass.

A cement foundation had been poured around the well.

Gates thought she was a loose end he could trim off and sweep away. She wasn't a loose end. She was a poison he'd breathe in, and she'd shut down his heart, his lungs, his veins—until all he had left was her.

She worked her way around the clearing until she was closer to the garden. The graves were still there, the river rock with their handprints tilted and smeared with dirt. But if the stone was still there, they were still there.

Gates had ignored them. The graves were almost lost in all the mud from drilling the well deeper.

Dinah crept closer, picking her way through the vines and branches closer to the graves, the section of the garden closest to the well.

Even after the rain, cracks ran across the ground, marking dried-out puzzle pieces in the dirt. A few yards away, she stopped.

Tire tracks. On their graves.

He wasn't bothered by those graves at all. He was so unconcerned with them that not only had he not moved their bodies, he'd driven the truck over them.

Dinah stepped out of the woods. Her boot touched the grass of the yard and she couldn't go back. Pulling the gun out of her belt, she strode to the house.

She skipped the creaky middle step and walked across her porch. Holding the gun steady, she knocked on the door. Whoever Gates had living here wouldn't be an errand boy. Footsteps crossed the floor and the door opened.

She looked into the face of the stocky, vested white guy who'd chased them through the woods.

Dinah pushed the barrel of the gun into his chest. "Let me in."

He backed up and slowly raised his hands, holding one of her mother's tea mugs. "Nothing worth stealing here."

He didn't even recognize her.

"Put the mug down." Dinah stepped through the doorway and kicked the door shut.

He set it on the table, glancing around the room.

"Who are you?" she asked.

"Alan Fry. Who're you?"

If she gave him any more time, he'd figure out how to get that gun away from her. "Sit down." She kept the gun leveled at his chest.

He sat down in the chair by the table. Dinah backed up to the kitchen sink, hooked the bottom of the cabinet door with her boot, and nudged it open. She crouched and grabbed the roll of duct tape from under the sink. She carried it over to him, pressed the barrel of the gun to his temple, and dropped the tape in his lap. "Tape your wrists together."

"Come on now, you're not actually going to shoot me—" He lifted two inches out of the chair.

Dinah whipped the gun around and struck his cheekbone with the handle. The skin split and blood trickled down his cheek. He was the third man this week to see a weapon in her hand and think she couldn't use it. "Tape your hands together, or your dying thought will be how wrong you were about what I'd do."

He picked up the duct tape and unrolled a length of it. Once he'd gotten it started, Dinah took the roll and wrapped several more lengths of tape across his wrists and then between them to tighten it. She shoved up his pant legs and taped his ankles to the chair.

There wasn't any limit to what she'd do for Warren. He'd trusted her. He'd run when she told him to. He'd waited for her to come back.

She stood up. This man's things were all over her house—his dirty coat on the braided rug. Mud tracked across her mother's floor, the sink piled full of his dishes. A cell phone on the counter.

"You're that girl, then." His cheekbone was red and swelling already, blood oozing from the split.

This man was one of the reasons Warren had died. His forehead was sweating, drops rolling into his eyebrows. Another in a whole string of chicken-shit men.

Every time she looked at his face, she saw herself watching him from the tree as he searched the forest. Saw Warren dying among the rocks, by himself. Suffocating while he waited for his sister to come back.

Dinah turned his cell phone over on the table. It looked sleek, new. It did not belong in her house. She slammed the butt of the gun down on the phone. Alan screamed. The phone shattered.

She walked over to the woodstove. The big metal box radiated heat. With the cloth mitt they'd always kept hanging on the fire poker, she wrenched the iron door open. The fire he had going was hot, leaping hungry orange and red. She tossed the pieces of the cell phone inside. When she turned back to Alan Fry, she left the stove door hanging open.

Her skin and clothing were dirty. Branches had snagged her braid and pulled wisps of it loose. She probably looked unhinged and desperate. "Gabriel Gates killed my mother. He stole my house and my land and my family's well. And you ran down an eleven-year-old kid with asthma in the woods, and he died, too. What do you think you deserve for that?"

The man didn't answer, simply watched her with terrified, bloodshot eyes.

Her voice went up an octave. "I don't have time for this. You've got one chance to answer my questions, and if you don't, I'm going to shoot you in the head and be done with you."

Alan Fry made a sound, a gurgling gasp. "I—I don't know."

She was going to end up killing this man if she didn't do something different. With Denton Marlow, Johnny had been right about having to use the gun if he pulled it out.

She didn't want to kill him. She wanted him to talk.

Dinah set the gun on the table behind her, then turned around and backhanded him across the face, hard enough that he grunted.

A drop of sweat dripped off his chin and splashed onto his taped hands.

"What's he done to the neighbors?" she asked. "Did he talk to them? Did they come here?" Heat from the open woodstove radiated against her jeans, carrying the chemical smell of the phone's melting plastic.

"I don't know," he said.

Dinah braced her hands on either side of her, back to the table, and hoisted herself up. Sitting on the edge, she put a foot on either side of Alan Fry's knees on the chair.

"Think of something." She rested her forearms on her knees and dangled her knife, blade down, over his knee.

"They—some of them showed up wanting water. We can't give it away. It's bad business."

She pressed the tip of the blade through the denim of his pants. "Stealing someone's land is bad business. And that's our water to give away if we want. Did he or anyone else go to their farms looking for me?"

If he'd threatened Kara's family. If he'd threatened Laura McCaffrey, who already brewed worry into her tea.

The man shook his head.

"Say it out loud," she said.

"We haven't been there," he said. "Gates wanted the well drilled farther down and an electric pump put in right away."

But her neighbors had come here, expecting to see her family. And instead they'd found the drill and an empty house and a stranger telling them everything was over. "You know this is my land. Admit it."

He stiffened, looked out the windows.

Help would not come for him right now. She dug the tip of the blade into the denim high on his thigh and jerked it toward his knee. The leg of his pants split, leaving a thin, bloody trail down his leg.

Alan Fry squealed. "Fine! Fine, it's yours. The well is yours."

"You stole it. Gates stole it. You're taking what's not yours and you killed for it."

"We stole it," he whispered. "He—he killed for it. I'm not a bad person. I grew up in St. George. My parents worked on his parents' ranch my whole life."

"You killed for the well," she said. "And you drove over their graves."

He was silent.

Dinah slid the knife back into its sheath and grabbed the gun. She'd had it with him. She'd had it with Gates thinking this was over and she had been handled. She aimed at the large glass bowl on the counter—not her mother's, so it belonged to this man. She fired. The bowl ruptured into fragments and her ears rang. Needles of glass showered them, splinters hit the walls and cascaded to the floor. Alan Fry screamed and nearly tipped his chair over.

"Damn it, girl! What do you think you're doing?" A scratch bled down his neck and fragments sprayed his clothing.

She would not let Gates believe he'd gotten away with this.

Dinah moved closer and bent down so her face hovered next to his. "You tell him something for me. You tell him he's going to pay for this. His days of sweeping us away are over. Tell him I am his angel of death, and the next time he sees me, he's going to wish he'd never heard of the Caldwells."

He stared into her eyes, completely still, like a beetle she'd pinned to cardboard.

Alan wasn't the man she wanted. Not this panicked, sweaty human.

She stood up, strode over to his coat. His boots sat in a crust of mud by the door. She grabbed them and the coat. She threw his boots into the woodstove and crammed his coat in with the fire poker.

Smoke poured out of the opening. The fabric had probably blocked the chimney. The flames would burn it away soon enough and make room. She let smoke billow into the kitchen as she headed for the sink. Fry choked on the smoke and yelled at her, but she ignored him and loaded all his dirty bowls and mugs into a big mixing bowl.

Dinah carried them out onto the porch and heaved them onto the driveway. The glass and porcelain shattered against the packed dirt. She carried her mother's bowl back inside. Looked around for his other things.

The bedroom.

She almost couldn't cross her mother's threshold when she saw his clothing tossed on her quilt.

Her bed. This man was sleeping in her mom's bed. She tore around the room, picking up everything of his she could find. His wallet was on the dresser, so she grabbed that, too. No cash in it, just cards. She hauled the overflowing armload to the kitchen. The smoke hung so thick, trapped by the low ceiling before flowing like water out the open front door, that she gave in to the burning and coughed until her lungs ached.

Alan coughed and gagged, leaning down in his chair for clean air. She wrenched the fire poker through the burning coat until the chimney cleared, then crammed all his clothing and his wallet inside.

Dinah rose from her crouch by the fire and left the woodstove open. She dragged Alan's chair out of the worst of the smoke into the living room.

"You can't leave me like this. At least untie me," he said.

Dinah checked the front yard from the window, glanced at the road. Clear. She headed for her bedroom. Pried up the board near the doorway. Fished around to pull out the tablet and charger beneath the floorboards. She plugged in the cold, dead tablet and wiped the dirt off it. The "charging" symbol winked at her. When it started up, twenty-one messages flashed across the screen.

Three from Mrs. McCaffrey, two from Kara's mom, and one from Mr. Franklin, all asking where they'd gone. If they'd be back.

Fifteen messages from Kara.

Hon where are you? What happened?

I'm really scared, where are you?

Dinah

Dinah, reply to me right now. I'm worried you're dead or something. My parents are beside themselves. I know you wouldn't leave like this if something wasn't really wrong

Dinah, please

Mi cielo, dónde estas?

Dinah pressed her hands against her eyes, then typed as fast as she could.

It's me. My tablet will be broken after this so don't reply. I'm okay. Don't go to my house anymore. Gates has the well for now. Don't move away—I'm not letting him keep it. More soon.

That was all she had time for. As soon as she got the "delivered" stamp on the messages, she unplugged the tablet and propped it in the doorway against the corner of the doorframe. Just as it flashed "critical battery," her boot cracked the tablet in half.

She wouldn't even give Gates the option of messaging the neighbors, pretending to be her. She threw the pieces of her tablet into the woodstove, too.

Dinah scanned the yard out the window. Time to go. She couldn't risk being here any longer. Closing the door behind her while Alan Fry yelled for help and smoke flowed out of the windows, she glanced around the yard again. No movement.

Except for the guy walking out of the woods, right by the graves.

Johnny stopped on the grass. Tall, quiet, waiting for her.

He shoved his hands in his pockets and looked around at the muddy yard, the well drill, the torn-down henhouse. His gaze drifted to a standstill right in front of him, on the graves and the river rock.

Obviously he knew now.

He was too far away for her to say anything. She walked down the steps and over to him.

"Are those—" He nodded to the grave. "Is that your family?"

All she could do was look at the grave, the dirt scarred by tire tracks. She'd lifted herself out of that trench to kill Gabriel Gates.

"I'm sorry," he said. "Your brother, too?"

She couldn't say it. Johnny had been able to put his life back together after being kicked out of town. His family was still alive. He had money and a motorbike and a home and everything she didn't. Telling someone who wouldn't understand meant she'd have to explain, and she just couldn't do that. "How'd you find me?"

"I saw Lissa coming back up in her truck. Said she'd taken you this way." He sighed. "The guy in your house?"

She wasn't going to apologize for leaving. It wasn't his business and he shouldn't have followed her. "He'll be fine. What are you doing here? Why did you follow me? For the second time now. You think I can't handle myself, or what?"

He snorted. "You stole my gun. I want it back."

"I didn't steal your gun. I told you I'd return it."

His eyebrows lowered. "Oh, sure you were going to. That .22 rifle is a crappy trade for a 9mm Glock. You know how long it's been since I've shown anyone where I live? This is why I live alone on the side of a mountain. It's never worth it to get involved in other people's shit. It always goes bad, and it never changes anything."

"You're just pissed your gun got downgraded a little. I needed it, and you probably wouldn't have given it to me."

He rubbed a hand over his face. "No, I wouldn't have. I nearly had a heart attack when you fired that shot. What the hell were you doing?"

Dinah pulled the holster off her belt and thrust it at him. "You don't have any right to question me. And I'm leaving before anyone shows up, so here's your gun back."

Johnny didn't take the gun. His frown disappeared and he reached for her arm as she turned away, but he lowered his hand before he touched her. "Wait. Please. Hey, I'm sorry. I had no idea your family—I mean, obviously there's a lot I don't know."

Dinah stopped where she was.

Johnny shoved his hands into his pockets. "You don't have to explain anything, but I do want to understand."

She searched his eyes. "Where were you? I woke up and you were gone."

But he didn't answer.

"I have to go." She headed for the line of trees, past the well with the fresh cement foundation. She'd left Gates a pretty clear message, and she needed to be farther away when he received it.

Johnny followed along, like there'd never been a question of whether he would. "I parked my motorbike about a mile past the house. If we head this way, we'll come out at the road."

She knew where the road was. When she didn't reply, Johnny kept glancing at her like he wasn't sure what she might do.

Dinah stopped at the edge of the forest. The dirt road ran east and west in front of her.

The tire tracks shouldn't have shaken her this badly. They were only prints in the dirt. It didn't make her mom and Warren any more gone.

Johnny checked up and down the road before looking back to her. They were a mile from the house, and no one ever came this way.

He sat down on the bank beside the road. After a second, Dinah sat down next to him. "I'm sorry I stole your gun." She carefully set the Glock in its holster on the grass between them.

After a moment, Johnny's shoulders moved and his hand covered hers. She didn't pull away.

He shook his head slowly. "It's yours if you need it that badly. I'm sorry."

She drew her knees up to her chest, rested her forehead on them, and tried to slow her breathing. Johnny gripped her hand, and the pressure helped. His skin was warm, and she could feel the calluses on his thumb when it brushed the back of her hand.

His words were slow and heavy. "I didn't know you were this desperate."

If the last four days had condemned her, the last hour had been a fragment of a pardon.

Johnny picked up a stone and rolled it in his other hand. "What do you need?"

She fiddled with the grass but then her hand stilled. "I don't even know. I need something that works."

Johnny tossed the stone into the road. "I have some things you can use. And I know some people."

She pulled a blade of grass out of the ground. "That's getting involved."

It hurt to look at his smile. "Yeah," he said.

Neither of them said anything more, and after a minute they both looked back to the road.

"Let's go," she said.

Johnny stood up. She followed him over to his motorcycle and slid on behind him. He gave her the helmet again, and she hung on around his waist with both hands. Her body was cold, but his was warm, and the motorbike rumbled to life.

CHAPTER

NINE

THE BACK ROADS TOOK THEM THE LONG WAY AROUND TO Johnny's cave. She'd asked him to stay off the highway, and he'd done what she asked without question. He chained up his motorbike, and they walked up the steep, rutted path to his cave.

She should tell Johnny why she'd left him that morning, what she'd done in her own home, but for a moment, she could take a breath.

"This place is really nice." A functioning kitchen, actual carpet, ventilation, even a bookshelf.

Johnny glanced over his shoulder at her as he shrugged off his coat. "You think?"

"Of course." He seemed so unsure, but he'd clearly put so much time and care into it. She'd be proud if she'd made a home like this, with its warm light and soft gray paint. "You must get bored, though."

"Well, I spend a lot of time in the caves. They're pretty cool.

Huge, winding systems up here." He pulled bread and a jar of peanut butter out of the cabinet. "Want a sandwich?"

Peanut butter? She hadn't had peanut butter in a while. "Sure. How long did it take you to find this place?"

He slid a knife through the coarse bread. "I lived in a tent for a few months. Summer, thankfully. But I needed a place I could fix up and make secure, and I had nothing else to do, so I hunted around for weeks and covered miles of forest before finding this."

His words made it sound like it hadn't been that big a deal, but she couldn't imagine being thrown out of town at sixteen and expected to survive in the woods. After only a day, she'd been seriously injured. She took the sandwich he handed her. "Why this spot?"

"Well, inside like this, it's about sixty degrees year-round, since caves stay the average temperature of the area. But that's still pretty cold to live in forever. The hot spring keeps this one a little warmer. Plus, you know, water."

"A hot spring?" She'd been thinking about too many other things to wonder about the heat.

He ate a quarter of his sandwich in one bite and then talked around it. "Wanna see?"

Dinah followed him to the back of the cave, passing crates she hadn't bothered to look at before. Potatoes and onions. Random tools. A propane heater.

The plywood wall he'd built in the passageway had a door. Hinges, a bolt, everything. She glanced at the wall as they walked through. Two-by-four studs.

He lifted an oil lamp off the wall by the door. "This cave system has a few entrances, so I built the wall to keep animals out. There're a few other rooms I use, but mostly I come back here for the water." He closed the door and the light reduced to the yellow circle the lamp threw around them.

Now that they were in the tunnel, she could hear faint bubbling. The tunnel dipped down and widened into a cavern. The ceiling vaulted up, and steam rose in wispy fingers from a creek trailing through the cavern. Damp warmth seeped into her skin. All this water. So much of it.

"Wow." Dinah glanced at him. His shoulders were squared, but he kept giving her sidelong glances.

If he was so nervous, he must really consider this place home.

When he held the lantern higher, she could see a rough wooden bench sitting on a large woven mat.

"So, yeah, the water keeps the caves warm and it makes a pretty good bath. It's deep enough that I can go swimming here, too."

No wonder he'd picked this spot. The stream cut up through the rock, bubbling and gurgling into a wide pool in the center of the cavern. She walked up to the edge. Heat from the water saturated the cave, smelling like minerals and earth.

"The soap probably isn't great to be putting in the water, but I don't really have a choice." He moved up beside her. "You can wash clothes and hang them on the line outside, too, if you want."

"I can't believe you have hot water." Maybe she could—no, that was silly. But she really wanted to. "Can I put my feet in?"

He smiled at her, and just kept smiling. "Sure."

Her legs ached. Her hands ached. This week had bruised her entire body. She sat down on the mat and pulled off her boots and socks, then rolled her pants up to her knees.

When she dipped her toes in the spring, it was almost too hot.

Johnny sat down beside her and pulled off his shoes. "So. This morning."

She'd been hoping he wouldn't ask questions.

"Gates killed my mother while I was at the neighbor's—I came home to him smoking on my porch. And he stole my house and our well. But it's not his, and I'm not going to let him keep it."

Johnny rolled up his jeans, too. "You were trying to make the guy there leave?"

The water reached almost to her knees. She disrupted the current by swirling her leg through the stream. "No. I just tied him up."

Dinah raised her legs out of the spring and flexed her feet, trying to stretch her calf muscles. Johnny's gaze drifted over to her legs, so she lowered her feet back to the water. "I was afraid Gates would have messed with the graves or thrown out all our stuff or something."

Her voice sounded quiet even to her. The hot water swirling around her calves was too relaxing. It made her want to take off her clothes and sink all the way in, but Johnny was right next to her. She kept her eyes on her toes to avoid looking at him. "I don't care if he's mad. At least then he'd be noticing us instead of sweeping us under the rug."

Johnny didn't say anything. He pulled his legs out of the water. Dinah lifted hers out too and let the water drip off.

His calves were toned but not huge. He just looked healthy. Not gangly or underfed. Trim, but he had some muscle on his shoulders. Living out here, he probably had to work pretty hard. Bright eyes, suntanned skin.

How in the world had he gotten a tan, living in the forest?

The fine, dark hair on his legs reminded her that she hadn't shaved in a long time. She liked having her legs smooth, liked wearing shorts because she liked the feeling of hot sun on bare skin. The status symbol of shaved legs wasn't one she and Kara could afford, though, and for most of middle school, she'd avoided shorts, even though everyone knew why.

She pulled her socks on. The last two years, she'd gotten a pack of razors for Christmas and made them last all summer. Winters, she didn't shave. Kara always complained she had it worse because her hair was so dark, but even so, it didn't show up as much on her brown legs as it did on Dinah's peach-white skin.

"I don't blame you for wanting to kill him. You're not going to get justice any other way." Johnny's voice was hesitant, like he wasn't sure if he was allowed to say that or not.

Justice.

Dinah stared into the darkened, swirling water rippling by her. "Probably true."

Justice had not even occurred to her before. She wasn't sure she'd ever seen justice in Charlotte County, other than in the form of bonds between neighbors. A friend showing up with a cartload of fruit, a man with a heated basement inviting twenty-three neighbors to sleep on his floor.

Johnny rolled his pant legs back down. "Look. You need help. I can talk to my friends. All of us together, we could do something."

Maybe if they lived in St. Louis, she could have reported her mother's murder and Gates could have been arrested. But they didn't, and the St. Louis police had nothing to do with the sheriff in St. George.

Dinah shook her head. "I can't drag more people into this. You've done plenty already."

Here, justice had warped into the right of the rich to be pardoned.

And that was why she'd gone back home. To let him know he had not won.

It had lifted the fog. What she'd done had burned away the haze that nothing else had cleared. And she was a little shocked by what was left. She felt the littlest bit brave. Unafraid.

She was not afraid of what Gabriel Gates would do. She wasn't even afraid of dying. Her only fear right now was failure, and she would not let that happen.

This rising feeling inside her was so close to freedom.

"You do need help, though." Johnny stood up, brushed off his pants. "At first I thought you were just kind of bananas and going to get yourself killed. But maybe I was wrong. And if you have help, it might work."

She'd already told him no once. She wasn't risking anyone else's life.

He tapped her head gently with his pointer finger. "Don't be so stubborn about it."

This new feeling of being unafraid was a little intoxicating, something light but potent bubbling through her. And he had no business telling her how to be or not be. "Are there big rocks or anything in the bottom of this spring?" she asked.

Johnny shook his head.

"Is it pretty deep?"

Standing right by the edge, he held out a hand to help her up. "Oh yeah. Over my head."

"And you said you can swim?"

"What?"

Dinah shot a hand out to his leg and pushed him backward. He yelled, but his feet slipped and he landed in the water with a splash that echoed through the cave. She stood and backed up a step.

He came back to the surface immediately, bobbing in the waves he'd created. He ran a hand over his face to wipe off the water. "You," he said. "*You* are lucky you're sitting back from the edge right now."

A huge grin cracked her face. "One, don't patronize me. Two, don't tell me what I need. Three, I will tell you if I decide I need help. Don't decide it for me."

The light from the oil lamp on the waves collected and broke, washing toward her, then away. Johnny swam over in two strokes and pulled himself up on the rock ledge.

Water streamed off him and he pushed his hair back with a hand. "Okay, one, I accept your declarations, or whatever. Two, how dare you shame me like this in my own house." In the lamplight, she could see the smile in his eyes, even though he was holding his mouth in a straight line.

"They're not really for you to accept or reject. They just are," Dinah said. "So is this the end of the tour?"

"No, but my three is that we will have to call intermission, on account of how I need to take you outside next. I had planned to be very dry for that." Johnny led her back up the path and into his living room. His t-shirt clung to his skin, the light blue showing transparent where it stuck to his back. He stripped his shirt off, facing away from her. A trail of water slipped down his spine.

"I'll wait outside." Dinah grabbed her coat.

She deserved to stand out in the cold and think about what she'd just done.

She never would have pushed Kara into the water like that. Teasing wasn't really Dinah's thing. Kara teased her a lot, but it took a kind of lightheartedness. Positivity. Things she hadn't been since her dad had left.

Of all the moments for that to surface, right now just seemed like irresponsible timing.

Johnny stepped out of the cave behind her, mostly dry and wrapped in a heavy coat. "I've got a trap line you can see in the morning when I check it if you want. Otherwise, I've got a garden I can show you."

"A garden?" She swung the cave door shut behind him.

"Sort of. Fruit is so expensive, it's a good thing to grow." He led her down the hill away from his cave.

She couldn't believe how well he'd survived out here. A lonely home, maybe, but he was set for years.

"Sunlight is a bit of an issue, so I had to find a place where the trees were thinner. Here we go." Johnny held back a branch so it wouldn't slap her in the face.

Sunlight dappled strawberry plants, spread out like a blanket through a small clearing, framed by raspberry canes and blackberry bushes. "This must have taken years." The strawberries had escaped the clearing and spread far beyond it into the trees.

Instead of moving away or giving up, he'd done this. He'd started over, and it made her want to sink down to the forest floor and cry.

Johnny shrugged, like he was nothing. "You'd be surprised what a guy can do when he's bored out of his mind. It wasn't that hard. I had to cut back some branches at the top and build up the soil, but after that it was just watering them."

Strawberries were so expensive that her mom had never bought them. "This is really cool."

He rubbed the back of his neck, like her awe made him uncomfortable. "I'm usually working on a project of some kind. It keeps me from dying of boredom."

"What project are you working on now?"

He grinned and bumped her foot with his boot. "Well, this girl crash-landed in my cave so currently I'm pretty busy with that."

"How'd you get the money for all this?" Rude question, but this did not add up. The plants, the lumber, his motorbike. The antibiotics, the suntan. How he presented himself as so careless and aimless, but every single thing she'd seen so far showed razor-sharp goals and a deep, subtle intention she could not figure out.

He turned back and started up the hill. "I had a little when I left town, and it snowballed. I traded for stuff. My friends helped me out a few times."

Dinah hiked beside him in silence. Trading and snowballing didn't account for all this.

And even though she'd asked, he hadn't told her where he'd been when she'd woken up in the middle of the night.

He walked beside her, a little ahead, occasionally glancing her way. "Careful." He held back another branch she'd almost walked into. "Those must be deep thoughts."

"What?" She looked up.

"You're frowning. And marching along at, like, thirty miles an hour."

She stopped where she was.

Her heart thudded and her chest felt hollow. "Where were you last night? And where did all this money come from?"

His face became guarded. "It's just one of my projects. It didn't have anything to do with you."

She could not stay here if he wouldn't tell her. "I can't trust that."

He leaned against a pine and crossed his arms. "Well, you'll have to."

"Look, you're entitled to your secrets, but there are some things I absolutely cannot risk right now. You could use a favor from Gabriel Gates. Everyone could."

His expression hardened. "I wouldn't turn anyone over to that man. And regardless, I don't need a favor from him. I need to stay off his radar. Like, I can't explain to you how much I need him to forget about me." He pushed off the tree and ran a hand through his dark hair, leaving it standing on end. "Fine. It's not worth you thinking that. Follow me."

"Where are we going?"

Her distrust must have shown, because he reached out and untucked a strand of her hair from her jacket collar. "Just up the hill. I swear to God, I'm not going to betray you. But you won't believe me unless I show you."

She followed him.

They hiked down the trail, scrambled up the hill near where he kept his motorcycle, and then followed another trail around to an opening in the rock.

In the entrance to the cave, he paused for her to catch up. He climbed a lot faster than she did, mostly because she didn't know where she was going. Dinah stopped next to him and looked into the cave.

Nothing. She raised an eyebrow.

He turned on a flashlight and kept walking. In, around a corner, down a trail. Set back in a maze of tunnels stood a two-by-four plywood wall, painted dark, and in the wall, a door. A sharp, sour smell permeated the tunnel.

Johnny unlocked the door and shone the flashlight around inside. "I'd light the oil lamps, but I think it's pretty obvious."

The air smelled strong and yeasty. Water bubbled somewhere.

Stainless steel drums and barrels on feet stood around the room, connected by long copper coils. Sealed tubs and wooden crates lined the wall. Glimmers of green glass shone through the slats in the crates.

She wanted to go in and look around, but he didn't move, so she stayed where she was.

Johnny turned his flashlight toward the copper coils. "As far as he knows, I went to another city or maybe even died. I'd like for him to keep thinking that. He's got some of his ranch hands searching for the source of the moonshine, and if they find it, I really am dead."

"Why would he care about moonshine?"

Johnny looked pleased with himself. "He and Mitch Harding control most of the supplies in and out of town, right? He does the contracting and the shipping, so he gets a cut of everything, all through the whole process. He even sells the liquor that the bar serves on a big markup. But my liquor undercuts what he brings in, so it sells way more, and he doesn't get a cut of it. He hates it. It's great."

She could barely see his silhouette in the dark of the cave. This was too strange. The moonshine in the green glass bottle she'd had in Denton's store had been Johnny's. What she drank that night had been made here.

Johnny was the source of the money coming through town that Gates couldn't control.

He locked the door and led her out of the cave. She blinked as her eyes adjusted to the daylight. "So if you aren't allowed in town, how do you sell this stuff?"

"I make night deliveries to my distributor. He sells it to the stores for me. And there's . . . more to it. My friends and I have a thing going."

"Why can't Gates stop people from buying from you?"

Johnny shrugged as he made his way down the steep trail. "It's a big product for the small stores. There's no good way for him to stop everyone from buying products that aren't his. So instead he wants to figure out who sells it and either buy the business or get rid of the source."

As they walked back to the cave, a little beam of delight settled inside her that he was taking his own revenge this way.

And suddenly she couldn't be around him anymore. He'd seen her worst fear and her worst failure today. Everything she needed to do, he'd already done so much better than she had. He'd started over, somehow built a new life—which she couldn't even do—and he was defying Gates in a manner so clever and effective that the man couldn't even get his hands on Johnny.

"Do you mind if I clean up?" she asked once they were inside.

He waved at the door to the spring. "Go for it. Don't swim downstream—there are rocks in places and eventually it becomes a waterfall through the cave floor."

"Got it. I won't swim anywhere." She grabbed her backpack and the oil lamp. A bath, a hot bath, sounded like an otherworldly miracle. He handed her soap and towels.

This guy even had towels.

Down by the pool, she stripped off her clothing and sank into the water, making sure she could still touch the bottom. With the lakes and ponds mostly being murky sludge, she'd never had a good place to learn to swim. She and Kara and Chrissa and Alex and Dylan had taught themselves how to float and doggy paddle in the big watering tanks for the cattle, but the tanks weren't big enough for much more than that. Her dad had grounded her for a week when she and Dylan had started roughhousing in the tank and splashed a wave of water into the pasture.

The heat seeped into her muscles as she tried to let go of everything she felt and figure out what she knew. She floated on her back and watched steam chasing the light of the lamp up until they were both lost somewhere between her and the ceiling of the cave. The hot water washed against her sides, drifted over her toes.

Dinah closed her eyes. She couldn't divorce the two. She couldn't separate the water she was floating in from the wetness she felt against her skin, she couldn't keep what she knew about Johnny apart from the feeling that she could trust him, and she couldn't separate Gates breaking her mother's neck from her own loss.

She tensed her muscles and let herself sink down. Until her head was covered and not even the light or the air could come down here with her. Just black and water and rock.

Not a grave, but definitely a disappearance. At this particular moment, she was rid of the world and the world was rid of her.

She let go, let herself float back to the surface and emptied her lungs with a sigh.

She trusted Johnny.

No matter how raw and ashamed it made her to see his success stacked up against her failure, if she trusted him, then she could let him help.

If he helped and she was not alone, the axle she'd been turning around since that silver truck had pulled into her driveway had tilted just a bit.

Dinah swam over to the edge and grabbed the soap. She scrubbed her hair and her body and swam a little ways up and down the wide spring to rinse off.

She finally—wonderfully—pulled on her pajamas: cotton pants and a tank top that was a little too small but worn to familiar softness.

She went back up to the cave-house with her hair towel-dried but down and still damp. Unbraided, her hair was a mass of half-dried, wavy blond strands, some dark, some lighter. Circus blond, her dad had called it. Red strands, a few black strands, brown strands mixed into all the blond. He used to tell her it meant she had the whole world inside her, but what must have been inside him for him to walk away, knowing this could happen?

He'd always played the lottery, her dad. Bought the tickets and believed he might strike it rich. Even though he knew the lottery preyed on people, he'd still believed he could be the winner.

Johnny glanced at her when she opened the door, but immediately turned away and shuffled things around in the cabinet.

"What?" she asked.

He shook his head. "Just making room for you to put some of your stuff in here. If you want. So you don't have to live out of the backpack."

"You looked like I scared you." She set her bag down on the bed.

Johnny snorted. "You didn't scare me. Sorry. I'm just—not used to . . ." He waved his hand vaguely at her. "You, like that. Girls in pajamas. Or whatever." He finally turned away from the cabinet and his face was stained pink, his blush turning his tanned cheekbones a shade she could hardly stop herself from reaching out to touch.

Dinah bit the inside of her cheek to keep from smiling. "I

hate to tell you this, but girls wear pajamas a lot."

He ducked his head and stepped back. "Shelf's empty for you."

She rubbed her hands back and forth on her thighs. "You were right. I need help."

His head lifted. "What kind of help?"

Dinah sank down on the mattress. "I'm not sure. I just know I can't carry out any sort of effective plan alone. I need some way to get around that's faster than a motorbike. I need supplies. I need a better gun and a plan that will actually work."

He waited, standing by the table and looking down at her on the bed. After a moment, he finally spoke. "My friends could give you some . . . options."

She tilted her face up to him. Options. She could use options. "How so?"

"They know people, they can get things shipped here, they can travel."

That was enough for her. "Can I trust them?"

Johnny snorted. "The last thing they would do is turn you in. The hard part will be getting them to agree to help. But they might point us in the right direction or something."

"How soon can we talk to them?"

"First thing in the morning."

She couldn't do much about the fact that it was dark out and they should be sleeping now. "That works. What's safe to tell them?" Everyone in Charlotte and Wright counties either wanted to be Gates or wanted revenge on him. But very few would say which side of the fence they took.

"Tell them whatever you want. They're no friends of his." Johnny unrolled his sleeping bag near the table. "But they stay out of it, like I should be doing," he muttered quietly.

"Sorry," Dinah said.

Johnny stretched out on top of his sleeping bag and put his hands behind his head. "Don't be. I made my choice."

On the grassy hill behind her house, Johnny had made a decision, and in the water of his hot spring, she'd made hers.

Her one chance to fix her own failure was to accept help. And the damage Gabriel Gates had done was bigger than her family, so she could not be the only one who wanted revenge.

 EARLY-MORNING SOUNDS OF JOHNNY MAKING TEA WOKE HER from the gritty slide of a shovel.

"Do you want oatmeal or toast?" Johnny said quietly.

Dinah rolled over with a sigh and sat up. "Whatever you're having. How soon can we leave?"

Five days ago, her mother had made their last breakfast. Five days ago, Dinah had peeled pears beside Kara and let the juice trickle down her arms.

Johnny pulled peanut butter out of the cupboard. "When you're ready. It's going to be tough to convince them to have anything to do with this." He stirred sugar into a mug of black tea and brought it over. His big hands wrapped all the way around the cup. When she took the hot ceramic from him, his skin brushed hers.

Five days ago, she'd torn her hands open on a shovel, and now hands that were strong and whole were serving her tea that was far too hot and far too hopeful.

Kara. She wanted Kara here. But it was this boy instead, and there wasn't even a choice for her to make about the two of them, because there was only one thing left for her.

The surface of the tea washed back and forth as her hands trembled. She didn't look up, but Johnny's hand touched her own, took the mug back from her. She pulled in a slow breath, trying to loosen her throat and keep the trembling inside.

She wanted her guitar. Strings under her fingers. Hard, sharp things she could pull sound and meaning from.

His hand touched her knee.

Not this. She couldn't do this right now. Dinah stood up. "Should we go?"

He stood up too, looking startled. "Yeah. Maybe we should. I'll—I guess I'll go outside so you can get dressed. Come on out when you're ready." He grabbed his gun and the water jug and headed for the door, glancing over his shoulder at her.

She picked the mug back up and closed both hands around the warm ceramic. Maybe drinking something, having something in her stomach, would help, even if it was still hot enough to burn.

All she needed to do was focus on Gates. After today, he would not be able to get away from her.

Dinah finished her tea, pulled off her pajamas, and dressed in her cleanest jeans and shirt. She wrapped a ponytail holder around her hair and noticed it didn't hurt as much to use her arm anymore. Good.

When she shoved her hands in the pockets of her jacket, she felt something crinkle. She pulled out a five-dollar bill.

Kara's money. Johnny had given it back. She crumpled the bill in her fist, then smoothed it out and slid it into her sock.

This gift was more than five dollars, and she was so desperate for the things it meant that she could hardly breathe.

Johnny waited for her outside, leaning against an oak. "Are you okay?"

She was not okay, but she had things under control. "I'm fine. Where are we going?"

"Not too far." He led her south, away from the caves.

"We're not using the motorcycle?" Big cats, dogs, bears—everything was out here. She didn't see Wolf anywhere, but she could be around here, too.

"It's shorter to hike than use the road. We've got my gun and you've got your knives. Are you any good with those?"

"Better than you could ever hope to be."

He snorted. "What about with a gun? How good of a shot are you?"

"Decent." She pulled a dried leaf off a maple and twirled it by its stem. "Warren was better than me."

Johnny reached for the water. "I'm going to need proof about the knives."

She looked up to see him grinning. "Fine. Give me a target."

He looked around. Freckled patches of sunlight splashed the pine needle floor. Trunks and heavy branches and scrubby brush surrounded them in protective clusters. "That." He pointed to a broad, low-hanging branch of a pin oak. "To the left of the big knot."

"That's too easy." She could hit that in her sleep.

"Then do it." He crossed his arms.

Dinah pulled the knife out of the sheath in her boot and tested the weight. She aligned her body, checked to make sure Johnny was behind her, and threw the blade.

It sank into the branch, right beside the knot.

"Hey, nice. But now you have to go get it."

"You made me throw it. You go get it."

He laughed and jogged the half-dozen yards to the branch and pulled the knife out. He stopped smiling when he handed it back to her. "How did you get that good?"

"A lot of time and a lot of anger." Dinah tucked her knife back into her boot. "So these friends. Did you meet them after you left town, or before that?"

He kept walking, following some trail only he could see through the trees. "After. I'm lucky they found me."

"You never said why Gates threw you out of town."

The ground turned to mostly rock, tilting upward even steeper. The trees thinned as they climbed. Small saplings and shrubs grew sideways out of the rock, their scrubby fingers bending toward the light.

Johnny sighed. "So, remember Gates has a daughter? Olivia. I'd been with her for almost eight months by the time he caught us."

Dinah almost tripped on a jutting ledge of the rock. "You dated his daughter?"

He reached to steady her arm. "Yep. He called me into his office and gave me twenty-four hours to leave town."

Not drugs. Not the moonshine or something else illegal. Johnny had been thrown out of town for dating the man's daughter. "I'm surprised that's all he did."

"Well, he also had Shaw break my nose." He gestured to his face and tried to smile, but it didn't quite work. Brian Shaw, the red-bearded man who had chased her and Warren through the woods. Once Gates was dead, she'd handle that man, too.

But eight months. For eight months, he'd been with the daughter of the man who killed her family.

But maybe daughters weren't guilty of their father's sins.

"Did you ever see her after that?"

"A few times. He told me I wasn't supposed to see her ever again. But I had to tell her good-bye and let her know what happened. Then she got sent to some boarding school up north. I don't know, maybe it helped her, to get away from him. She was so unhappy when I met her. And then I went and made everything worse."

This should have made her even angrier at Gates, at the callous and cruel way he'd torn Johnny's family apart. At how he'd acted like the town was his to ban people from and that this boy's life and his daughter were his to limit.

But all she could do was picture Johnny, barely sixteen, getting his nose broken and having to say good-bye to his girlfriend and home and family.

His eyes watched her uncertainly. He still had a half smile on his face, but his stance was awkward, his shoulders too straight. Dinah stepped close to him and reached a hand up to touch his cheek, then traced a finger down his nose, over the ridge where it had been broken. "I'm sorry," she whispered.

His eyebrows drew together. He didn't speak, but when the look in his eyes changed and he lowered his head not even an inch, she backed up a step.

Gates. Going home. Nothing else.

He froze. Shoved his hands in his pockets. "C'mon. We're almost there."

Dinah followed him. She tightened her ponytail then played with her fingernails to avoid looking at him. He kept to himself, though, staying a few steps to her left and only checking to make sure branches didn't slap back at her and that she saw the roots rising out of the leaf cover.

Kara must be so worried. That one cryptic message was all Kara had heard from her, and it had not been a comforting one. If she knew Kara, that girl would not take her message as an answer. She'd be searching the woods, watching the house, rounding up people to find her. And Gates would hear about it.

The baying of hounds and a distant, urgent buzz reached her before she saw the persistent little shack clinging to the side of the mountain. Three loose-skinned, slack-jawed hounds bayed and barked down the rocks at them.

Johnny finally led her onto a road, a narrow clay trail, really, that came in from the north and wound past them, switching back to dead-end at the tin-and-clapboard shack.

Three tall Black men in bulky coats were running chainsaws near the house. Someone yelled a warning, and a dying tree crashed to the ground.

Across the yard, a big, bearded white guy and the Lakȟóta woman who had driven her down the mountain—Lissa Thomas, Johnny had said—were splitting wood.

Dinah kept an eye on the hounds as they walked. These dogs looked a bit too much like the one who'd bitten her.

"Boys! Knock it off!" The bearded man set down his axe to yell at the dogs. Lissa kept right on splitting logs, her axe blade finding some trick inside the wood and popping it in half like she'd pulled a lever.

The man slid a giant cigar out of his pocket. "Johnny, huh?" His voice was harsh and rumbled in his chest. A low forehead and bushy eyebrows frowned at her.

Never in all her life had she seen a man who looked like this guy. Gray and white hair stood straight up from his head, only a shade lighter and barely longer than his sideburns and beard.

He practically had a mane. Fingers as thick as his cigar tugged up denim pants. A flannel shirt with rolled-up sleeves hung over the waistband. Somewhere in all that hair, his mouth moved. "You've got a girl there," he said, as if Johnny might not have noticed. Smoke curled up from his cigar.

Johnny gave her a strange sort of half smile and shrugged.

They reached the patchy grass of his yard—a few hundred square feet of cleared forest—and stopped next to him. Tires, barrels, and scraps of sheet tin littered his yard. A shed clung to the rocks near the treeline. The hounds circled them, tails whipping, sniffing their shoes.

"Uh, yeah." Johnny looked from him to Dinah. "Dinah, this is Burns Holloway. Burns—Dinah Caldwell."

"Ohhh." Burns took a drag on his cigar. "I know that name. Kwamé picked up something on the CB. Bet you're that girl, aincha?"

Dinah glanced at Johnny. "I'm hoping you can help me with something."

He laughed, a slow, deep chuckle like a bear grunting. "You musta made that man pretty damn angry, girl."

Johnny broke in. "We need to talk to you about something. You got time?"

The saws surged and whined in the distance, split only by the pop of Lissa's axe.

"Well." He looked them over. "Well, I suppose I got time, yeah. C'mon in." He led them to the house and up three steps that creaked as if they might split. "Kwamé! Lissa!" he bellowed across the yard.

Lissa set her axe down and whistled loud with her fingers at her lips. One of the chainsaws stuttered out.

Dinah and Johnny followed him into the house. Two rooms, it looked like. One a combination kitchen and living room, and the other closed off with a heavy wooden door. A bedroom, probably. A radio crackled on the sill of the lone window, right by a box of shotgun shells.

A redheaded woman stood near the stove, stirring a giant stock pot of chili. She looked up briefly and smiled.

"This is Alice." Burns gestured with his cigar. "And in the corner, that's our girl." A high cradle beyond the fireplace. A bundle of blankets fussed inside the wooden slats. The cradle was the nicest item in the room, sanded and polished and intricately carved.

Dinah nodded. "Nice to meet you, Alice."

"You, too. Can I get you tea?"

"No thanks. We're fine." She wasn't here for tea.

Burns led them over to a couch, and he sank into an old rocker. Everyone waited in silence until Lissa and a man who must be Kwamé walked in. He had to be nearly six foot five, dressed in worn jeans and blue flannel that pulled up the cool tones in his deep black skin, his hair a neat tapered afro. "Kwamé Adu," he said.

"Dinah Caldwell." She sat down on the couch.

Lissa raised her eyebrows at Dinah but didn't say anything about that morning.

Burns spoke around his cigar. "On the CB radio today, we heard that man is looking for you. So why you in trouble, Dinah girl?"

Dinah was sitting a bit closer to Johnny than she would have if this man and his house hadn't seemed so odd. Johnny nodded at her, so she took a breath. "Gates killed my mother."

Burns blew smoke out his mouth and rocked back and forth. "Killed her how?"

Strange thing to ask. "I—I was gone. He broke her neck. He

claims she just fell. And he's taken over my farm now, too."

He shook his head. "You got another parent, girl?"

Being called "girl" that way was fast getting annoying. "He's been gone for years. Went to St. Louis and never came back."

Lissa sat down on a stool by the fireplace. "So why are you here? When I gave you a ride, it didn't seem like you planned on returning."

She was starting to feel something so familiar here. This living room had six seats, in a one-bedroom house. Alice's chili right there, floating the scent of roasted tomato and peppers through the room, could feed thirty people. The chainsaws still running outside, how Burns had waited for Lissa and Kwamé to come in, Lissa giving her a ride down the mountain without a second thought.

It felt a lot like loaf after crusty loaf from Laura McCaffrey on bread day, hot canned apples with cinnamon in December, huddling in the windy truck bed on the way to the Christmas Eve service with the Franklins; like water for free.

"So you want a job? You need a place to stay?" Kwamé asked.

"No. I want him to pay for what he did."

Burns shook his head and just kept shaking it, back and forth. "You don't be messing with him. The only reason Johnny has territory in St. George on his own is because we don't want in on it. He's a ballsy, foolish kid for tryin' it, and I'm almighty surprised he's not been caught so far. You leave that man alone."

Oh. Burns was a moonshiner, too. Of course he was. Johnny wasn't distilling by himself. His friends were a ring of bootleggers.

Dinah leaned back. "I'm aware he's dangerous, but I don't care."

He kept shaking his head and rocking. "Just forget it, girl."

She brushed off Johnny's touch on her knee and stood up. "What would you do if Gates killed your wife and little girl over there? Would you forget it?"

His bushy eyebrows went up. "You lay low with Johnny, and then get the hell outta the county. That's what you oughta do."

Johnny muttered something on the couch behind her, but she ignored him. "I'm the only living person left in my family, and I don't care what it takes or how dangerous it is. I should have killed him the moment I saw him on my porch and I didn't, and now my brother is gone, too. Everyone needs to stop telling me that it's dangerous. I don't understand why you think that would even matter. There's nothing to argue about here. All I want to know is whether or not you'll help me."

Burns Holloway's eyebrows stayed up. His eyes tracked over to Johnny, and for the longest time, they looked at each other and said nothing.

Kwamé was the one to finally speak. "Why'd he take your land?"

"We have a well. He's going to charge for the water, and it will mean all my neighbors have to sell their farms."

Burns stopped rocking. "Water's too valuable. He'll fight hard for it."

"That's why I need you."

He started rocking again. The eyebrows went down and the smoke curled up.

By the fire, Lissa pulled off her jacket and unlaced her boots. "You have every right to want revenge. Fighting for your home when someone else takes your land and your livelihood away is your right. It's a threat against your life, the Oglála oyáte can tell you that. But vigilante justice usually doesn't bring actual justice."

"She'll never get justice, though," Kwamé said. "Not from these people."

Dinah sat back down on the couch and ran a hand through her hair. Justice herself should strike her down if she was ever the person who could help but wouldn't. "I don't care what it is. Justice, revenge, vigilante justice—I want him dead and I want my home back."

"Did you see him kill your mother?" Burns asked.

Her hand fell to her lap. "I—I walked in after. She was on the floor. He was the only other person there. He said she fell but she didn't. And he'd bruised her the day before."

His face turned a little softer. "Her body. Where is it?"

"I buried them," she said. "I had to."

"Them?" Lissa asked.

"My brother. He had bad lungs. After Gates killed my mother, he sent people after us. Warren had an asthma attack in the woods." Her head felt clear enough, but her hands had started tremoring and she couldn't get them to stop.

"So not a clear-cut murder. Not an accident, but no single man to prosecute for the brother and not a clear intention with either of them? This would be multiple cases, years in court, lawyers you can't afford."

Dinah lowered her head to stare at her fingernails. She was not responding to that.

"Burns. What the hell are you doing?" Johnny said.

"What's his claim on your land? Was it outright theft, or did he have some claim on it?"

Her silence was answer enough.

Johnny leaned forward. "Burns. Stop."

"My point is, I'd want to know a lot more about what happened before I step into someone else's revenge. And a court would see a shaky case here at best. He'd claim an accident during a rightful foreclosure," he said.

Kwamé snorted. "What court?"

Sheriff Anders and Judge Harding were judge, jury, and executioner for Charlotte County. Judge Harding had gotten elected because Gates campaigned for him. And Gabriel Gates's big donations every year to the town council and sheriff's department always got written up in the paper, which Judge Harding's son Mitch owned. *Local son gives back. St. George's own funds city law enforcement.*

"You know why I'm asking," Burns said. Kwamé fell quiet.

Them doubting her like this was worse than them saying no.

Johnny braced his forearms on his knees. "We don't need you to help kill him. We just need to develop a good plan, get some supplies, transportation. That's all."

Lissa just sighed. "Johnny, hon."

Burns ground out his cigar in a tin cup on the floor by his rocker. "Thirteen years ago, I went after one of those Amazon farm engineers—the ones who handle the big computers that run the whole farm. It was the Oklahoma farm. My friend was a mechanic, he managed the whole fleet of combines for the state. But the engineer's programming error caused an accident and my friend lost his arm and then his job. I went after that engineer, wanting that eye for an eye. He saw me coming and drew on me, so I had to draw, too. I was the better shot." He leveled his gaze on Dinah. "But the programming error wasn't made the day of the accident like I'd figured. It was another guy, the week before."

"Revenge gets messy," Kwamé said.

But this was different, and Kwamé and Burns did not need to be saying that to her. She knew exactly who had killed Ellen Caldwell. "You don't want to help, fine. But I'm fixing this. He's a plague on this whole county, not just me. I'll wait in town for him if I have to, but I'm getting this done."

Burns rocked backward. "Don't you go into St. George for nothing but the apocalypse, girl. People are starving, and those who aren't are still broke as dogs. If you piss that man off and he decides he really wants to get ahold of you, he'll make you everybody's get-rich-quick scheme."

She looked from Johnny, who'd gone pale, back to Burns. Fine. Bring on the apocalypse. She'd take it right to that man's door.

Burns held up a hand, the creases in his face deepening. "I can't say I blame you, but you're asking a lot from the folks around you, and mostly for people who're already gone. You keep that in your mind. Now, we want to talk to Johnny here, by himself. How about you give us a few minutes and then I'll send him on out to you."

Dinah set her jaw. Fine. She'd tried, and they'd shut her down. She needed help, but she didn't want it from people who wouldn't even try.

"It ain't about you, girl. We got other business." He stuck his cigar back between his teeth and rocked back and forth.

Whatever. "I'll be outside." Dinah stood up and walked outside to the porch.

But instead of heading down the steps, she waited by the open window.

Johnny spoke. "You do so want to talk about Dinah."

Burns grunted. "Whatcha doing with her?"

She wouldn't have listened in if it had turned out to not be about her, but like she'd thought, it was, and therefore she was going to.

"I met her in town," Johnny said. "She helped my brother out in a fight, and she had no place to go, so I took her back with me."

"Well. She's something to you, though," Kwamé said.

Johnny huffed.

Burns's rocker creaked. "That girl is gonna get you killed, Johnny boy. I can't say I'd do any different was it me, but that girl can't see past her revenge. Can't you hear how she talks like it's her fault? She thinks she's atoning for something, all mixed up in her guilt. People like that ask too much and go too far. Who knows what she's missing about what happened. Plus, you kill Gates, and Mitch Harding swoops in and we have the same problem all over again, just a different name. If you follow her, you're gonna die, too."

"Too?" Johnny's voice went tense. "So you think she's going to get herself killed."

"Yeah. Yeah, I do. You think so, too."

A sigh that sounded like Johnny's.

"She ain't wrong that something ought to get done," Kwamé said. "Last time I all but missed the connection with the combine fleet because that deputy had the spot staked out. Woulda had to drive up to Nebraska to make the delivery."

Lissa's voice. "We don't know her. She might be able to end that man."

"But sure as anything, she's gonna get herself killed and take Johnny with her," Burns said. "And Johnny here is already breaking his rules. I thought you was done with other people's business."

"So all of you think I shouldn't be helping her?"

Of course he shouldn't be. She'd told him that several times.

"Well, now, we didn't say that. You do what you gotta do, and if that's getting yourself killed, then that's that. You did what you had to," Burns said. A long pause. "But I want you to think about it. And I got a baby now, so I can't be mixed up in this."

Dinah stepped off the porch. Even in the middle of the day, it was cold now. Especially up here, where the wind was harsher.

A field-dressed buck hung by his head from a white ash over by the barn. The hounds circled below it hesitantly, muzzles high and sniffing.

The still was tucked back a few yards into the woods, a huge system of drums and barrels framed by cords of tarped-over logs.

The door creaked open, but she didn't turn around. Footsteps came out to her, and when a hand touched her shoulder, she expected to see Johnny, but it was Lissa, boots untied. Her light brown skin was warm in the sunlight, the glow of golden hour on the fields at home.

"I'm sorry about your family," Lissa said. "My mother died, recently. Just old age. But it still wasn't easy. I hadn't seen her in a while because she's up in South Dakota and I'm down here with my wife. So I felt a lot of guilt about it, too."

Dinah looked up. "I'm sorry." The wind whispered cold against her skin.

Lissa slid her hands into her coat pockets. "Will you be happier, be able to let go, if he's dead?"

"Happier?" Dinah said. Let go of what? Let go of Warren?

"If you leave, will you be able to start over?"

Start over with what? Start over for what? "I don't really plan on doing that."

"Then do what you need to." Lissa touched her shoulder

again. A tattooed cottonwood tree rested on her wrist, fluffy seeds floating up her arm. "Just don't let him or what happened or your own guilt make you someone you don't want to be. Keep yourself, okay?"

But who she was had already been taken. She was not a daughter anymore, she was not a sister anymore, she was not Kara's neighbor or a nighttime guitar player or a high school student or even a resident of Charlotte County anymore.

When Gabriel Gates had killed her family, he'd killed her, too.

# ELEVEN

"I'm sorry," Johnny said. "At least we tried."

Dinah pulled off her coat and sank onto the bed. "Don't be sorry. We'll figure something out."

It was understandable that his friends didn't want to put themselves and their families at risk. A month ago, if someone had come to her desperate and wanting to kill Gabriel Gates, she would have taken one look at Warren and sent that person packing.

Johnny smiled as he poured two glasses of water.

"What?" she asked.

"Nothing," he said.

"Something."

We. She'd said "we."

She'd started depending on him too much for him being the boy who'd insisted all he would do was give her food he was already going to eat. And then he'd said he'd do what he could, but that was when he thought his friends would come in as backup.

If it was just the two of them, Burns was right—she'd get him killed.

"I can see on your face what you're thinking," Johnny said. "Stop it."

"I can't," she said.

They'd have to find others. Anyone else who might want the world to be rid of that man.

Kara's family, Mr. and Mrs. Hernández. No, they had little kids. And they might have sold the orchard already.

They better not have. Kara had better not be gone.

The Franklins. Maybe they could help. Mrs. Franklin and Chrissa, their oldest daughter, were better shots than even Warren. But Alex and Dylan, their eighteen-year-old twin boys, were basically the smartest guys in the state and planning to go to college for engineering and chemistry on scholarships. First kids in the county to go to college since the depression. She couldn't ruin that.

Mr. and Mrs. McCaffrey didn't have kids, but even through the motherly front Laura McCaffrey always put on, Dinah had been able to see her fear of everything from a long winter to inevitable drought fires to Warren's coughing. And Mr. McCaffrey's bad heart meant he wasn't supposed to be exerting himself. Their nephew sent them money sometimes. The one who worked for Gabriel Gates.

Everyone was too busy surviving.

"Like you said, we'll figure something out." Johnny finished his water. "I have to go work for a few hours. If I don't go run that batch of moonshine, it's going to be a big waste."

Dinah stood up from the bed. "I'll help." After everything he'd done for her, she wanted to give something, anything, back to him.

He pulled on his coat, trying to hide his smile. "If you want. Sure."

The sky was grayer now, the wind carrying a sharp chill. Winter weather was unpredictable this high in the mountains— snow would make her plans a whole lot more difficult.

"So Burns and Kwamé got you into distilling?" she asked.

He nodded. "We share costs so we can buy bulk, out of state. Corn, malt, yeast. Propane, sometimes. I prefer to use locust wood since it burns so hot and doesn't cost money, but sometimes in the winter dealing with wood is a pain. When I make a fruit batch, though, the fruit is mine. Kwamé and Burns only do straight moonshine."

His garden. Strawberries, blackberries, raspberries. Back at the store in St. George, Denton Marlow had mentioned fruit moonshine.

"Problem is, Gates knows one of our vehicles, so we can't use it anymore." He lit a lantern that washed the cave in light. Something scurried down the tunnel ahead of them. "About every other time we deliver, he's got someone tailing us that we have to shake off."

"What happens if he catches you?" She could smell the mash way out in the tunnel—sharp and sour, smoke and fermented corn.

Johnny unlocked the cave door and she followed him into the room he'd walled off. "Well. He's got Sheriff Anders so in his pocket that the tail is almost always a deputy. They'd arrest us and seize it all, probably. It's illegal, technically—but that law's almost never enforced anywhere else. The government's too over-loaded as it is, and no one has time for it."

No one except a man who wanted a share of their business.

She lit the lanterns on the walls as he opened the ventilation shafts. The room was warm and muggy from the fire and the water she heard bubbling somewhere. When he slid the lid off the drum, thick foam covered the top of the whitish liquid.

The size of the steel drums surprised her. "These things are huge."

Johnny stirred the contents of the largest drum with a long-handled paddle. "Small, actually. The mash-to-moonshine ratio is about ten to one. So a hundred-gallon pot makes me a ten-gallon batch." He glanced at the thermometer on the side of the tank. "Grab a couple logs over there? It will boil quick if I get the fire a bit hotter."

Beside the door, a neatly split stack of logs climbed the wall of the cave. She grabbed several and carried them over. While he built up the fire, she finally found the source of the bubbling water. It trickled in a thin stream down the wall of the cave in a miniature waterfall. She tipped her head to look up at the ceiling. "Did you drill that out?"

He glanced over. "I used a sledgehammer and a chisel. It was too thin of a stream, just a leak from the hot spring, but I really wanted the still inside a cave. Much harder for people to find." He stood up. "Gotta have cold water. Most of the streams in these caves have dried up, but not all of them." He shoved the end of a narrow trough up against the wall. The rubber end pressed into the rock so it fit tightly. Water trickled down the trough and emptied into the third drum, a barrel that the copper coils curled into, which was already full of water.

He nodded to the barrel. "See the tap on the bottom? The second one? Twist it enough that water trickles out about as fast as it's going in."

Dinah crouched down and twisted the handle of the little faucet. Tepid water splattered into a groove on the cave floor that ran back to the waterfall and emptied into the eroded gap in the cave floor where the waterfall disappeared.

If the water was cold enough to use for distilling, it must have traveled far enough through the rock to have cooled down.

He swished his hand around in the barrel with the coils. "Getting there. Okay. Let's get the jugs."

The three barrels, tubs of cornmeal and malt, and crates of jugs and jars nearly filled the tiny room. "So all this only makes about ten gallons?"

"I'd love to do bigger batches. Burns has an eight-hundred-gallon pot. I don't have room for that kind of thing, so I run a batch a few times a month, and by the time my distributor is ready, I've got enough."

Dinah reached out a hand and ran a finger along one of the copper coils. The color and the curve together were so pretty. "It's warm."

Johnny glanced at the thermometer. "Okay. It's ready." He grabbed a crate of sturdy plastic jugs. Hissing and a gentle *thunk-thunk* sounded, and a few minutes later, plinking, trickling, bubbling.

He had her hold the jug under the first tap on the last barrel. When he twisted it, clear liquid streamed into the jug.

"Basically, I soak the cornmeal in hot water with malt and yeast to ferment in the big pot. When it's ready, I heat it like this, and the steam rises from the pot into the copper coils. The steam collects in the coils and gets forced through that second barrel, the thump keg, which is basically a big filter." He traded out her jug for another, brushing her shoulder with his and crouching down next to her. "The steam rises out of the thump keg and gets piped into the worm box—this barrel with the water. It's just called that because of the copper coils; no worms are involved, so don't look like that. The water drops the temperature of the coils so the steam condenses into liquid again, and it runs out the tap here."

Dinah shook her head and watched him work. The liquid coming out the tap turned from a trickle into a stream.

The faint, high whine of a small engine broke the silence. "Hey, can you hear that?" Dinah said.

Johnny stood up. His hand went to the Glock on his belt as he strode down the tunnel. She pushed up from the ground and followed him.

The mouth of the cave showed the forest had darkened already; the trees turned to shadows masking the stars. The engine grew louder down the trail—coming from the wrong direction. Johnny's cave.

A motorbike bumped to a halt below. Someone killed the engine and a voice called, "Johnny?"

Cole. Dinah took a step back into the darkness of the cave. Better for him to not know.

He swung off the motorbike. "Getting up this path is almost impossible on one of these. It's gonna kill the suspension."

Johnny stepped down onto the rocky trail with the lantern. "Where'd you get that?"

"Borrowed it." A yellowing bruise marked the boy's jaw.

"What's wrong?" Johnny's voice went tense. "Is it Dad?"

He shook his head. "I haven't seen him in almost three days, though, so who knows. Worked late and spent a few nights in Mr. Gates's bunkhouse." He looked around. "Where is she?"

"Who?" Johnny crossed his arms.

Even from ten feet above them in the cave, she could see the skeptical look on Cole's face. "Dude, come on. I know she's here. I looked for you first in the house and her stuff was there."

Johnny's arms fell to his sides. "What's going on?"

Dinah stepped forward. "It's fine, Johnny. What's wrong?"

Cole climbed up the rocky steps into the cave. "I don't have long. I shouldn't even be here, but I owed you." His scruffy hair hung in his eyes. Dirty clothes, sharp cheekbones, shadowed eyes. A kid whose body and posture and words were all harsh angles. A tenser, paler version of his older brother.

And clearly Cole knew what his brother did for a living, even though he worked for Gates. He must be able to keep that secret, so hopefully he could keep hers.

"I have to keep running this batch." Johnny led them back to the still, and in the lamplight, Cole looked far too haggard for only twelve.

Was this what would have happened to Warren in a few years? Had Cole ever been that young, that hopeful, making little creatures with his whittling knife?

Johnny switched out the jug under the tap and leaned against the wall. His shoulders tensed, stretching tight the fabric of his t-shirt. "How did you even know she was with me?"

"When I left, you guys were together in the alley, and your bike woke me up when you rode out of town. I saw a girl on it and figured it was you." He nodded to Dinah.

The place he'd stored his bike in town. That must be his dad's house. "So what's wrong?" she asked.

Cole met her eyes. "Mr. Gates has posted a ten-thousand-dollar reward for anyone who can find you. He's charging you with property damage, assault, and violation of your eviction."

Dinah moved toward him so quickly Cole backed up and bumped into the rock. "What did he say?"

"I—I only talked to the barn manager." His gaze fell to the floor.

She backed off a step and put her hands carefully in her pockets. No need to jump on him like that. "Sorry, I didn't mean to scare you."

His glance flipped to Johnny then back to her. His chin tilted up. "You didn't scare me."

"What did you hear?" she asked, softly this time.

"Well." He shrugged. "The barn manager wouldn't shut up about it. When Mr. Gates and Shaw and Adwell went out to check on the well drilling and building the pump house yesterday, they found Fry tied up. After that Mr. Gates and his foreman were locked in his office for hours, yelling about a public challenge. He said the guy had been carved up with a knife and left tied there for three days."

"A public challenge?" Johnny shoved off the cave wall. "Dinah. What did you do?"

"I told Alan Fry to tell him he wasn't going to get away with this."

Cole narrowed his eyes. "That's all?"

Gates had heard her. She should probably be scared—that was a lot of money. She should regret what she'd done, drawing his attention like that. "I didn't hurt Alan Fry that badly, Cole. I mostly just scared him and burned all his stuff. Which was in my house. And it was yesterday morning, not three days ago. Three days ago I was basically unconscious and slept the whole day—I was so sick from that dog bite I could hardly move."

Johnny moved up behind her and touched her shoulder briefly in warning.

Gates was Cole's boss.

"I'm not going to hurt anyone else. It's just between me and him now," Dinah said.

Cole looked from her to Johnny and back again. "Mr. Gates reported it to Sheriff Anders, and they talked to a bunch of teachers at the school and your neighbors and everyone. They put up reward notices in town, tried to find your school tablet. And the notices have your school photo."

The teachers? That could mean Kara. "Thanks for telling me."

That kind of money could change someone's life.

Cole rubbed the back of his neck. "I can't risk my job. If anyone found out I knew where you were, it would be over for me. He's so mad. You gotta leave town. Just leave and don't come back. If I see you around again, I won't have a choice."

Dinah didn't have a choice either, but Cole didn't need to know that.

"She's just staying until her arm heals. She's leaving this week." Johnny's voice had an edge she hadn't heard before. Dinah turned toward him, but the miniscule shake of his head stopped her words.

"She'd better." Cole ran his hand through his shaggy hair. "If he finds you, he'll make you into an example."

Hard as he looked now, the younger, frightened version of him she'd seen in the alley still had to be in there somewhere. "Take care of yourself, okay?"

He brushed his hair out of his eyes. "I've been doing fine. Worry about yourself, not me. Everyone is looking for you. I wouldn't even leave this cave unless you're leaving for good."

Johnny stepped over and held out a hand. "Thanks for letting us know. Coming up here took nerve. I'll make sure she gets out of town okay."

Cole shook his brother's hand, a stiff, unfamiliar gesture. "No problem, dude." He headed for the door. "I gotta return this bike. Stay low, guys. See you around." His steps echoed faintly down the tunnel.

Dinah turned on Johnny. "I am not leaving town."

"Shh." He held up a hand. The whine of the motorbike sounded. Johnny walked over to the door and checked to make sure Cole had actually left.

Then Johnny came back, sat down beside her, and put his head in his hands. And then he scrambled up to check the temperature of the pot. "I have to do the first cut. We gotta throw out the first jug—it's lethal. Methanol is what comes out first because it boils at a lower temperature than ethanol."

Dinah sat down on the floor in silence, watching him work.

Taunting and threatening Gabriel Gates had been a terrible decision.

Maybe Burns and Lissa were right about some small part of this. Maybe she was letting her judgment be clouded by her grief.

The fire underneath the big pot snapped and fogged the air with smoke, but it dissipated into the tunnel. The campfire smell lessened the bitter smell of the mash, and the thumping, bubbling, trickling of the still was its own strange kind of music.

There was a whole system here. The biggest drum with its water and fire, the copper coils leading to the thump keg, to the worm box, to the tap. To Johnny. To Burns and Kwamé and Lissa, to his distributor, to the stores, to people who knew it didn't belong to Gates but bought it anyway. This whole system, tucked away like this.

Some people were willing to work against Gates, or this still wouldn't even be here. There were people all along the chain who weren't brainwashed or asleep. They were just waiting.

But the person to change that was not her. Because right now, even if she could undo her threat to Gates, she'd still make that same terrible decision all over again.

The final jug was full. He stood up with a sigh and shifted the water trough over to the big tank that held the mash. The stream splashed into the bottom.

"Ten thousand dollars." He spread the fire out and raked it down to coals.

The entire town had an opportunity now. It wasn't just people working for Gates she had to stay away from; it was every single person who'd heard about that reward.

"You really shouldn't have done that," he said.

What she did was only his problem if she stayed here. "I'll find another place to stay. I'm not leaving the area, but at least you won't be involved."

He put the rake away neatly in the corner. "You have to leave the county. Your life here is over. Even if you manage to kill Gates, which isn't likely, he's going to kill you, too."

Not happening.

"Seriously, Dinah. Maybe he deserves to die. But *you can't kill him.* You're not the first person to want him gone. You think you're the first person to go off half-cocked and hell-bent on revenge? Want him dead and be as angry as you like, but it won't happen whether you try or not, so just move away. You can go study music. Get a job in the city, maybe. You don't have anything keeping you here, and you have to find a place to live anyway, so why not use the chance to do what you always wanted, instead of dying for no reason?"

Never. Even if those things were actually available to her, she could never, ever use Warren's death as an opportunity. "I'm sorry you don't love your family, but I loved mine. I still love them. That land is mine, and they're buried on it, and I can't leave. They didn't just die, they were murdered, and I should have—" She stopped herself and stood up. Walked out of the cave, down the tunnel.

Johnny strode after her. The door to the still slammed shut. "You are absolutely unhinged. You're going to get both of us shot. And actually, if Gates catches either of us, a good clean shot to the head will be too much to hope for."

She spun around at the mouth of the tunnel. "If I die too, then that's what happens. It's what should have happened in the first place."

The light from the lantern swam in waves around them as he walked toward her. "You can't mean that."

Oh, but she did. In the dark, she hiked down the hill. Brush cracked under her feet. He scrambled after her.

"Stop. Please stop. You're going to break a leg. You don't have a light." His words echoed off the rocks around them, disappearing into the pines.

When she reached the path, she turned on him. "I mean that more than I've ever meant anything in my life. Mom had been waiting, years of misery because my dad was a coward, and then she died. She kept saying things would get better, but things never got better, and then she died. And Warren might as well have been mine. He *was* mine, for all it matters. I taught him to walk and climb trees. He came to my bed when he had nightmares. I was the one feeling guilty and scared for him when he went to school, because he was getting bullied because of his asthma. He should have had his dad there to help, he should have had his whole family, and so I tried to fix my dad's mess. But no matter what my dad did, at least he didn't just *stand there* while someone killed his family."

Johnny ran both of his hands through his hair. "I'm sorry. I'm so sorry."

"When I came home and found Gates in our living room, I had my knife. I should have killed him right then. And when Warren came in with the gun, I should have taken it from him and shot that man in the head as he was leaving. Even when he sent his men after Warren and me, I should have sent Warren into the woods and stayed behind with the gun. I had three chances, and I didn't do anything."

Deep lines settled on his forehead. "You can't blame yourself for that. If you'd tried any of those things, he would have killed you, too."

He understood her, he just didn't believe her. She was so sick of people not believing her. "That's the point. I should have tried!" She was yelling, but now she couldn't stop. "Maybe trying would have killed me, but I should have died trying. They needed me, and I should have given everything for them. And I didn't."

Johnny closed the distance between them and set the lantern down. The pool of light circled them both. He put his hands on her shoulders. She stared into his eyes, daring him to say something. His face was inches from her own, but she'd be damned if she was going to step back.

"You didn't abandon your family, Dinah. Your mom and brother were murdered, and it's not your fault you didn't die, too."

She couldn't answer him. She had abandoned them, no matter what he said.

He dropped his hands from her shoulders. "Okay. If you want to figure out a way to take him down, then that's what we'll do."

"I can't stay here. I'll leave in the morning." It didn't matter that she'd miss the company and his music. Those things barely mattered.

He shook his head. "You need a place like this. You aren't going to find anywhere else you can be relatively safe."

"I can't stay." If she left as soon as it was light outside, she'd have several hours to find somewhere. Maybe she'd have to stay in her tarp tent for a few nights, but that would be fine.

"You don't have other options. You can't go anywhere with people because of the reward. And you can't stay in the woods; it's not safe, either." Johnny shoved his hands in his back pockets. "Dinah. I want you to stay here. It's a risk, but that's okay. Please. Just stay with me."

The risk he was talking about was his life. If he died, his cave would be empty. The still would sit there abandoned, rusting away. Wolf would come by, looking for scraps, and there'd be nothing. His dulcimer would sit on top of the cabinet, collecting dust and eventually rotting in the damp cave. Johnny would never have the chance to fix whatever had gone wrong between him and his brother.

She started walking down the path so he wouldn't see her face.

"Why?" she said. He obviously felt bad for her. He'd feel guilty making her leave. That was no reason for her to risk someone else's life.

"Because." He kept pace with her, lantern swinging. "It's nice having someone around."

Also not a good reason. "You really should find someone who doesn't have the whole county looking for them."

They hiked up the rocks to his cave in silence, and he stopped at the door. "Maybe. But you keep saying you abandoned your family, and you so clearly didn't. I am the one who left my family."

"So you want me to stay because you feel bad about your brother."

"No." His voice was tighter, the words clipped. "I want you to stay because at one point, I wanted to kill him, too. And back then I probably could have. This wouldn't have happened if I had. But I didn't."

She stopped by the door to look at him. He looked away, like he was embarrassed. "I'm not worth you dying," she said.

"Fortunately, you're not the one who gets to decide that." He opened the door and held it for her, then locked it behind them. "He won't find us up here if Cole keeps his mouth shut. You can wait out the initial frenzy of everyone hunting for you."

"It's a huge risk."

"I take a lot of risks. And I'd do just about anything to get Cole away from him." Johnny set the lantern on the table.

It would be such a relief to not have to find somewhere else. To concentrate on planning and doing this right, rather than worrying about being discovered.

She stepped closer to him to make him look at her. "If you're sure, I'll stay here just until I know what to do next."

"Good. Yes." Hands shoved into the pockets of his jeans again, he didn't move away from her. She was tall enough she didn't have to tilt her head back at all to see his face. He had a nice jaw, actually, sharp lines.

She wondered if he'd ever kissed someone before. If he'd kissed that man's daughter. Not that it mattered. She just wondered.

She didn't blame him for not having done more for his family. It sounded like he'd tried as best as he'd known how, and honestly, what kind of parents would let their son be kicked out of town and not go with him? If she'd been exiled like that, her mother and Warren would have gone with her, not let her wander off into the forest and disappear.

If she'd met Johnny before all this, maybe they could have been friends.

She didn't know what to say, so she let the silence stretch out between them.

Friends. Wondering if he'd ever kissed someone before.

If she was one thing, it was honest with herself. If she could kill a man, she could admit it when she liked someone.

This wasn't the scared-but-curious feeling she'd had when she'd kissed Sarah Maxwell in sixth grade. And she didn't feel like she had on her first and only date with Luis Cruz, attracted but not really sure to what, because she'd barely known him. They'd gone to school together, sure, but she hadn't really known him. And it wasn't even the way she felt about Kara, because how she felt about Kara was a life of its own.

Johnny probably wasn't aware of her in the same way she was aware of him. But either way, it didn't matter.

He stretched his neck like it was stiff and changed the topic. "What do you want for dinner?"

Maybe sleeping on the rock floor was messing with his shoulders. One more thing because of her.

Also, dinner? How did he remember to think of these things? "Anything's fine."

He tossed her a bag of trail mix and poured some for himself into a bowl.

Dinah tore open her own packet. "I can't stay with you for free. It's not fair for you to have that risk when I'm not doing anything for you in return."

"I have pretty much everything I need, and you're overly concerned about things being fair. Don't worry about it."

She sat down on the bed. "But I can't use you like this."

"I don't think you're hearing me." He sat down on the bed next to her. "I've never met a more reckless, wholehearted person than you. Everything has gone wrong for you, so just—let me be something that goes right."

She narrowed her eyes and studied him. He looked so serious, so completely focused on her.

How could this be the boy who wouldn't get involved?

Dinah looked away for a second and then back to him. She played with her nails again, but then stopped.

Even if he meant what she thought, she couldn't do this. It didn't matter how he'd said exactly what she needed to hear or let her have the bed or built a home and a living out of the side of a mountain.

Anything else would be smarter than this. "Why did your family let Gates kick you out of town?"

Johnny pulled back like she'd splashed him with cold water. He slumped back against the wall.

Hopefully that abrupt little rejection hadn't embarrassed him too much. "I'm sorry I said you didn't love your family. That wasn't fair. You obviously do."

He opened his mouth to say something, and then didn't. She stared at his legs, stretched out next to her. Worn spots at the knees, frayed hems.

Johnny wouldn't look at her, instead glaring across the room at the table. "My dad is really sick. My stepdad spends all his time helping him—neither of them can take care of Cole anymore."

"I'm sorry." She was saying that a lot today.

His face flushed darker. "It's been years. Inoperable lung cancer. Keeps returning. They go to St. Louis for treatments, and he comes back so sick he can't stand up. I quit school to work so I could help pay for the treatments, even though Adam yelled and yelled about it."

"When did you drop out?" Her voice went softer without her meaning to, and he flinched.

"Eighth grade. As soon as I legally could."

"That sucks."

"I didn't mind." He crossed his arms.

Maybe she'd pushed it too far, because his expression turned from tense to annoyed. "They really needed me to be making money, no matter what Adam said. When Gates fired me, Adam had to take a second job and it left Dad alone twelve hours a day. But you know, a normal person would just let it drop, since I clearly don't like talking about it."

She'd never been good at masking what she felt, and right now neither was he. He didn't want to talk about this, but he needed to. Alone up here, all these things had rusted into place inside him. "But—your business does well now, right?"

"It does. And I sneak into town once a month to give them everything I can. It helps some. Adam was able to quit his second job and start saving a little."

"Is he getting worse?"

Johnny just shrugged. "They don't tell me as much anymore."

"I didn't mean to upset you."

"I'm not upset."

But his arms were crossed, tensed until his arm muscles strained the sleeves of his t-shirt. Dinah rolled her eyes. "Yes, you are."

"Fine. I'm angry because it sucks, and if I had been able to stay away from Olivia, I never would have gotten fired, Cole wouldn't be dropping out, and we might still have some kind of family. Do you know what that was like for my parents? Adam having to decide if he should move his dying husband to the city where he couldn't get work just to stay with their irresponsible son who'd be moving out in two years anyway? For my dad to know his cancer was the reason I had to leave alone? And Cole. His family just fell apart, all because I picked the wrong girl. I'm sorry I don't want to talk about my greatest personal failing right now, but I really don't." Closing his eyes, he thumped his head back against the wall.

Maybe this was better, because now that they were both frustrated, neither of them would start something that shouldn't happen.

He was right, though. It wasn't her issue to push, and being taken apart always hurt. He clearly needed to talk, but whether or not to do that was his choice.

She shifted over beside him, closer, and his jeans brushed her knee. "Okay. We won't talk about it."

Johnny opened his eyes. "I shouldn't have said it that way. It's not your fault I tore apart my own family."

Somehow she'd managed to both hurt and embarrass this guy in under two minutes. "Gates was the one who kicked you out. His actions are his fault, not yours. Do you know what most people would have done if they'd been thrown out of their homes like that? Given up. Died in the woods. Anything but what you did. You're so smart. And resourceful. And incredibly loyal to your family, even if you won't admit it."

The side of his mouth twisted down, but the annoyance left his voice. "Please don't do that. I don't need you to fix my feelings."

Dinah leaned back against the wall again, her shoulder touching his. He shifted, but he didn't pull away.

Every time she moved, he reacted.

"Well, just turn me in," she said. "I'll sew razor blades into my shirt or something, and as soon as he hands you the money, I'll kill him, then you can use the ten grand to move your family to the city."

He rolled his eyes. "That's not funny."

"But you're not frowning anymore."

His one-shouldered shrug brushed her arm. "I didn't know I was."

Living should not have to be this hard.

"It's just," he said. "Dad got fired from the general store the second time he had to take a week off for treatment. It was this bomb that made me realize life is just unfair—it doesn't matter who you are or how good you are or how much your family loves you. Doesn't change how things turn out. None of that means anything."

"Of course it means something. It means everything." Dinah moved her thumb, felt the stone in her jeans pocket. It had worn a home for itself by the seam. "Some of us are just fated to bad ends."

He snorted. "I don't believe in fate."

"Why all this, then?"

Johnny tipped his head up to stare at the low rock ceiling.

"I think there's a predictable pattern to how life behaves. It's all micro- and macrocosms of empires. Everything from cancer to economics—people and trees and cells consuming so they can grow and growing until they choke out everything else. But then something revolts, and either the empire crushes it or collapses. And it happens all over again, all these little bubbles of power rising and bursting. It just depends on where you land in the cycle. We landed at the shit end."

"So it's not fate, it's just our nature?" Whether it was fate or human nature, it wouldn't matter to Gates when she was done with him.

Johnny nodded. "When I was thirteen and quit school, I discovered, hey maybe life isn't fair but look, I can earn money. I can provide something. That meant Dad could pay for his medication and stay on it longer. He's had a few remissions, times where we thought things would be okay, you know? It seemed like we could be okay, and even when I first started seeing Olivia, it was like that would be something good, too. And then it all went bad. I can still earn money and send it to my dads, sure, but I can't change the world. And every time I try to help, I make things worse. We're just stuck mopping up, forever. That's why I don't get involved in other people's stuff. It doesn't change anything."

But it had, for her. "Then why are you insisting on helping me?"

His sigh sounded hopeless. "I'm trying to figure that out."

She leaned her head back against the wall. "You don't ruin things, you know. You've done nothing but help me and asked nothing for it."

His glance flicked over to her and then away.

She should not say this, either. "So was Olivia your first broken heart?"

Johnny smiled faintly. "She didn't break my heart. Why? Who first broke your heart?"

To give herself time, she drew her knees up to her chest and pulled a thread from the frayed hem of her jeans. She broke the thread. "My dad."

He didn't say anything, and she couldn't bring herself to look at him. Dinah rested her forehead on her knees.

"You do know it was never your job to make up for what he did, right?" he said.

She couldn't even tell if that was true. "Well. I have no idea why you believe you ruin things, because you so obviously were born to help people and make all these beautiful things. You made your own dulcimer. And look at your house."

Total silence.

Eventually, she asked, "What are you thinking about?"

"You."

She pulled back a little and turned to face him.

Now he was the one looking like he wanted to take her apart.

It wasn't a choice between him and Kara, because there would never be a life in which she could have Kara. And whether she was fated to a bad end or born into a little empire ready to burst, she wanted to kiss this boy. She barely had to lean toward him, but it felt like a long distance, and like crossing it was changing something.

Her lips touched his, and he immediately froze. She kissed him for the briefest second, his mouth soft under hers, and for a moment it was embarrassing to be kissing so one-sidedly. It made her so nervous she couldn't keep herself from laughing. Her lips still close to his skin, she said, "I'm sorry. It's not funny. You just look like—"

He put a hand on either side of her face and kissed her back. She stopped laughing. He pulled her body up against his. Her hand rested on his chest, and his too-fast heartbeat was the only thing she could hear.

Johnny pulled back for a second. "I thought you didn't want me to kiss you."

So that had been what he wanted, all of those moments. It was more than she knew how to handle. "I changed my mind. Is this okay?"

Can I touch you like this, she meant. Can I see how you're made?

"Yes." His breathing slowed. "Yes. It's okay."

He didn't seem like he knew what else to say, but he lowered his head and kissed her again. Her hand touched his face, traced his jawline. She felt his stomach muscles tighten through his shirt, and she touched him there, too, because she couldn't not.

Watching him struggle to tell her who he was, hearing him say what he had about his dads and brother and the last two years, she'd seen something too familiar—that dead-certain knowledge that you were the only one holding your family together, and you were the one telling them life would turn out okay. And no one, ever, was telling you that, and no one likely ever would, and so the question of whether you were lying grew bigger and bigger until somewhere along the line, you realized that God and life and fate had just lost you.

She wanted Johnny to know one person, at least, had found him.

Moving to his lap, one knee on either side of his legs, Dinah leaned her forehead on his. He wasn't smiling. His face was more serious than she'd ever seen it.

"What?" she asked.

He shook his head. "Nothing."

"What kind of nothing?" She touched his neck, hoping he didn't mind. He had such a handsome face. Maybe not handsome, actually, but she didn't know what else to call it. His cheekbones and his jaw were sharp, giving his cheeks slight hollows and throwing shadows around his eyes. His cheekbones were where he blushed, and she ran a finger across his left cheekbone like she'd been wanting to. Uncut dark hair, wiry and thick, not quite black, hung to his eyebrows when it wasn't standing on end. A slight curve in his nose, the ridge where it had been broken. Light brown eyes, a fascinating contrast to the sharp lines and shadows.

The serious lines on his face softened a little. He lifted a hand and brushed her bangs to the side. "So—is it just me?"

She knew what he meant, and she didn't stop to weigh it. "No." Whatever change this was, she needed it.

Her mouth was only two inches from his, so she moved closer, her lips barely touching him, waiting for him to come the rest of the way to her.

He closed the distance. His hands gripped her waist, his thumb stroking her stomach over her tank top. She wouldn't have moved, didn't want to ever move, except this wasn't close enough. She slid off his lap onto the mattress, hooked a finger in the collar of his shirt, and pulled him down.

Johnny followed her. She'd thought kissing him would hurt too much, that something good and something only for her would be too heavy.

His left hand suddenly tightened on her hip; his right hand wound itself in her hair and didn't move. "What?" she asked.

Johnny spoke into her hair. "Don't do it. Please. I'll take you to St. Louis. Or send you. Whatever. Make sure you have a way to start over."

It was okay for him to ask. But. "I can't."

He traced the fringe of her eyelashes with a finger. "Then tell me why people do self-destructive things."

She blinked against his fingernail. "It's part of having a choice."

His hand slid from her hip to her lower back, underneath her. He pulled her onto her side, facing him. She touched his chest, his ribs, and his eyes caught hers.

Her hands found the small of his back and she pulled him closer. Her stomach touched his, warm through their shirts, and they stopped talking. He ran a finger down her arm until he found her hand, and he threaded his fingers between her own.

She'd never lost track of time like this before. Around midnight, Johnny got up to make tea, and they only drank half of it, because he made hers way too sweet, and when she couldn't stop laughing at it, he set his down, and took hers away, and kissed her again.

They lay there for hours, sharing the single pillow, and so much had changed inside the cave that it certainly must have changed the world outside it.

# CHAPTER
# TWELVE

OR THE FIRST TIME, SHE DID NOT DREAM ABOUT DIGGING A grave. Instead, she shot Gabriel Gates between the eyes. Over and over, she sighted down the rifle barrel and pulled the trigger. The kickback hammered her shoulder, but Gabriel Gates stood up again, blood running into his eyes. He stood there and let her kill him, as many times as she wanted. So she pulled the trigger again. He stood up, fell, stood up, fell. Until finally he stood up and walked down the driveway, a bag over his shoulder. He walked down to the blacktop highway, turned south, and kept going.

When Dinah opened her eyes, she didn't have an answer to her dream. Even after hours of killing him, she had no idea how many times would be enough.

Dinah rolled over and glanced at the boy next to her. Even though he was asleep and had rolled toward the cave wall, her face flushed.

At some point, she'd crawled under the covers, but he was on top of the blanket, still in his clothes.

And her shoulder hurt like she'd bruised it. Dinah sat up and rolled her shoulders to stretch out the stiffness.

She hadn't been close to a single other person in over a week. It was unfamiliar, craving someone's touch like this. And if she'd missed human contact after a week, what must two years be like?

The blankets rustled, and she turned around to see Johnny watching her. He blinked, then sat up. "Sorry," he said. "I didn't mean to sleep here."

Her face felt warm. "It's okay. I don't even remember falling asleep."

Johnny ran his hand through his hair and straightened his shirt, but it didn't help. His clothes were unbelievably wrinkled. "Yeah, you fell asleep while I was talking to you."

"I did?" She didn't remember him talking. "Sorry. What were you saying?"

"I don't even remember." He stood up. "Did you sleep okay?"

No. But she couldn't really say she'd kissed him for hours, then had fallen asleep and shot a man in the head for the rest of the night. "Mostly. You?"

He glanced at her while he reheated the tea from last night on the propane stove. "Yep. The mattress is a lot nicer than the floor."

She didn't mind that he'd fallen asleep on the bed. But she didn't know if he did. He liked being independent, liked having his space, and here she was, messing with all that. Taking his bed was one of those things she was sure he minded but didn't want to admit.

He brought her a mug of tea and sat back down on the mattress, farther away than he'd been last night. "Did I get it right this time?" he said.

Dinah stared into her tea. She shouldn't feel like this about him after only a few days. It was unrealistic. And desperate.

When she looked at him, when she kissed him, she felt like she knew him. Not the details. Not all the facts and the quirks. But she'd never before looked at someone before this and known who they were, what they wanted and the reason they were alive, underneath all the superficial stuff people packed around themselves.

"It's okay," she said. "It's good."

The primary revelation of her teenage years had been that romantic love was flimsy. Her father had walked down the road and left behind a woman who had given him nineteen years of her life, and he'd left her to face what should have been the next fifty years alone. And Dinah had loved Kara to distraction— which was still not enough to make her do anything about it or to make Kara love her that way, too.

Strong emotions, but brittle ones. Prone to cracking, like the peppermint canes the teachers gave out every Christmas.

Even if Johnny wanted something with her—and she didn't know if he did; he might just be lonely for company and con- tact—it was already so tempting to stay here, curled up on the mattress with him, until the deadness inside her went away.

But dead things didn't come back to life.

"Dinah." He touched her hand.

She met his eyes, but she couldn't wipe the fear and guilt off her face in time.

Johnny pulled his hand back. "Hey. If you don't . . . it's fine.

It's okay." He tried to grin. He stood up, changing gears as fast as possible. "I have to get that last batch to my distributor. So I guess I'll . . ."

Shit. "Johnny, stop. I didn't mean that the way you took it."

His back to her, he spun the sugar spoon around and around on the table.

"It's not you. It's not. I just don't know what to do."

Johnny faced her. "About what?"

She couldn't think, looking at him. "Maybe everyone's right. Even him being dead won't be enough."

His lips parted a little. He dropped down into a chair by the table. "So what, then?"

Dinah pulled on her socks and shoes. "The problem is you're distracting me. I need a minute."

"I'm distracting you?" He looked a little too pleased by that.

"You know you are."

"I knew no such thing. You're overestimating me again."

She flicked the back of his head as she walked past him, and his laugh warmed the tunnel up to the door.

It wasn't at all funny, though, and she could not let him cloud her judgment. He was too much change, too fast, and probably too late. Wild longing for something outside her constant grief had spiked through her last night. And like making Alan Fry scream and burning all his things, falling asleep beside Johnny had lifted the haze of her anger.

Outside, she sat down on the rock ledge by the door. The ledge was about two feet deep and ran along the face of the slope like a step. The cold sky was sunny above the treetops, but their branches held most of the morning sun out of the forest. She buttoned her coat and flipped up the collar to cover her ears.

A squirrel leaped from a dogwood tree to a spruce, leaving the branches shivering.

Last night Johnny had said it hadn't been her job to pick up her father's slack. That she hadn't failed her mom and Warren.

Even the idea of it made her eyes sting. She had tried. She had tried to kill him, then tried to escape, and tried to protect Warren. She hadn't failed them on purpose.

Her mom would say she hadn't failed them.

Even if that was true. Even if she had done everything she could and there was nothing for her to need forgiveness for—how could she start over, after this? There was nothing left for her if she wasn't Warren's sister and her mother's daughter and the girl with the well.

There was no way for her to start over. Even after Gabriel Gates was dead, she'd still want to kill him. She could spend her life looking down that barrel and tearing his world apart.

What she wanted was for him to feel what she felt, and he never, ever would. It wasn't inside him to take away. He could not lose someone the way she had.

And he'd taken two people from her. She could not take two lives from him. She couldn't have an eye for an eye.

So she couldn't have true revenge and she couldn't even have justice.

A shadow slipped through the trees. Dinah squinted in the morning dark. A dozen yards away, the gray glimmer of Wolf eased through the sumac.

Maybe living on the borders of each other like this, coexisting, was a tension people had just quit trying for. Last night Johnny had said people survived by consuming each other. And he was right. The human relationship was predator and prey.

Wasn't it?

What did justice even mean, with Gates? Convincing Sheriff Anders to arrest him, charging him with murder, him going to prison if everything could be proven beyond doubt, and only if everyone involved refused the bribes that would be passed along under the table?

Not only was that not what she wanted, it didn't even seem like actual justice. Even if he got a life sentence and wasn't released early due to prison overcrowding or yet more bribes, Brian Shaw and Mitch Harding and his business managers would certainly get away with whatever they had done—and they'd still be running his little kingdom, collecting rent and foreclosing and price-controlling everything that came into town and raking in extra for his businesses by shaving away at people's survival margins. What Burns had said last night was right—even if Gates was gone, someone else would step into the gap he'd left, and the machine would keep rolling.

Sending Gates to prison wouldn't undo or even stop his damage.

Go to Kara's, ask the neighbors for help, her mom had said.

But she hadn't. She'd let shame and pain and fear of what Gates would do to them turn her the other way.

Dinah rubbed the frayed hem of her jeans between her fingers. She pulled another thread from the fabric and tugged on it until it started unraveling.

She stared at the thread in her hand, at the weakened hem of her pant legs, and then she tugged on the thread again, kept unraveling it until it broke off.

Dinah jumped to her feet. She ran back inside, leaving the door to bang shut behind her. "Johnny."

He whipped around, nearly dropping the mugs he was holding.

"I figured it out." Actually, her mom had figured it out.

Johnny thunked the clean mugs down in the cabinet. "I thought bounty hunters had seen you or something."

"Oh. No. But we need to go back to your friends." Dinah grabbed her backpack and shoved trail mix inside, then started filling the water bottle.

"Hold up, what? Why?" Johnny took the bottle from her and started filling it himself because she was spilling water everywhere.

"He wouldn't have gotten where he is without a sheriff and a judge who took bribes, without people who would enforce whatever he said, without the money from one scam to fund another. I was pulling threads from my jeans when I figured it out."

Johnny stared blankly at her.

"I'm not just going to kill him. We're going to unravel his whole system." Dinah slung her bag over her shoulder. "Ready? Let's go."

His mouth fell open. "Where? His ranch?"

"What? Of course not. To the other bootleggers. We were talking about the wrong thing. They need to hear this."

He thumped the water bottle down on the table. "It doesn't matter what you figured out. It won't change their minds." The resignation in his voice stopped her.

"Sitting in this cave won't change their minds either, Johnny. Sometimes you just have to fight harder. We need to hurry; come on, let's go." She gestured to his coat, slung over the chair by the table.

He narrowed his eyes at her like he was thinking, a hand resting on the back of the chair. Then he shook his head. He grabbed his coat and pulled it on. "Okay, you weirdo. But if you want a different answer, we better talk to one of the others. Burns will be stubborn. Our best chance is Kwamé—the Ghanaian guy you met. And if we're going to Kwamé's, we'll have to take the road, which means possible bounty hunters."

Dinah couldn't stop her smile.

Johnny pulled his Glock out of the cabinet. He ejected the magazine, loaded three more rounds into it, and clicked it back into the hand grip. "Put on your sweatshirt with the hood and pull your hair back. No blond showing. Get rid of the bag—put everything in your pockets. We can put water in the saddlebag. And make sure you have both your knives."

Dinah rolled her eyes. "I always have both of my knives. Sometimes I even carry the third."

Johnny looked her over, like he was wondering where else on her body she could carry a third knife.

"Stop that."

"What?" He slid the Glock into his holster.

She yanked the sweatshirt over her head and pulled up the hood. "Stop looking at me that way." She'd meant it mostly as a joke, but he moved away anyway.

He grabbed the water from her bag. "Ready if you are."

Dinah bent to check the knives in each of her soft leather boots. "Ready." Her heart was a chime in her chest, because she wasn't ready, but Kara and Laura McCaffrey and the Franklins all needed her to be. Warren and her mom needed her to be.

Johnny padlocked the door behind them. Outside his garage, he started the little green and black Kawasaki and waited for her to climb on.

She slid on behind him, but she hesitated with her hands

hovering over her knees. There was nothing to hang on to. He glanced over his shoulder at her. Before she made it any more awkward, she reached around him and held on to the strap on the seat in front, instead of wrapping her arms around his waist. Her forearms rested on his thighs this way, though, so she wasn't even sure that was better.

The cold pre-dawn wind rushed faster as they sped up the mountain road, ruffling her hair and filling her ears with sound. Her whole body tensed, but not from the ride. Ahead lay yet another thing she could not take back—and she was hurtling toward it.

But this, it felt so different. It felt alive and like it came from every piece of who she was.

The curving, narrow road lay bare and quiet. A doe sprinted across the road ahead of them, and Johnny slowed down. Hitting a deer would total the bike.

A left turn took them to a gravel road, then a dirt road. Curving, winding up, circling around outcroppings and rocky spires marked with spindly pines. The knobby tires on the Kawasaki handled it just fine, but this road, the forest spreading out below them, the ground falling away on either side of the dirt path all made her heart slam in her palms against the leather strap. She almost asked Johnny to stop, not because of the distance she'd fall, but because he might, too.

They hadn't seen a single other set of headlights yet. Living this far up the mountain was a good idea. Gates probably didn't even know these people existed.

Because they stayed out of town business. And here she was, asking them to change that.

A light burned through the morning in a small riverstone

house. Johnny braked on the path. A tiny stream, drying up in a larger creek bed, bubbled behind the house and wandered around the side of the yard by the barn and down the mountain.

Burns and Lissa and Kwamé had retreated to the peaks and folds of the mountains. No one could want anything or take anything from them way up here. And maybe that was part of the problem.

Johnny parked the motorcycle, and the engine cut out.

"I like this place," she whispered. A pair of hounds loped down to them, followed by a mountain goat, big-eyed and nimble.

"What is that?" Dinah stared at the creature. It was a goat, of course, but why was it in the yard?

"I think he's pretty tame. He's not a pet, but he likes the dogs, I guess."

Dinah shook her head, keeping an eye on the animal's curving horns.

The door opened. Kwamé came out to stand on the porch with his hunting rifle. "That you, Johnny?" he called.

"It's us," he yelled.

They climbed up the sloped yard to his porch. Kwamé spit tobacco juice over the railing. "Lot of suspicious traffic around today. How you been?"

"Alright," Johnny said.

Kwamé set his rifle down against the house. "People are a-runnin' all over, down a bit farther, looking for you, Dinah. Ain't come up farther than the blacktop, but they will."

This spinning, rushing feeling inside her must be whirling toward some kind of drop. But right now, all she could feel was the rise. "That's part of why we're here," she said. "I changed my plans. I need to talk to you about it."

"Really." Kwamé looked to Johnny.

Johnny raised his hands. "That's about all I got out of her."

"Well. Lissa and my sister are on their way here from running this batch. Supposedly. They shoulda been here nearly an hour ago. Burns and my brothers are already out back." He nodded his head toward the barn. "Alice and the baby are inside."

Dinah glanced at Johnny. He lifted one shoulder half an inch in a shrug meant only for her to see.

She'd wanted to talk to Kwamé alone, but maybe it was better to just get this over with.

An engine shifted into a lower gear on the road somewhere below them, and a moment later Lissa's truck came into view. It pulled around by the riverstone house and jerked to a stop on the grass, the bed loaded with plastic crates. Lissa jumped down from the passenger's side, and a petite Black woman in a green coat closed the driver's door. The hounds charged over the rocks toward the truck, baying a song while their tails whipped the air. The mountain goat stood self-importantly on a ledge above the path, watching them while placidly chewing the frozen weeds he'd picked from between the rocks.

"We were tailed," Lissa said. "Had to go all the way into Wright County to shake them." She pulled jerky from her pocket and tossed two pieces to the dogs.

Kwamé immediately put two fingers to his mouth and let out a piercing whistle. His brothers and Burns came out of the barn, and the women headed for the porch, too. A barn, for a man who didn't have crop land or livestock, as far as she could tell.

"Lissa and Akosua were followed," he said.

One of his brothers turned right around and bolted the barn doors.

"Could you see who it was?" Burns asked.

Akosua pulled gloves out of her coat pocket and slid them on. "Sheriff Anders and two others in that blue Chevy of his." Her glance flipped to Dinah.

Kwamé's gaze tracked over to her. "Dinah. These are my brothers, Yaw and Kobe," Kwamé said, as the two men stopped by the steps. "And my sister, Akosua—Lissa's wife."

Dinah leaned against the porch railing, next to Johnny. Clearly they already knew who she was. She could feel everyone watching everyone else—Johnny glancing at Kwamé, Lissa studying her, Burns staring unblinking at Johnny.

"You sure you lost that truck?" Kwamé said.

Akosua nodded. "They could find their way up here anyway, though."

"We oughta sit quiet for a while. Run this batch but stay put for a few days," Yaw said.

And here she was, putting a bigger target on them. "Sheriff Anders might have put out this reward on me, but it's because Gates told him to. And his only reason is that I threatened a trespasser, in my own house, after Gates seized it. I still even have the deed." She pulled the folded papers out of her pocket and handed them to Lissa. Lissa unfolded them and read, then passed them to Akosua, standing right beside her. "I'm not asking you to participate in my revenge. I'm asking all of us to pull together to cut out his entire system. For all of us. His loans, his ranch hands, his businesses, everything."

Johnny grabbed her hand and squeezed it hard.

Yaw said something to Kwamé in a language she didn't recognize. Then Kobe and Akosua chimed in.

"Asante Twi," Johnny said quietly to her. "It's Ghanaian, an Akan dialect."

Kwamé looked from one of his brothers to the other, then sighed. "We've all got family and friends who work for that man. My aunt and uncle run his barns. Burns's sister married his cook. We can't kill each other."

Dinah nodded. This was nothing if not a family matter, and that was both the reason to fight and the reason they had not.

Akosua looked at the papers then handed the deed back to Dinah. "That deputy nearly ran us off the road last time we went to pick up supplies. Y'all were there. Sooner or later, he'll find us. Even without people looking for her, he's making himself our problem—"

Kwamé held up a hand. "Quiet. The dogs."

Both hounds had turned toward the road, folded ears pricked and hackles on end.

The whine and surge of engines climbing a steep grade rose in the air. It bounced off the rocks around them—either coming from the east or west, she couldn't tell which.

The sound broke through the echoes to the west. "Go," Kwamé said.

Yaw and Kobe ran to the barn and Kwamé went for his rifle on the porch. Lissa bolted to her truck. Johnny grabbed Dinah's hand and ran for the trees.

Unlike the woods around her house, this high up the mountains, there wasn't much underbrush. Tall pines and spruce, some scrubby bushes and downed, rotting trees. A thick layer of pine needles deadened their running, instead of the dry crunch of fallen leaves.

Two trucks surged over the hill to Kwamé's house—one a blue Chevy, one silver.

"Stop," Dinah said. "If we keep moving, they'll see us." She crouched down by two fallen trees crisscrossed on the ground. Decent cover, at least for now. Johnny sank down beside her on the pine needles.

The engines cut out and doors slammed.

"Stop." Kwamé's voice cracked like a gunshot. "You ain't welcome here."

"The law don't need permission." Sheriff Anders's voice drifted back, over the growling of the hounds.

"Where's your warrant?" Burns, this time.

Another truck door slammed. "We have cause to believe you're illegally making and selling moonshine." That voice. He was here.

His voice froze her from the inside out. Surely Gates could hear her breathing, recognize her heartbeat among every other sound.

"Why do you care? You ain't any part of the law," Kwamé said.

"Call it civic duty," Gates said.

"You can stop pretending," Lissa said. "Even if someone was running a still, it's a dead law courts leave alone all over the country. You just think you're owed a piece of anything someone else's got."

Johnny gripped her shoulder. "He might send his goons into the woods to look around," he whispered. Strain lined his eyes. He couldn't be seen, either. Gates could not know Johnny was still alive.

"We can't move," she said. They could see well enough to know if someone was heading their way. They'd make a run for it if they had to.

"I hate that I left them standing there," he said.

"You had to." It would have been worse for everyone if Gates and the sheriff had made the connection between Johnny and the other bootleggers.

Brian Shaw was with him, the bodyguard with the shaved head and a russet beard who had chased her and Warren through the woods. Another white guy she didn't recognize was with him, too. "Who is that?"

"Don Adwell," Johnny whispered. "He and Shaw have worked for him for years. Not from around here. They were both rovers before that."

She had no idea what a rover was, but Adwell did not look like good news. He was short, wiry, and mean-looking, with a long neck and a small head. If Shaw looked like an angry bear, Adwell looked like a snake.

Sheriff Anders's voice drifted over. "We ain't here to talk about if you are or ain't selling moonshine. Since you're so concerned with the law, we're here to let you know the St. George town council has declared anyone doing business within the county needs to apply for a local business license from the newly formed St. George Business Association."

Gates pulled out a pack of cigarettes and lit one. "Getting all our local businesses to work together will give the tri-county area a big economic boost. Neighbors helping neighbors and all."

"You on the town council now?" Burns asked.

"No, no, politics isn't my field," Gates said.

"But Mitch Harding is, right?" Lissa kept her rifle aimed at his feet. "And you started this business association."

"As one of the chief business owners in the area, it seemed time we all started working together."

Johnny cut a look toward Dinah, shook his head slowly.

She could hardly even listen to that man's voice.

"Well, we don't have a business. We're farming for ourselves and trading, like most folks," Kwamé said.

Sheriff Anders stepped closer to him. "I hope that's true, because anyone without such a license come Wednesday will be fined, and unpaid fines could result in arrest and forfeiture of property."

Johnny's lips parted in shock. Dinah touched his arm. That wouldn't happen. That was why she was here, hiding in Kwamé's woods—to keep that from happening.

Yelling erupted from the yard—Burns and Kwamé and Gates, a torrent of words she couldn't make out. One of the hounds started baying, then switched to barking, sharp and ceaseless.

The yelling kept going, voices run over by others and the constant, urgent barking of the hounds. The crack of a pistol broke the noise. A woman screamed.

"That's Akosua." Johnny pulled his feet under him.

Dinah caught his hand and yanked him down again. He landed half on top of her where she lay on her stomach in the pine needles.

From here, all she could see was a brown shape collapsed in the driveway. "That's one of the dogs," she whispered.

Johnny's hand clenched hers. "He's a dead man," he said hoarsely into her hair.

Breathing dirt and pine, hearing that man's voice, the gunshot itself—she might as well be digging that grave again. Dinah half expected her palms to have blistered, but when she uncurled her fists there was nothing but pale skin and scars.

Gates, Anders, and his deputies strode for the trucks. Doors slammed, engines cranked, and the trucks backed out of the driveway, then disappeared down the dirt trail.

Johnny helped her up and she kept his hand tight in hers. She'd come here to shift her revenge to something bigger. But now all she could smell was grave dirt, and someone was crying over a dead dog in the driveway.

God would have to forgive her for her revenge, because she was not certain she could change it.

When she and Johnny reached the house, he crouched down by the body of the hound and stroked its floppy ear. Dinah made herself look at the bloody fur on his chest.

She'd stabbed a feral dog in the neck in order to live, but that wasn't why this dog was dead. "Which one of them did it?"

"Anders." Akosua's voice was rigid. "He said Duffy lunged at him. He was just protecting me and Kwamé."

The other hound, Duffy's sister, lay crouched next to him unmoving, her big eyes watching his body. Dinah knelt to stroke her head and didn't wipe her face when tears stung her eyes. Anger uncurled in her stomach. It was always there, now. A desperate, bitter anger so combined with her grief she didn't know how to separate the two.

"What's her name?" Dinah asked.

"Dandy," Akosua said.

Burns sighed. "I'll bring my dogs over for a bit, so she ain't alone."

Kwamé crouched down by his dog's body, scooped it up in his big arms. The dog was gone, likely had died immediately, but Dinah could hear him talking to Duffy in Twi as he walked toward the barn and then behind it, a soft, steady murmur.

"That license," Johnny said. "He knows we won't pay for one."

Burns nodded. "Probably requires disclosing how much cash

we make, who we sell to, and all kinds of information he'll use for his own private ends. And notice we have to apply for it—meaning he can reject it. His little committee could tell us we ain't allowed to run our own business. And they'll know everything they need to make sure we don't."

"Say he does grant a license." Lissa slid the safety on her rifle and leaned it against the porch railing. "All of us playing into his system just gives him more power. If he has every cash stream in the tri-county area by the throat, it doesn't matter what business he technically owns or doesn't. He'll own the chokepoints, and therefore the people."

The county was already one giant foreclosure.

Dinah glanced at Johnny, who nodded at her, so she took a deep breath. "Gates knows he can get away with having people disappear now, killing my mom without anyone blinking, forcing people to abandon property just because he wants it. He's been using loopholes and bad loans to get what he wants, but now he's figured out he can just take it. That's why he's doing this."

Kwamé came back, his brothers following him. "I don't want my livelihood seized because the town council has new legislation catering to that snake in the grass. We gotta do something—but lynching ain't it. Civil war ain't it."

It was too hard to care about something so distant and huge as justice, when she cared about someone who had been so small and so good and so hopeful. If she had to pick between justice and Warren, she would not pick justice.

"It won't be lynching," Dinah said. "I want him dead. But I also want more than that."

It woke the guilt in her stomach to look beyond putting a bullet between that man's eyes. But these strangers, standing in a half-circle around her on the porch and in the frostbitten grass, could be enough to change everything.

Because Kara. Kara was a truth she cared about.

So was Johnny.

So was Mrs. McCaffrey, with the life she worried smooth between her fingers.

If someone had stopped that man earlier, her family would still be here. And if she didn't stop him now, someone else's family would be next, and to that person, the world would have ended, too.

If she needed this so badly right now, someone else did also. She could not be the only one.

"I want to get rid of his whole system. Gates himself, Mitch Harding, Sheriff Anders, his stolen farms and businesses, the men who work for him, his liquor business, his trucking company. I want us to collapse it all and take it back."

Only the wind through the treetops answered her.

"Well," Kobe said dryly. "Thanks for sharing your hopes and dreams."

Kwamé leaned against the porch railing. His voice was lower and tenser than Kobe's. "No one's sayin' that man shouldn't be strung up in the street. You and Johnny just ain't the people to do it. Neither are we. Too many people here don't have a real say in who they side with if it comes to guns. It'd be a slaughter."

If you see it and can do it, it's your job, her mother had always said.

She had misunderstood that to mean she had to fix what her father had done. But she hadn't seen that wasn't what her mother had meant. She'd meant for her kids to be part of what was happening around them.

Something was coming, and pieces of it lay all around her. When she'd worked with Johnny at the still, she'd thought the person to bring it all together could not be her. She was too rash, too unswerving and unconditional. Too flooded with grief and regret. And she always would be.

The person to pick up all these pieces and do something right with them would never be her. No single person alone could ever be the answer.

Dinah turned toward Kwamé. "We can figure out the right way to do it, but it is the right thing to find a way."

Burns pulled up his overalls straps with callused fingers. "You know what you're asking for, with some kind of tri-county revolution? Like Kwamé said, the first thing that man is gonna do is pull close the people who depend on him to survive. You wanna make the whole county decide between high ideals and feeding their kids? Because I gotta tell you, it won't swing your way."

The gray sky and the sharp wind made the cold settle through her skin. Most of the plants had already died to make way for winter, the grass letting its roots dry up, leaves giving up hope and letting go.

"It's not high ideals. It's our lives. What happens, Burns, when your kids have their choices and futures determined by his prices and his jobs?" she said quietly. "You think you're staying out of this, but you're not. It does affect you. And you're letting it happen. We're the ones to do this because we're the ones who can. Killers and loan sharks and thieves destroy lives, but bystanders do, too."

"She's right," Akosua said. "And it doesn't have to be a slaughter. If we want a plan that limits loss, then we find one."

Kwamé pinned his sister with a steady gaze. Akosua lifted an eyebrow at him, and then slowly raised them both.

Kwamé broke eye contact with his sister. His sigh floated through the cold air. "Well. If we're gonna do that, we'll have to lean all the way in. Sweep out his trash. Replace that gutless sheriff and Judge Harding with someone who gives a damn."

Lissa nodded. "Waiting just means what happens won't be on our terms. The longer we wait to do something, the worse it'll be. Akosua and I were already tempted to move with my family to He Sapa when the Sioux won the South Dakota land claim. This gets worse, and it won't be much of a choice."

Burns grunted something that everyone else seemed to take as agreement.

"So we figure it out," Johnny said. "We create new options. We figure out how to get Gates's money out of law enforcement, for starters."

"Well." Kwamé spit into the grass. "We'll need to get a few of those old radios fixed. Yaw, Kobe, we'll need our gas reserves so we can stay outta town. And we'll need to order things in from the Oklahoma outposts. Maybe Kansas, too."

Dinah flipped her collar against the cold. "There have to be more people who want him and his friends gone. I'll talk to my neighbors. I don't know how many of them would help, but they'd all agree it needs to happen."

Every additional person they involved was a risk, but this needed to be more than a small group of outcasts bent on revolt.

Johnny spun around. "You *cannot* talk to your neighbors. If someone sees you, if one of them turns you in for the money—"

"We're all taking risks here," she said. Her mom had told her to go to Kara's. She hadn't listened then, but she could now. Someone else couldn't do this for her.

His expression turned into that stubborn one she was starting to recognize. "No one else has a ten-thousand-dollar reward on their head."

"He's right," Akosua said softly. "I don't know you, so forgive me if this isn't wanted, but we all just pitched in for this. Risk to you is risk to all of us."

Dinah shook her head. "We need more people. And we need some way to vouch for those people. It's a risk for me to go, but it's a definite liability if we don't have the numbers to take on him, his ranch hands, Anders, and his deputies. Especially if we're trying to not kill people who don't have a choice in whether they defend him."

Johnny's gaze could have scorched her skin, but she refused to look at him. She'd been all in from the start, and he knew that.

"Well," Burns said. "Time to hit the CB, I guess. Gotta call some folks."

The way to solve this wasn't righting the past. It was changing the future.

Starting over wasn't something she could do. There wasn't enough left of herself to start over. But there could still be some kind of future for others, and that meant doing what she should have done in the first place.

# CHAPTER

# THIRTEEN

**T**HEY'D TALKED THE SUN DOWN ON THE ADU FAMILY'S PORCH, everyone divided over what to do and how to make it happen. They'd reached a fragile consensus, barely, by the time dusk fell. They weren't in agreement about how and when to seize Gates, but the only way forward seemed to be to capture him when he was away from his ranch and with the fewest ranch hands possible. It would be Shaw and Adwell with him, Johnny was certain.

With Gates held and Shaw and Adwell dead or seized too, a raid on the ranch would cut off all payments and temporarily stop his business operations. With the money to the police department choked off and Gates unable to retaliate, within a few weeks they'd get enough signatures to recall Sheriff Anders. They'd install someone trustworthy as acting sheriff and hold Gates in the county jail until a new sheriff could be elected. Judge Harding was in the last year of his term for the county, and a new election would be happening anyway. Without Gates funding the campaign for his candidate, they could get someone into the office who could oversee a fair trial. Active loans Gates had given out would be forgiven, and with his assets seized, property could be returned as best as possible to people he'd stolen from. As legal as possible, as little loss of life as possible, as little power vacuum as possible.

It wasn't until Dinah and Johnny were back in the cave that she let herself close her eyes and draw a full breath, and when she did, she suddenly felt sick.

"You okay?" Johnny sat down at the table beside her.

"Just . . . adrenaline, I think." A surge of gut-twisting nerves combined with the raw, overexposed feeling of having talked out her soul to total strangers—that was all.

He moved his hand like he was going to touch her, but then abruptly stood up. "I can make you some tea?"

She would have smiled if she'd had the energy. Always with the tea. "Sure. Thanks."

The soft gray walls of the cave lit by warm lamplight were somehow making her shoulders relax, her spine sink back into the chair. This was not home, it couldn't ever be her home, but it was already a place she felt safe. Safe enough for now.

Johnny came back over with two mugs, and his arm grazed her shoulder when he set hers down on the table.

"Sorry," he said, and sat down in his own chair, at least two feet away from hers.

Last night, they'd been so close. They'd made out for hours and he'd slept next to her. All the way up to Kwamé's place and all the way home again, her chest had pressed against his back and her forearms had rested on his thighs. And at Kwamé's, he'd stood next to her and touched her hand without hesitation.

But around other people, it seemed more casual. And on the motorbike, it was necessary. Here alone in this cave, maybe something was different.

If he wasn't acting this way, pointedly staying out of her personal space, she might have grabbed his belt loop and pulled him close, thanked him for sticking close to her all day, standing up for her, gripping her hand so tight when that man had stood in Kwamé's driveway.

A lot more had been okay with him last night, so she didn't know what this was.

He'd said things that had made her think last night wasn't just a one-time thing for him, but maybe he'd re-evaluated. Maybe everything that had happened at Kwamé's had changed his mind?

But. After hours of talking logistics, in the middle of Burns's heated argument that they should hire some of the gunmen roving the empty Midwest to back up their little revolt, and Kwamé demanding a first attempt using county-wide nonviolent action and business strikes, Dinah had crouched down against the porch railing and pulled Dandy's head into her lap. She'd stroked the poor hound's fur during the whole argument, wondering if Dandy, too, felt like she should have done more. When she'd looked up, she'd caught Johnny staring at her. She'd never seen him with that intense an expression, and for a moment she'd thought he was angry. But then the corner of his mouth tipped up and his face turned pink. He'd looked down, away, at someone else, and she'd wondered if that was what she looked like when she was staring at Kara.

Banging broke the silence. She nearly spilled her tea when

she jumped, and it took her a moment to recognize the sound as someone pounding on the locked door to the cave.

Johnny held a finger to his lips and grabbed her bag, shoved her things inside it. Dinah leaped up and closed the cabinet doors on her shelf of things. He opened the back door to the spring and motioned to her, but she doubled back at the last second to grab her mug. Two mugs at the table wouldn't go unnoticed.

He closed the door behind her and sprinted to the front tunnel.

Dinah stood alone, in the dark, and lowered her bag to the ground.

The CB radio Kwamé had given them had stayed silent since they'd gotten home. One of the bootleggers surely would have used that before coming all the way down here. But it would be so much worse if it was anyone else.

"But why now? It doesn't make any sense." Johnny's voice drifted to her as footsteps echoed in the cave. "He was doing okay. What happened?"

"Nothing happened." Cole. Of course it was Cole.

Dinah bit her thumbnail, waiting to hear if the footsteps came too close to the back door.

"They never wanted to move before. Just tell me what it is." Johnny's voice sounded pained.

Cole's sigh was heavy. "He got accepted to that clinical trial. Turns out it has a good chance of stopping his cancer from spreading. So really, it's great news. But it's too much travel back and forth, and there's extra expenses the sponsor for the trial doesn't cover. If they sell the house and move, they'll have the money to cover the extra costs and live for a bit while Adam looks for a job."

Johnny should go with them. Leave this mess behind and move with his family. Dinah leaned her head back to stare at the darkness hiding the ceiling from sight. She could live with that. Knowing he was safely away from Gabriel Gates, able to be with his family, finding a new way to start over. That would be okay.

"When are you leaving?" Johnny asked, his voice quieter.

"I'm not."

"What?" Johnny's voice dropped an octave.

"They're moving to St. Louis. I'm staying here," Cole said.

"There's no way Dad and Adam agreed to that."

"They didn't have a say. Mr. Gates offered me a promotion and said I could live in his bunkhouses. The guys there are okay, and I can send my savings to Dad and Adam, so I took it."

"Cole." Dinah could hear every thought in Johnny's voice.

"I'm almost thirteen."

"Live here with me," Johnny said. "Quit your job. You can make just as much helping me."

Silence, for a long time.

"Move here," Johnny said again.

At the lift in his voice, Dinah sank to the ground. She knew that desperation, and from his tone, he knew it wouldn't change anything.

A chair scraped. "Guess who's buying the house."

Johnny's sigh filtered through the door.

"If I quit, I'm worried he'll back out of the sale, and then they couldn't move at all," Cole said. "He probably wouldn't do something like that, but I don't want to risk it."

"That man is so much worse than you think he is. If you keep working for him—"

"You always do this!" Cole's voice rose, tense and furious. "Why can't *you* see that just because he's successful doesn't mean he's bad? Your job with him and now mine have fed us for years. That's how our dads paid off the house in the first place. He's willing to buy it back just so Dad can get better treatment. His family has lived in this area longer than we have—he's a fifth-generation Charlotte County farmer, not some violent dictator. You say I can't see who he is, but you're just hung up on him kicking you out of town."

Dinah crept over to the door, to the gold sliver of light shining between the door and the frame. Cole paced the carpet while Johnny leaned against the wall, arms crossed.

"He's done much worse things than that. Did you know when I was working for him, he had me looking into which families only had one income and what their assets were? Figuring out who his competitors were in debt to, so he could pressure them? He had me make stun grenades to force homeless people out of abandoned—"

"That's just business, Johnny," Cole said. "Everyone does stuff like that. No business deal is fair to everyone, and if I want a job, I have to deal with it. Maybe once I get promoted, I can help change some things."

Now Cole was starting to sound the way her dad used to.

"Wait. Where'd you get that?" Johnny asked. "That's a really nice handgun."

"I bought it." His voice immediately gave away the lie.

Judging by what she could see from here, it was an expensive pistol. Too nice for Cole to buy as an errand boy. If he'd earned the gun from Gates, she didn't want to know how.

"What's that look for? You really want to push this? You want me to tell you why he gave me this gun?" Cole walked toward Johnny.

"Yes," Johnny said.

"You don't give a shit, do you? I should tell him you're out here and be done with it." He took a step back toward the tunnel to the door.

Johnny grabbed his arm, but Cole twisted and threw a punch. Johnny caught his fist. His brother's foot shot up and kicked him in the kneecap. Johnny grunted and went down to his knees, Cole struggling to get out of his grip.

This boy was clearly so hopeless and floundering, and if him seeing her wouldn't have made the problem worse, she'd be pulling him off Johnny already.

The boys twisted out of sight, but she could still hear them fighting. And then they rolled back onto the carpet and knocked over a chair.

Johnny flipped his brother over and shoved his shoulders to the ground. "Stop it! What's wrong with you?"

"You. You don't know. You don't even know." Cole swung again and the blow landed on his jaw and slammed his face sideways.

Johnny jerked his head back and sucked in a breath. "I'm not gonna hit you, Cole. Knock it off or I'm not letting you up. What's going on? Why do you really have that gun?"

Cole finally stopped struggling. "He knows. Okay? He knows, and he thinks I know, too."

Johnny slowly pulled back and let him sit up. "He knows what?"

"Denton Marlow from the general store. He saw you with Dinah."

No. In the alley. Denton had seen Johnny right before he swung the pipe.

Johnny got to his feet. "He told Gates?"

"Of course he did." Cole brushed off his pants. "The day after I came here to warn Dinah, Gates wanted to talk to me. He said he knew you were still around town and she was with you. He raised my pay, gave me a gun, gave me a bigger job. If I see you, I'm supposed to tell him. Turning you in would get me another promotion." His voice broke, so he cleared his throat before he spoke again. "I'd be able to live good on it, take care of Dad. Adam would be able to take care of him all the time instead of working constantly."

Dinah sank down to the ground by the door. Gates knew Johnny was alive. He knew Johnny was still here.

And if Gates knew she was with Johnny, then that was why his men hadn't found them yet. People from town were searching, but Gates would know she wasn't in town if she was with Johnny.

Gates was waiting for them to make a move.

They didn't have to search for her at all. He knew she'd come to him. Just like he knew he didn't have to catch the bootleggers in the act. He had a bigger trap waiting.

Johnny moved back a step from his brother. "You can't do that."

That was not what his brother needed to hear, but Johnny was clearly too stung to see it.

"You did it to me."

"What?"

"You left me. Us. Just up and left."

"I didn't have a choice. You know that."

Cole's face was still red. He said the words slowly. "You could have taken me with you."

No wonder. Dinah turned from the crack in the doorway to stare down the dark tunnel to the spring. She shouldn't be listening to this.

Johnny's voice softened. "I could have died, Cole. Most people tossed out in the forest would have. I couldn't have taken you with me."

"Was this better? Staying home with Dad while he blamed himself and I wondered every damn day if you were dead yet? And you know who they talked about constantly, every day? You. The kid who left. Not me, the one who was always working and handling everything. But you know what? It doesn't matter. Gates is giving me a chance, and if I do well enough, I'll be set. I won't have to deal with this kind of shit ever again."

"I'm sorry. I should have done something. I could have figured out how to take you with me. I should have been there for Dad. I shouldn't have left you."

She could hear the hardness in Cole's voice from here. "Don't worry about it. I'm fine now."

"I didn't know you needed me. You've barely talked to me since you were like, nine years old." At Johnny's voice, Dinah couldn't resist turning back to the crack in the door.

Cole stared at him. "Yeah. I was nine. You should've tried harder." His face was so hard and old and bitter it hurt her to look at him.

"Maybe, but you weren't easy. You've been pissed for years. I'm sorry I wasn't there, but my life has been shit, too."

"Yeah, whatever. Everything turns out fine for you."

And then Johnny sat down in a chair and his voice lost its edge. "I missed you, you know. I guess you're too old for it now, but when I was working on this place, I kept thinking I'd like to teach you how to do that stuff."

Cole's expression didn't change. "What stuff?"

"Setting my trap line. Painting. Putting in the doors and sink. Whatever."

Cole shrugged. "Some of that I guess I don't know."

Johnny's shoulders relaxed. "I can show you sometime, if you want."

"Maybe."

"I'd like to," Johnny said.

More silence.

Then Cole coughed awkwardly. "I have to get back before anyone wonders where I am. It won't be good if they get suspicious."

The boys moved away from the crack again. Two sets of footsteps went out to the door, and she could hear Johnny's voice but not his words.

And then one set of footsteps came back. Johnny sank down on the bed and buried his head in his hands. Dinah opened the door, and he jerked his head up like he'd forgotten she was there.

He collapsed backward, bonelessly.

Dinah pulled her shoes off and sat on the edge of the bed. "Do you think he'll tell Gates?"

Johnny rolled over and spoke into the mattress. "I'd say no, but with Dad needing the money for this move, he might feel like he has to pick between them and me. See? This is what I told you. They're better off without me. Now I'm being used as leverage against my own family."

"You can't keep thinking that. You should go see your parents. Tell them you think you ruined everything and see what they say."

Johnny flipped over and sat up. "No way. I can't do that."

"You need to see them before they leave. Send them a message to meet you somewhere outside town." She lifted a hand to gingerly touch his jaw, where Cole had punched him. No ice here for swelling.

"It's not worth it. It won't change anything."

"How could it not be worth it? Your dad is sick."

His mouth twisted. "I'm aware. But if I see them, it will make them all upset, they'll want to know what's happening with Gates, how I'm getting my money, why I can't move with them to St. Louis—and I won't know what to say about any of it, and Dad doesn't need that stress."

"They do need to know how much of a mess Cole is in. He shouldn't be dealing with that at all, let alone by himself." That boy's utter desperation for a way out had been creased into every word and motion.

"Cole won't listen to anyone. Not them, and definitely not me."

"He needs someone to stand up for him. He thinks he's completely alone," she said.

"You don't know him."

But she knew feeling abandoned. "He's scared. Really scared."

"What do you want me to do about it? I tried to help him. He doesn't want help."

"You might have to try harder, for longer."

"It won't do any good."

Dinah threw her hands into the air. "Not if you keep doing this, it won't. Your family is still alive, do you get that? They're *right here*. You can see them and talk to them and fight with them and almost anything you want. It's hard, but you could, and it makes me so angry that you won't. I would give anything to have that."

Johnny's mouth fell open. "Hey, your issues don't make mine irrelevant. What if I try to help Cole and Gates takes it out on him? What if me helping you means Gates screws over my parents? And you know what makes *me* angry? You deciding to risk your life to get your neighbors on board. With everyone looking for you, you want to cross the county just on the chance some of those people might help. Sooner or later, always doing the most reckless thing possible is going to get you killed."

Her spine stiffened. "This is something worth fighting for. Surely you get that."

He snorted. "I do and I don't. Objectively, yes, Gates and his buddies and his whole system should be thrown out. We should get honest law enforcement installed and no one should be poor and I shouldn't have grown up with my neighbors constantly asking whose kids Cole and I *really* were and people would understand men can be bi and that's why my dad married a woman first. But that's not the world we live in. And in the process of fighting for all this justice, say you and Kwamé and Lissa all get shot. Are we really better off? Or have we just lost the people who made life tolerable? What if me picking the wrong girl *again* means the people I care about lose everything?"

Dinah pressed her palms to her eyes. Wait. He'd picked her? But she was the wrong girl?

And he couldn't actually see eliminating Gates that way, could he? "It's not just about us. It's about the people who come after us, too. You agreed we needed to do this. You helped plan it."

"I helped with part of it. Your crash-and-burn ideals just aren't possible for most people."

She ran her hands through her hair, pulled on the roots. "What's that supposed to mean?"

He rolled the pillow into a ball on his lap. "When your family's still alive, it's harder to take massive risks."

And maybe that was why her mother had stayed. For her and Warren. For the well and the garden and the place they'd always lived, the place her dad might come back to.

Her thoughts turned to static. "Are you backing out?"

"No." He let go of the pillow and it unrolled. "It's not Gates, really, that's the issue. It's you, taking unnecessary risks, jumping at things that will get you killed, just for the chance at another chance. If we're going to get the big thing done, we have to be smart about the little things, or we won't even be alive to try at the big thing."

"So the problem is just me wanting to go to my neighbors."

"Yes." He tossed the pillow to the other end of the bed. "And no."

"Johnny, that is me being careful. The more people we have, the safer all of us are. More people increases our chances of having Gates back down without a fight."

But that wasn't entirely true. She could see it now that she'd said it. It could help—but it was not her being careful.

His shoulders dropped. "Maybe. Sure. The end result will be safer, if you live through it." He spoke to the floor instead of to her. "Just explain it to me. Okay, we and everyone after us would be much better off with him gone. But why is the life of future people worth more than yours? They don't even exist yet, no one loves them yet, and you are here now and people do care about you. Why don't you think your own life is worth saving?"

It wasn't that, exactly.

She touched his hand, ran her fingers over his callused knuckles.

Johnny pulled away from her and stood up. "It's okay. I get it. I just don't like it."

He took his dulcimer down from the shelf, sat down on the sleeping bag, and started to mess with the tuning pegs. He played for an hour while she watched him, and neither of them said a word.

"Good night," Dinah eventually whispered.

"I guess so," Johnny said.

# FOURTEEN

WHEN JOHNNY PUT HIS DULCIMER AWAY AND TURNED THE lamps almost all the way down, she assumed he was going to bed. But the rustling did not sound like getting into his sleeping bag. She rolled over and peered through the dark. He was lacing his boots.

"Are you leaving?"

He looked up, long shadows cast down his face by the dim light. "Sorry. Didn't mean to wake you."

"I wasn't asleep."

"Oh."

Dinah sat up. "Where are you going?"

Johnny slid his Glock onto his belt. "I have to meet Martin. My distributor."

He'd gotten mad about her taking risks he thought were unnecessary, so what was this? "After Gates and Anders drove into Kwamé's yard and shot his dog, you're going out by yourself, business as usual?"

He zipped up his jacket.

"Johnny. Stop this. Talk to me."

His mouth twisted sideways. "You were considerably less bossy the first few days you were here."

"When I was dying of an infection? Yes, I was less bossy then."

He shoved a lighter and a pocketknife into his coat. "You can cross a county crawling with bounty hunters and people who want you dead just to talk to your neighbors, but I can't do my job? I still have to make money. My parents are moving. This whole mess is expensive. And I like eating sometimes."

Fine. If that's how they were going to do this, then fine. Dinah kicked her way out of the blankets. She snapped the hair tie off her wrist and pulled her hair into a ponytail. She was pulling on her boots before Johnny even noticed.

"No way, absolutely not. You're staying here."

"Bullshit I'm staying here. You can't tell me what to do." She yanked the laces on her boots tight and stood.

Johnny picked up his helmet by the strap. "I could ride off and leave you here, which amounts to the same thing."

Dinah strode toward him. She grabbed the collar of his coat and yanked him close. His pupils flew wide, trying to focus on her so close. Lamplight threw fringed shadows of his eyelashes up to the heavy lines of his eyebrows.

These details of him only made her want more.

"I know you don't get it," she whispered. "I'm sorry it hurts you. I didn't want that. You're so hopeless, about everything, and sometimes I think that's worse than grieving. Or maybe it's its own kind of grief. You think you're better off alone, but you're not. You need someone with you tonight if you're going out. I'm the one who's here, so that's me."

She let him go, but he didn't step backward. The fabric of his jacket uncurled where she'd crushed it in her fist, but Johnny didn't move. And then he handed her the helmet. "If you're coming, you have to wear the helmet."

Okay. She'd wear his helmet.

After he put the lamp out, she followed him out the door.

Up the trail at the still, they carried the jugs to the mouth of the cave, and Dinah looked down the slope to his little garage. "So we have to make a few trips down to your bike?"

"Nope. Wait here a second." He pulled out his keys and jogged back into the cave, but he went the opposite direction of the still. His flashlight beam caught the flat black paint of something at the end of the tunnel. Something clinked and then an engine gunned, the rumble reverberating against the rock walls. Johnny rolled down the tunnel on a different bike, a much bigger one, leaning down to avoid the low ceiling.

Dinah's mouth dropped open. That was an actual motorcycle.

He grinned, and she'd missed seeing him smile like that. "Gotta have something fast for bootlegging. And some people know my little motorbike, so I can't use it for deliveries or pickups."

It was a low-slung, hunkered-down model with knobby tires for off-roading, a black paint job, and a matte finish for low reflectivity. Every bit of chrome was blacked out, and no plates, either. Way more horsepower than the little bike but still lean enough to handle well, probably good suspension, and custom leather saddlebags.

Johnny swung off the bike and grabbed one of the sturdy two-gallon jugs. Dinah grabbed a second and they tucked them into the saddlebags. Once the bike was loaded, he slid onto the broad leather seat—so broad his legs had to spread wide, thighs extending over the leather until it pulled his jeans tight against him. He tapped her helmet. "Let's go, lady."

She slid on behind him and wrapped her arms around his waist.

"There's a grab bar behind you, if you want," he said.

She looked down at the bar. "Do you want me to use it?"

"Nah," he said. So she tightened her arms and hung on as Johnny let the bike roll slowly over the bumps and ruts on the path.

When they hit the mountain road and opened up the engine, she sucked in the cold air of the November Ozarks. Night-blackened branches whipped past them. No one on the road in either direction. Wind noise so loud they couldn't speak at all, just ride close and fast with nothing between them.

Maybe he'd take her out for an actual ride on this sometime. Just for fun, because they wanted to, with nothing at the end of it but an eventual sunrise.

And then far too soon, he braked and the engine slowed to a gentle rumble. He pulled to the side of the road near an empty field where an abandoned combine sat there rusting. It was twice the size of her house, an enormous green metal box. No wonder they'd had to clear the trees back from Highway 65 and fill in the ditches to move these things. The header was even wider, and there wasn't a cab or a visible control system or any way she could see for a human to guide it, only a number of doors and panels leading into the box. This single machine must have cost more than every farm in the county. And here it sat, and it had clearly been here for months.

Johnny turned off his headlight before rolling into the field and backing a ways into the trees. They were covered by darkness and could see in each direction.

"Where's this guy from?" she asked.

She could hardly see him in the dark. "He lives in his truck. I hired him to help two years ago, and then he started buying entire batches, dividing them into those green glass jars, and selling it at his own markup. If he breathes a word of it, he'll lose his job, so it removes one of the riskiest parts of the process for me."

Headlights bore down the highway. At the split tree, the headlights cut out, then blinked back on.

"That means everything's normal. Better hop off." Johnny blinked his own headlight. Dinah slid off the leather seat and moved back a few yards behind a growth of vines and wild raspberry canes. The truck pulled into the field and the lights died again.

She settled down into a spot in the grass where she wouldn't have to move. Martin turned around in the field and backed up toward Johnny at the treeline. Johnny lifted a hand when the tailgate was close. He swung off his bike and flipped the tailgate down. A cat jumped up on the seat back in the cab; she could see the animal's silhouette through the rear window. She liked that Martin had a cat.

Johnny unloaded the moonshine into the crates in the truck bed. The money must have been in the bed because he counted out something from a pouch and shoved it into his pocket. Through the raspberry canes, she could see Martin's silhouette shift to scratch the cat's head.

Johnny slammed the tailgate and slapped the side of the truck.

The engine still idled, and Martin rolled down the window. "Got a second?"

Johnny hesitated.

Dinah held completely still, hand braced on the hilt of the knife in her belt.

Johnny walked the few steps to the cab door. Their voices carried to her mostly, but Martin was speaking quietly. Something about Gates and the license law. She couldn't make out most of the words, but Johnny stiffened.

"What about it?" he said.

Martin's voice was tenser, a little clearer. "I can tell which way it's going. And the grapevine says something's happening."

She could tell just by Johnny's posture he didn't like this.

Before they'd left Kwamé's place, Burns, Lissa, Akosua, and the Adu brothers had been reaching down through their network by CB radio, by word of mouth, by methods they wouldn't tell her about. Reaching through their channels into the vast, unsupervised fields of Missouri, Tennessee, Kentucky, Oklahoma. Looking for people who had been choked out of Charlotte County, Wright County, Chester County. Calling up their friends down the network, asking anyone who had local ties to reach back for instructions.

Martin kept talking out the truck window, but she couldn't see anything except the motion of his silhouette. When Johnny stepped back, Martin said something and the truck rolled forward. The headlights flicked on and Johnny stood watching them disappear down the highway.

Once the night faded to silence, Johnny came back and swung onto his bike. He held out a hand to help her onto the motorcycle. "You good?"

"Fine." Dinah brushed the leaves and dirt off her pants and slid on behind him. "What did he want?"

"He heard from someone who talked to Akosua and Lissa. He wants in."

"Do you trust him?"

"Enough." He eased the bike through the little field and back onto the highway.

Dinah rested her helmet between his shoulder blades. Tomorrow would tell her how many people felt like she did and were willing to do something about it. Pooling their ideas and resources and skills would give them more of a plan. Maybe she wouldn't need to go back home to convince the Franklins and McCaffreys and Hernándezes. Maybe Johnny was right that she didn't have to take that risk.

But if she didn't give everything she had right now, and the plan failed—she could not live with that. These recalls and elections, to say nothing of kidnapping Gates and somehow avoiding a fatal shootout, were the best-case scenario. And she'd never seen a best-case scenario be the way things happened.

She had to see Kara one more time.

Sometimes it felt like Kara had died, too, like she'd disappeared along with everything else. She had been so woven into every part of Dinah's previous life, it didn't seem true that Kara could exist without it.

Her house and yard and the road to Kara's had been welcome boundaries. The gravel road, the struggling green grass, the geraniums sifting the breeze by the screen door. They'd all said *here's your life. These are your roots. This is as far as you will go.* She'd grown up in it, and the broken heart she'd been born with had told her it was true.

But then she'd walked right past that into the woods to violate everything her mother had ever taught her—everything except that it was her job to do what needed done, and she was to be kind, and to be strong, and to take care of her brother.

Her arms clenched tighter around Johnny. He reached a hand down to touch her fingers, and he left it there until they reached the turn up into the mountains.

The gravity of those boundaries had held her pieces together, and without them, there wasn't much to keep her atoms from flying apart.

WHEN JOHNNY AND DINAH PULLED UP TO KWAMÉ'S HOUSE the next morning, people were already working in the yard. Sorting guns, rifle rounds, shotgun shells, hunting knives, butcher knives.

Dinah had to spin away for a moment after seeing the pile of weapons everyone had pooled on Kwamé's porch. What about this wouldn't grieve her mother into a grave if she hadn't been put there already?

A separate pile of nonlethal weapons lay in the grass—someone had brought a riot gun, a Remington 870 that Akosua was examining. They were for town, when they went to take Sheriff Anders's gun and badge. Townspeople Gates employed would likely try to fight for him—draining the county or not, people depended on him for work. And she wouldn't have them killed because they were afraid.

"Please don't get carried away with these," Akosua was saying.

"Riot guns can still kill people or maim or blind them. The term is actually less lethal, not nonlethal. But they still have a much lower body count than other weapons. Hopefully this will allow us to pressure some of his ranch hands into giving up and leaving, keep it from being a total slaughter."

This violence was protection, right? This had been forced from them. It would still cause so much damage, but it wasn't for profit or simple vengeance.

Mr. Adu, Kwamé's dad, was sharing copies of a list of lawyers and judges in a two-hundred-mile radius who had a record of not taking bribes, or at least fewer bribes. It was a short list. "If you get into trouble, this is who you go to," he kept saying. "Jurisdiction will cause problems, but this is who you try for."

Lissa sat on the porch, programming thirty small plastic squares from a box that had come all the way from Ohio— texters, she called them. Alice's two sisters and her brother arrived and went inside with what had to be a hundred pounds of cornbread and chili.

More people were arriving slowly, so Kwamé motioned to the house, and everyone followed him inside. She caught the screen door behind Johnny and stepped into the moonshiner's living room with sixteen other people, even a young, newly married white couple who had come all the way from Kansas City.

The Adu family had lived here for three generations, apparently. The room was neat and spare. A thin-cushioned couch separated the eating area from the living room. People crouched down against the wall, settled on the couch, leaned against the riverstone mantel. A buck's head with a twelve-point rack hung over the fireplace. Underneath it, a needlepoint red, gold, and green Ghanaian flag with a black star in the middle, and beside that, a stack of books by authors from Ghana—*Our Sister Killjoy* and *African Love Stories* by Ama Ata Aidoo, volumes of poetry by Kofi Awoonor, and *A Voice in the Forest* by Efua Sutherland. They looked well-worn and passed down.

"Everyone," Akosua said from her spot by Lissa on the kitchen chairs. "This is Dinah Caldwell."

Dinah turned away from the books. Every face in the room was looking at her.

Someone else should be leading this. No quick comment from her could summarize what they were all doing here.

Johnny had said she was not responsible for what had happened. Her head knew that. Her gut still wanted to say I'm so sorry, Mom, for leaving you alone.

She explained the loan, the well, the reward he'd placed on her. What had happened. When she drifted off into silence, Johnny stepped in with what Cole had told them.

"And Wednesday, when we haven't applied for a business license, he'll be after most of us here to seize the stills and arrest anyone involved," Akosua said.

A car braked outside, and the whole room rose to their feet. Someone stomped up the porch and came right in, a Korean woman Kwamé shook hands with. "It's alright, everyone sit down," he said. "This is Jay. She works at the eastern outpost for the Oklahoma farms. She's the one who gets all the liquor we ship that way on the combine fleets."

The woman looked so familiar. "Jay Kang?" Dinah asked.

She nodded and pulled off her boots. "I graduated your freshman year. My family used to own the bar in St. George. Gates bought it from us and Mom ran it for him for a while, but we couldn't live on what he paid. He said like it or leave, so we left."

"I remember you," the blond twentysomething woman from Kansas City, Sarah DeVos, said. Apparently she was a great shot. "We used to have the farm next to Gates."

The room settled back down, and Jay nodded to everyone, unzipped her leather jacket, and took a seat on the arm of the couch.

People asked questions, tried to figure out who had actually chased her and Warren. She tried to remember details of faces, weights, height, facial hair. Alan Fry, Lissa said, had grown up a neighbor boy to the Gates family.

"Shaw and Adwell, his two main henchmen, have been working for him since before I was. He hired them from out in Kansas. They were rovers out there," Johnny said.

"Rovers?" Akosua asked.

"They're my job," Jay said. "Criminals, hired gunmen, escaped prisoners, anyone feeling lucky. Statewide farms mean no eyes, you know? No officer is going looking through millions of acres of empty Oklahoma farmland for one criminal. So they roam the Midwest, buying or trading at the outposts Amazon Ag and Tyson-Deere have for the mechanics and the ag engineers' families. But there's really only three or max four of those per state, so rovers mostly live on the roadside or in the rafters of machine sheds or the EPA zones. They wreck machines for parts to sell, make a mess fighting over shelter, pillage crops, sometimes rob the central hub for the farm. I'm in year four of rover security, and it hasn't gotten boring yet."

"So you're in law enforcement?" Johnny asked.

Jay winked. "Well. John Deere's law enforcement. But if those are the people he has as his ranch hands, it's not cattle they're handling. And they're not going to operate by some friendly neighborhood honor code. Seizing Gates may be a lot harder than you're predicting."

The woman who had chased her and Warren, Burns figured, was Gates's cousin. He ran his hand through his wild white hair, and it sprang right back up. "Something's far gone in that family."

"His parents were the nicest folks," Alice said. "Doesn't make much sense."

"We know he's been going to Dinah's house every other day to see how the pump house they're building is going," Johnny said. "He only takes a man or two with him. That's why we planned to do it there—surprise him, and we have the cover of the house if we can get inside. The last of the stuff should be in from Kansas in a few days, right?"

They'd pulled together almost every penny everyone could spare for this. For nonlethal—less lethal—weapons, ammunition, better scopes for the snipers. She'd added Kara's fifty-two dollars to the fund because it was all she had, and because if there was anything she should use it for, it was this. They'd tried to pull together enough money for at least one or two bulletproof vests, but each one cost hundreds of dollars.

Kwamé watched the conversation for a few more minutes, then disappeared into his back room and came out with two duffel bags. He took them out to the porch and started unloading. When Johnny went out to help, Dinah followed.

A bootlegger's stash was useful, dangerous, and strange. Boxes of shotgun shells. Duct tape. Bungee cords. Flares. A pair of two-way radios. A coil of thin wire and one of nylon rope. Two butane lighters.

Johnny looked over the bags. "Got any pipe?"

Kwamé sat down and pulled out his tobacco can. "Some. Could call up the route for more, but might take a while."

"Twenty steel, twenty aluminum. Maybe five inches long?"

He nodded. "I'll check."

"The steel will need cut-outs."

"I got a hacksaw." Kwamé stood up slowly, his tall body unfolding. "I guess this is your show now, Dinah."

"No, it isn't. That's the whole point," she said.

"It is and it ain't. We're here because of you. And it's going down at your house."

She knew what he meant. "Tomorrow, I'm going to talk to my neighbors." If this was going to happen so close to their homes, they had to know. She couldn't have Laura McCaffrey driving over in a panic because she heard gunfire.

Shaking his head, Johnny leaned back against the porch railing. "Fine. I'll take you. We can use my good bike."

Dinah couldn't meet his eyes. Her gaze caught on his hands as he nervously cracked his knuckles. She had yet to mention a word about Kara to him. At some point, it would be too late.

Kwamé glanced between them, and then his gaze settled on her. "When we found him, he was sick."

"Johnny was?" she said.

"He had a tent, and he was catching fish, but his nose was broke bad. Face all purple. Had a fever. We got him some meals. Burns took him up to his place for a week. Got his face fixed up." He turned and spit a stream of tobacco juice over the porch railing. "That was all he needed. This boy did more with less than most people I've ever known."

Johnny wouldn't look at either of them.

Dinah nodded. She knew why he was telling her this. "I tried to do this myself. He wouldn't let me."

Kwamé looked out across the hills. "Well, yeah, he'd do that.

He's tried to stop himself, but he can't quit helping people and fixing things."

"We'll be careful," she said.

Kwamé thumped off the porch. "I'll go check what I got for pipe."

Dinah pulled her gaze up to Johnny's face. "You're right, it's a huge risk. I just have to. I wish you'd go see your dads. I wish you'd fight harder for Cole. You don't want those kinds of regrets."

Johnny gestured to the house and the pile of weapons on the porch. "All of this is for Cole. He's one of the reasons."

"Does he know that?"

Johnny turned away. "It's cold out here. Let's go inside."

There was nothing that was anything without family. The family people were born with and the family they created with kindness and sweat. The worth of everything else in the world came from them. He should know that, out of everyone.

But what made her lean in harder seemed to make him pull away.

She strode into the house behind him, and the bang of the screen door behind her made her instantly homesick. Dinah leaned against the sink and looked out the window, toward the southwest, where her home would be if she could see through the mountains.

"Here's Martin." Johnny had crossed the room to stand with her in this place full of people she barely knew, and at least that was something. "Lissa is handing out these texters to everyone. They're all programmed with the codes for the others, so you can text anyone else here if you need to, or the entire group." He slipped the small, cool square into her hand. She flipped it over, glanced at the little digital screen, and slid it into her pocket.

His distributor's truck pulled up the dirt path and parked around the side.

Eighteen, now. A few more might show up, but so far they had eighteen people. Not enough.

The element of surprise was their only real asset.

People started saying hello when the door closed, so Dinah turned around.

"Martin," Burns said. "Been too long."

The driver.

Johnny's distributor.

Only her hand on the sink kept her from falling when her knees gave out. In the dark, yards away, she hadn't been able to tell.

"How long—" She choked. Her voice sounded like she was crying, but she wasn't. "How long have you known your distributor?"

"About two years." Johnny looked over at her, his glance asking.

Not dead. Not lost and helpless in St. Louis. Right here.

A spiraling, white-out rage. His name was not Martin, it was Neil. Her dad was alive, here. For so long. For years. He'd been *here.*

Her father didn't even see her.

Her hands started shaking. He'd bailed, and if he hadn't, Warren and her mother might be alive right now.

"Martin," Johnny said.

Her dad turned, smile on his face. Thinning blond hair, body gaunter than she remembered.

The smile fell off his face. "Dinah."

She couldn't speak. Not a word could she say to him.

"Dinah, sweetheart." He walked over, stopped right in front of her, like he was not a horror taking human shape.

And then she saw that Johnny understood.

"Stop," Johnny said. "Back up. She doesn't want you here."

But Neil sidestepped Johnny and crowded her against the counter. "I'm so sorry, sweetheart. We need to talk. I've regretted leaving so many times—I kept wanting to come back, but I felt like I couldn't. Not after I lost the garage, which was all my fault. Look. I've kept this, all these years." He pulled a worn photograph from the inside pocket of his coat. He thrust it at her.

She barely saw the faces before she dropped it like it burned.

And then she crouched down to pick it up. All four of them sitting on the porch steps, long ago: her on her dad's lap, Warren a toddler holding on to their mom's hands and balancing on the step below her with his baby feet.

He used to hold her hand like that, too, his entire fist wrapped around her index finger.

She gripped the photo in her left hand. She rose up off the floor and her fist slammed into his eye. Her father dropped like a rock.

She wanted to fight and scream and run until she couldn't breathe. Air had flooded her body; too much of it pumped through her and she couldn't get it out.

"You," she said. "I heard you that night, talking to Mom, saying you couldn't take watching us go broke. You couldn't take *seeing* it? You left us to live it, alone. Do you even know what happened to them? You don't deserve to know. And you don't get to call me sweetheart."

Dinah strode out of the house. She was halfway across the yard before someone pounded up behind her. She swung around and nearly punched Johnny in the jaw before he ducked. "Whoa, hey, it's me!"

She dropped to her knees in the grass.

"Dinah. Look at me." Johnny took her hands, closed his fingers around her wrists when she tried to stand up. "Hang on. Stay here. You're shaking."

She couldn't feel herself shaking. Just cold seeping in everywhere, like January frost spiraling up the windowpanes.

"I'm so sorry. I had no idea." Johnny tipped her toward him, circled his arms around her shoulders and held her against his chest.

Her knees pressed into the dirt. He kept his arm wrapped around her, his hand on her wrist, where she felt her pulse thumping against his thumb.

"Can we go home?" she asked.

"Yes," he whispered.

He meant the cave. Not the house where her mother and brother were buried.

She didn't look toward the house as they left. She didn't want to know if her father was watching. If he cared, if he didn't care—either was terrible and if she knew, she'd have to do something about it.

"Why was he even there?" she said when Johnny finally locked the door of the cave behind them. "He always said there was nothing anyone could do about Gates, and that it was his own fault we lost the garage."

"I don't know," Johnny said. "Maybe he finally got his head on straight?"

If he had gotten his head on straight, why had he not come

back to his family? The people whose lives they were trying to save—they'd worked for a terrible person in order to feed their families, to survive, because they didn't know or couldn't face knowing, because they'd been lied to and swallowed whole.

That was not the same as abandoning your wife and children to live or die on their own.

Johnny took her by the shoulders in the dark tunnel. "We *are* going to kill Gates. And—listen. If you can't do it, I will."

"What?" Dinah pulled back from him.

"I want you to know that if something goes wrong, I'll finish it. I'll make sure he doesn't get away with any of it."

If she died first. That's what he meant. If their plan went wrong and the next time it wasn't a dog he shot and she didn't even make it to the day they were going to bring him down.

In the morning they were going to visit her neighbors, so that could be tomorrow.

Dinah looked down at her hands, played with her thumbnail. She nodded, a quick, sharp movement.

She missed her mom fussing about things that didn't matter, like coffee. She missed Warren pounding up the porch steps, making as much racket as possible. Sometimes she wondered if he was a noisy child simply to counteract his size and his lungs, his way of telling the world that he was here and he mattered.

She missed her mother, craved her mother, because her mother was who she needed right now, and she wasn't here.

Hands touched her arms.

She couldn't talk to Johnny right now. The pressure of the stone she'd pulled from that grave was always in her pocket. She dreamed of digging, constantly.

The grief that followed her for every step had let up for the hours she was with him. She hadn't just ignored the grief, set it aside, like she'd wanted to. Johnny had taken the edge off it, made it somehow less painful. And she couldn't handle any more of that.

"Hey," he said. "I need to tell you something." He slid his hands into his pockets by the kitchen table.

There were so many things he could say to her right now that she had no idea which thing it would be. She leaned against the cabinet. "Okay."

"I'm sorry about your dad. He's a coward. You deserved better."

Like father, like daughter. He'd left when things were bad, and she'd been a coward when their lives were draining away.

How dare he think he could fight Gates now.

How dare she think she could make things right.

When she didn't reply, Johnny sat down in one of the small chairs, overwhelming it with his broad shoulders and long legs. After a moment, he spoke carefully. "I should wait till later to say this, but with how things keep happening, I keep wanting to . . . if I knew what you were thinking, and if I knew whether it was overstepping, then I could—" Oh, Johnny. Dinah lowered her head, put her face in her hands.

This kindhearted, foolish, lonely boy.

"I'm sorry," she whispered, and raised her head.

He rubbed his hands back and forth on the legs of his pants. Under the concern and awkwardness, his eyes looked hurt. "Why are you sorry?"

She scrubbed her eyes with her hands. Because she'd loved things before, and she couldn't anymore.

She'd loved her mother's geraniums. Their sturdy, resilient beauty. And like Warren, she'd loved birds, watching them burst up from tree branches. One moment they were fragile, vulnerable creatures, and the next, they left the earth, unbound by geography or predators or their own insignificance.

And she'd loved her music. Because it was such a beautiful, magical thing to pull notes from strings and place them together, making something of the whole that the notes could never be by themselves.

And she'd loved Kara. Still loved her. But she couldn't sign up for any more heartbreak.

"I loved all these things about my life," she said. "I never even paid that much attention to Gates and what he was doing. The only things I didn't love were my father and how weak I was, and now that's all I've got left. And I don't know if it can be right for me to love anything else."

He swallowed, reached out to touch her hand, but took it back.

"I don't want to move on and be okay, because it's not okay that they're dead. And if I move on and stop hurting over it, I'm saying it is okay." She would have become a monster if she ever reached the point she wasn't imploding with this loss. What kind of person could heal from that?

This time he reached for her hand and pulled her toward him. He stood up, so close to her their chests touched, and she could feel his muscle and warmth. "Losing your mom and Warren will always hurt. Nothing's going to change that. I promise."

No one could promise anything.

Dinah braced her hands on the table behind her, fingers curling over the edge. He'd pinned her up against the table, but she wasn't trapped. With him looming over her like this, he was blocking everything else out.

The braided rug in her living room, with the couch and the

lamp's circle of yellow light. At night, playing guitar on that couch, she'd felt like this. Like if the whole world consisted of this right here, she'd be okay.

But she didn't want to be okay, and she didn't want the world to be just her and him.

He touched her face, traced an eyebrow with his thumb. "I keep being surprised, kind of shocked, by how much you love your family, how much you care about everything. I lost that years ago."

She wanted him so much it felt like something inside her might split open. "You love your family like that, too." ·

Johnny lowered his hand from her face. He fell silent, like she'd just touched something raw and secret. He didn't move again until she rested her forehead on his, and then his arms closed around her.

He kissed her first this time, and it was so strange, so terrifying, to have someone want her like this. Someone touching her this way made her feel her own body differently. Like there might be something out there that could make her love being in this life, in her own body. And it kind of broke her heart that she couldn't have it.

Neither of them left the cave again that night, and on the blankets she held him so tightly it probably hurt him, but she didn't know how else to make this wish.

When she fell asleep, it was with him beside her. And when she woke in the dim hours of the morning with panic in her stomach and crying because even in her dreams those gray eyes and blue lips followed her, Johnny was still awake, and his arms circled her middle and pulled her close.

**SIXTEEN**

DINAH WOKE JOHNNY JUST BEFORE DAWN. THEY ATE WITHOUT talking, and while she got dressed in the cave, he went down to the hot spring to bathe, which she tried to not think about.

She'd never thought she could be this way about someone.

And maybe she wasn't. Maybe this was just because she'd lost everything and this boy had found her and he was kind and needed her, too. That was enough, that was more than enough, because it was only for now.

The point at which she should have told him about Kara had been last night. But she hadn't been able to sum up seventeen years and a girl who'd known both her mother and her brother like family and had hair that always smelled like the orchard.

The way Kara had taken shape underneath Dinah's ribs felt so private, it was some kind of exposure to say her name to Johnny. There wasn't much way to compare the two or how she felt about them. She held Johnny with her hands and Kara in her bones.

There was nothing to do about how she felt about both of them. In less than a week, it wouldn't matter anymore.

When he came back through the door, dressed in faded jeans and a thin white shirt with his hair all damp, she pretended to not notice those things. If it flustered her when he stared at her that way, he probably wouldn't like her doing it to him.

Except, she did like it. She just didn't know what to do with it.

"Is it very important to fold clothing correctly?" he asked.

She looked up from her backpack. "What?"

Johnny nodded at the shirt in her hands. "You've folded that thing three times."

Crap. She stuffed it back in her bag. "I can fold my clothing however I want."

He was smiling at her in that way again. "Ready to go?"

"I have to tell you something." She stood up slowly.

He waited, toweling off his hair and watching her.

"So. One of my neighbors is my best friend, Kara. I grew up with her."

He nodded encouragingly. "Okay."

And then that was all she knew how to say.

He kept waiting, sliding his arms into his coat. "So, she's your best friend?"

"Yes. And . . . " Her face was horribly hot.

Slowly, his face began to change. He pulled his lower lip between his teeth.

He'd figured it out, clearly, and her eyes were stinging for no reason other than all of it.

"So she's your best friend, and."

"Yeah," she whispered.

"Is she why you stopped me from talking last night?" He

sounded so hesitant. "Why you didn't want . . . want to talk about what I said?"

"No." She said it clearly, firmly. "Nothing's ever going to happen with me and her, and I don't want it to. I just didn't want you to find out the wrong way."

"Alright. Thank you," he said.

"Are we okay?"

"Yep. Let's go," he said, but he was standing too straight, shoulders back instead of a little slouched like usual.

The cold reached through the walls of the cave, sharp and insistent as they packed the bags. This wasn't a trip for the little Kawasaki. If things went south, they'd at least have a chance of escaping on the big bike.

Dinah checked her knives and filled the water jug. Johnny messaged her on the texters Lissa had programmed to make sure they worked. He kept glancing at her as they packed, but there wasn't anything she could say. She'd loved Kara since before she'd known what love was, and there was no point in picking between them because she couldn't have either of them.

Johnny only wanted to know if he was different, but she couldn't let him be.

The wind on the big motorcycle was bitterly cold. The fleece inside their gloves kept their hands from going numb, but breathing the air was enough to make her cough.

Ridges of ice and powdered snow clung to the roads. Johnny took back roads when he could, but most of the trip had to be on the highway. They passed a water tanker headed to some little town, but the rest of the world was still sleeping. Gray morning light shadowed the trees and hollows on either side of the road, and fine flecks of snow started falling again when they reached the dirt road to Kara's. They'd circled around to come up from behind her house rather than take the road past Dinah's home, since Alan Fry and probably someone else now were staying there.

No one appeared to be following them, and they waited down the road for a good fifteen minutes, watching Kara's yard. No one coming or going, no vehicles parked outside. It was still early, so the kids were probably asleep. Mr. and Mrs. Hernández were likely eating breakfast. Maisy was browsing through the frosted pasture grass just outside her shed by the pear trees.

Johnny hid the motorcycle in a part of the fencerow lined with saplings, and they walked through the orchard to the back of the house.

The sunrise scattered morning light on the ice. Walking across open yard this way made her feel like at any moment she could be shot. Some bounty hunter or one of those rovers working for Gates. She could fall dead on the snow-crusted grass, bleeding into the white.

Johnny was tense beside her, too, his hand resting on his gun. "I'll stay by the fence to watch the road. Text me if you need backup."

Dinah closed her hand around the little plastic square. "I won't need backup." This was Kara's family. She was safe here.

But morals only went so far when your family couldn't get enough to eat. She'd abandoned these people and they'd been forced to pay unaffordable prices for water because she'd left.

She climbed the steps of the back porch and glanced at Johnny. He was already half-hidden by the trees in the fence line, letting her handle her own job while he did his.

What she wouldn't give to have not stopped him from saying those things last night.

Dinah raised a hand to knock on the door. She'd never knocked here before. The door was always open, or she'd holler as she walked in, because Kara knew and was waiting already.

The door opened a crack, and then jerked all the way open.

Kara ran the three steps out the door. Her arms were around Dinah's neck before Dinah could move, Kara's hands grasping her shoulders, clutching the back of her shirt. "Oh my god it's you, you're okay, it's you," she kept saying.

She felt like home. Kara smelled like cinnamon from canning and a little like Maisy, so she'd probably been out to do her chores already this morning. Dinah pulled back so she could see Kara's face.

If she'd learned anything from this girl, it was that quiet love was not weak love.

"Can I come in?" Dinah said.

Kara pulled her into the house by the hand. "You shouldn't be out where people can see you, have you heard what's going on? What *is* going on? Dinah, what happened?"

They stopped in the kitchen. Her parents had frozen at the table, Mrs. Hernández with her coffee halfway to her lips.

Both of them shot out of their chairs. "Dinah, sweetheart, we've been terrified." Mr. Hernández pulled her into a hug and then Mrs. Hernández pulled her away from him.

"Ellen and Warren?" Mrs. Hernández asked.

She'd been able to tell strangers, but people who'd known them, she couldn't.

Dinah shook her head.

Kara's grip tightened on her hand, like she was afraid Dinah might run away. "I knew you wouldn't have left unless they were gone."

"Your mother wouldn't have left us in the lurch like that

without a warning, if she could have helped it," Mr. Hernández said.

"I'm sorry," Dinah whispered. "I took too long to come back. Please tell me you haven't sold to him yet."

Mr. Hernández sat back down at the table with a heavy sigh. Wisps of steam rose from a stack of golden, crispy potato pancakes on the table. He shoved the plate away.

Kara's mom went to the windows and pulled the curtains shut, flipped the lock on the front door. "We sold the orchard last night. It wasn't entirely the water problem. Living hand to mouth like this only works when there's still something for your hands to do. It was a bad deal, yes, but we're surrounded by bad deals and had to pick one."

She was too late. Kara was leaving.

"We wanted to sell last week, but Kara wouldn't let us," Mr. Hernández said. "She'd gotten that message from you and refused to let us even talk about selling for days. Kara, mija, I'm sorry, but eventually we just had to."

Kara avoided looking at him.

A hope simmered to life inside her. "You sold it last night? Have you given him the papers already?"

Kara shook her head. "They're right there, on the counter. Signed."

But not delivered. "Look. What does everyone who can't afford to live this way or anyone Gates screwed over do?"

"Leave," Mr. Hernández said.

"That's what I thought, too. But not everyone has left. I've been staying with these bootleggers, and they've found ways to keep going. They have a whole distribution system through this county and all the neighboring ones, even way out into Kansas and Nebraska, connecting to the outposts and the state's farm hubs. They're bringing in supplies and help."

"What does that mean?" Kara asked.

Dinah let go of Kara's hand. "It means we're done with Gabriel Gates. It will cost us to throw him and his system out, but it will cost us more to keep letting him feed off us. Now he's gotten that business association created, he can have anyone who doesn't participate arrested and fined. And anyone who does participate, he has under his thumb."

"We heard about that," Mrs. Hernández said. "The orchard qualifies as a business, so we would've had to pay that fee, in cash, every year for a business license. It's one reason we decided to sell."

"You have another option." Dinah slid her hand into her pocket to feel the plastic texter. "You could throw out the papers you signed. Help us seize Gates, recall Anders, and elect a new judge. We have eighteen people, but we need more, and I want you to have the chance to do this, too. I'm taking my home back tomorrow, and this time I'm not leaving."

"Dinah," Mrs. Hernández said.

"Okay," Kara said. "I'll be there."

Mr. Hernández's mouth fell open. "Kara, por favor. Think about it. Tu sabe——"

Kara walked over to the counter and gathered up the sale papers. "Papi, this is our home. And I'm nearly eighteen now. It's my future, too. Besides, I couldn't live with myself if we let Dinah do this alone."

Even though her parents were standing right there, Dinah turned and pulled Kara into her arms. She buried her face in Kara's shoulder.

Here was what she had not been able to explain to Warren or Johnny or even herself. No, she hadn't been brave enough to tell

Kara about her feelings and yes, Kara was straight, but beneath those things, it hadn't even mattered whether she'd told Kara or not. Because being in love with her hadn't been the main thing. It was secondary. It had always been secondary.

"We'll have to discuss it," Mr. Hernández said.

Kara's mom took the papers from her. "Come talk with me, Andrés."

He followed her into their bedroom, and the door closed quietly.

Dinah pulled away from Kara and wiped her sleeve across her face.

"Mi cielo. Tell me what happened." Kara pulled her into the living room, over to the couch.

Looking at her friend, this girl of her fantasies and childhood, she wondered why she had held romantic love with her so highly. As if it was somehow better or deeper than this kind of friend.

She chose friend. She chose loving her, and being here for her, and knowing her better than anyone because she always had been there.

Sitting sideways on the couch to face Kara with her feet tucked up under her felt so safe and so familiar that Dinah told her everything that had happened. This wasn't about planning or convincing anyone, just about the fact that saying the words helped, and seeing Kara nod, and hearing her questions, and watching her eyes fill with rage and tears. They talked for a long time, for too long.

Kara glanced toward her parents' bedroom. "I'll tell them what you told me, and they'll agree. They won't be able to leave after this."

The texter in her pocket vibrated. Dinah pulled it out and clicked the screen to read the message from Johnny.

Still clear out here. All ok?

She swiped up to engage the tiny digital keyboard.

Yeah, done soon.

"Who's that?" Kara asked.

"Johnny. The guy who found me and let me stay with him. He's watching the road outside." She slid it back into her pocket.

Kara narrowed her eyes. "Is he just a friend?"

Dinah shook her head.

"Tell me more."

A blush stung her cheeks. Dinah picked at her thumbnail. *I'll be there*, Kara had said.

Now or never. She looked up from her nails. "I used to have a crush on you, you know. Not just a crush."

Kara sat bolt upright. "Uhh, no. I did not know that."

Dinah pinned her gaze on the little coffee table with the bowl of misshapen apples and pears. "I was too scared to say anything."

"You were scared of me?" Kara leaned back. "Did I—I hate that you felt like you couldn't—hon, I'm sorry."

*Like* was such a small word. "It wasn't you," Dinah said. "It was mostly me being afraid of my own self."

Kara touched Dinah's knee. Her palm warmed the denim. "I've wanted to be more like you ever since we were six years old."

Dinah's mouth fell open. "That's ridiculous."

Kara snorted. "No, it's not. Don't argue with me." And then she sighed. "You told me you were pan what, six years ago? I just never thought . . ."

"If I had told you a month ago I had a crush on you, what would you have done?" The girl she'd been before needed to know.

Kara went still. "I guess—I—I don't know."

Dinah couldn't take her eyes off her. "What does that mean?"

Kara tilted her head back on the cushion to stare at the ceiling. "I would have thought about it. That's big. And it's you."

Quiet drifted between them while Kara stared into space and Dinah fiddled with the texter.

Ultimately, there was no choice to make, because Dinah was not free to ask.

"So," Kara finally said. "What's the deal with this Johnny guy?"

"I have no idea." Dinah flipped the texter over to stare at the screen.

"You have some kind of idea."

Okay, yes. She did know, and she couldn't help it. But so much was in the way, and there wasn't time. "There's so many problems."

She should give Kara this code for this texter. She held her hand out for Kara's tablet. Kara pulled it off the coffee table next to the fruit bowl and Dinah added her code to the contacts.

"Why is this happening?" Kara whispered.

Dinah glanced toward the curtain. "Microcosms of empires, apparently."

"What?"

"Johnny said it. Since people and trees and everything grows by consuming, eventually they choke out everything else. But then something finds a way to revolt, and either the empire wins or collapses. Us or them. It's all these little bubbles of power rising and bursting. The pattern of life. We just landed at a bad place in the cycle."

Kara snorted. "Come on, Dinah. That's the guy you fell for?"

"Well, he's right. If I eat an apple, you can't eat it, too."

Kara plucked an apple from the bowl on the table and threw it at her.

Dinah caught it. "What?"

"You can't tell me you really believe that."

"It fits."

Kara leaned toward her. "Symbiosis, silly. Consuming isn't the only way for life to grow. And people aren't just an environmental cycle. What happened to your family isn't natural or normal, regardless of whatever empire Gates is building."

"So why, then." Dinah's texter vibrated with a new message.

We gotta hurry

Kara shrugged. "Complicated problems with several reasons. I don't think anyone can easily sum up why, but that doesn't mean there isn't an answer. For as long as I've known you, you've been a person utterly defined by hope. And that's probably where we have to start."

Dinah could not meet her eyes. Hope that her father would come back, the well would last, she could keep Warren safe, her mother would find a way, she would find a plan, her neighbors would fight with her, she could kill that man, Johnny would talk to his family, the drought would lift, everyone could start over, and she could be enough.

"I think I've lost that," she said.

Kara reached out to touch her chin. "You're just tired."

Dinah leaned forward until her forehead met Kara's shoulder. "My dad came back. Just showed up. Acts like I should forget about everything and be happy to see him."

Kara's tone turned dark. "Are you serious?"

"He had this old picture of us, like he has any claim to it now."

"Do me a favor?" Kara said. "Don't let what your dad did have so much control. You deserve to make choices free of him."

Dinah sat up. "He doesn't control me."

"It's just, you're always punishing yourself for being human. Have a little mercy on yourself."

Mercy. On herself. After all this.

The bedroom door opened and Kara's parents came out, holding the sale papers, torn in half. Mr. Hernández cleared his throat. "We'll help."

Mrs. Hernández tossed the torn papers on the table. "Just let us know what to do."

This was the last of her family, but they were already in danger and the only solution was for all of them to pull together.

After Mr. Hernández checked the yard, Kara walked Dinah out to the back porch. "Do you want to meet him?" Dinah asked.

"Do you want me to meet him?"

Dinah lifted her hand and waved toward the trees. After a moment, Johnny's silhouette parted from the stark lines of the trunks. He walked toward the house.

This should not make her nervous. It was just Johnny. It was just Kara.

"He seems . . . confident," Kara said dryly.

Dinah stepped off the porch, but Kara stayed two steps up.

Johnny paused by Dinah and held a hand out to Kara. "Hey. Johnny."

"Kara." Kara stayed on the steps, eye-level with Johnny, as she shook his hand.

The two of them together like this cracked the barrier she'd kept up between her before and after. "Her family's gonna help. And she has the code for my texter now," Dinah said.

Johnny's eyebrows went up. "Good. We'll need an inventory and a headcount from you. There's a few specific things we haven't been able to find."

"Like what?" Kara asked.

Johnny smiled. "Don't have any capsaicin capsules for riot guns lying around, do you?"

"Darn, I used the last of them yesterday," Kara said.

Dinah rolled her eyes. "We—"

"Engine." Johnny spun toward the road. A glint of silver topped the hill from the direction of her house.

Dinah dropped to the ground in the snow on the far side of the porch. Johnny landed beside her.

Kara ducked back inside the house and closed the door. The slow, easy rumble of the engine grew louder as it motored toward the house, then the sound let up a little as it drew even along the road. Either he'd received some kind of tip, or else he was casually, randomly scanning people's yards.

Johnny was stiff beside her, his shoulder pressing hard into hers in the small triangle of slushy dirt hidden by the house and the steps. His hand rested on his gun, ready to draw, and she held the knife from her hip sheath.

If Gates pulled a gun on her, he could make her drop her knife. He'd search her clothes, find her two other knives, and then she'd have nothing.

Johnny's Glock only held fifteen rounds. Hardly anyone could hit a moving target under stress. Without time to reload, those fifteen shots would go fast. And knives and guns were so easily taken away and used against the owner.

The engine grew louder as the truck accelerated past the house and down the hill beyond it.

He was gone.

She couldn't be helpless like this. She needed something less obvious and more sure than a gun or her knives.

How many more times would she have to hide from that skeleton in a suit?

No one moved for another minute, and then the back door above her head creaked open. Kara stuck her head out. "Looks clear."

Dinah and Johnny dusted off their pants, and Kara walked out.

"We're pushing it," Johnny said. "We have two places left to go, and it's taking way too long."

Kara grabbed Dinah's arm. "Don't bother asking the McCaffreys. John's heart means he can't help with something like this, and Laura will just panic. Her nephew works for Gates."

"But I need to warn them. What if Laura hears gunfire—"

"I'll warn them. I go over there all the time. It won't be odd."

"Good plan," Johnny said. "Dinah doesn't need to be the one to do it."

Dinah narrowed her eyes at both of them. "Fine. We'll just go to the Franklins' place."

Kara crossed her arms. "Are you kidding me? Gates *just* drove by here. I'll talk to the Franklins. I'll tell them what you told me."

Dinah kept her gaze on the road where that silver truck had disappeared. "It needs to be me they hear it from."

"No, Dinah, please listen," Kara said. "You're risking too much. They might listen to me and my parents. They really might."

"If we get caught on the way over there, Dinah, it won't matter whether they would have listened to you," Johnny said. "We'll just be dead."

She'd already let so many people into this, she'd given up

chance after chance to kill that man; she'd waited so long Mr. and Mrs. Hernández had already decided to sell their home, and she couldn't sit around waiting one more day. She was the one who had failed. She was the one who had to do this.

"I'm going," Dinah said. "I need to. We'll be as safe as possible."

"Going at all isn't safe, so that's not true," Kara said.

Fine. She could concede that. Dinah shrugged.

"This isn't right. It doesn't all fall on you." Kara pressed her hands to her eyes. "I can't imagine what this has been like for you, but please, don't convince yourself you're alone. You're not. And you can't let what you're afraid of make your choices."

It sounded good. Except she had this photo in her back pocket, and she'd taken it from a man who had left all of them to live or die without him, and whether or not she actually had failed them before, she would not fail them now.

Johnny just looked at her. She could see in his eyes what he was thinking, and she wasn't going to answer it.

"Fine. Let's go," Johnny said.

Kara pulled Dinah into a hug. "This worries me. But you worry me more."

Dinah gripped Kara's waist tight. "I'm sorry." Not just for worrying her, but for everything that had already happened and was going to happen still.

Kara shook her head, and she suddenly sounded like her dad, twenty-five years older and tired. "Don't be sorry. Forgive yourself, and come back home."

They swung onto the motorcycle. Its size and deep rumble were comforting. She watched Kara until she and the house faded behind them.

She was trying. Why couldn't any of them see that she couldn't try any harder than this?

Forgive yourself. How could she do that if she left these things for others to do or left Gates alive or let his loans and fees and greed destroy anyone else?

There would be no forgiveness for her until everything that man had touched was ash.

# SEVENTEEN

THE FACES AROUND THE FRANKLINS' TABLE SHOWED EVERY BIT of the shock she'd expected. Mrs. Franklin had her hair tied back in a blue scarf, every worried crease showing around her dark brown eyes. Chrissa looking like a sixteen-year-old carbon copy of her mother but with a shy, thoughtful fear on her face. Mr. Franklin pacing behind their chairs, while his sons' twin gazes refused to leave Dinah. Their arms were crossed and their shoulders hunched in tension. The youngest sister was napping, thankfully, because she didn't need to hear this.

Johnny had come inside this time, his spine ramrod straight as he stood by the door, watching both the group in the kitchen and the driveway. The whole way from Kara's place, he'd tried to talk her out of coming here.

"You can take some time to think about it. It's a lot to ask," Dinah said.

Mrs. Franklin shook her head. "Putting a gun in my children's hands to kill those people? We're not doing that." The bright morning sunlight poured through the kitchen windows, lighting up her rich umber skin and the determination on her face.

"The only person who needs to die is Gabriel Gates. We're limiting the loss of life as much as we can. That's why we're going to take him by surprise." A few years ago, it would have been Johnny beside him.

This way, everyone but that man would have a chance. Hired rovers with no idea what this fight was could back down. They could leave. Gates could not.

"We're not really kids anymore," Dylan, one of the twins, said.

"Chrissa is." Mrs. Franklin leaned forward. "And she's the good shot."

Mr. Franklin braced his hands on the table, calluses creasing darker lines into the dark brown skin of his knuckles. "We can work that out later. Whether we participate at all is the issue. I don't know that this is the right way to start this fight."

"We can't wait for ideal circumstances. They won't come," Dinah said. The longer they waited, the tighter Gates drew his noose and the fewer options they had.

The board was set, and they could only move so many of the pieces.

"The likelihood of this working is too small," Mrs. Franklin said.

"If it doesn't work, we'll lose the house and have to flee. Even if we all live." Mr. Franklin shook his head.

Chrissa checked something on her school tablet and then set it on the table. "Some of that is inevitable anyway."

Dinah held her gaze. "Exactly. I felt that way a few months

ago and did nothing about it. If I had, I might still have my family."

An engine sounded. "Truck," Johnny said. "I don't recognize it."

Everyone froze as Mr. Franklin peered out the kitchen window. "Just Laura, back from town. She borrowed the truck to get John's prescription filled."

Dinah let her breath out slowly.

"Hello, hello." Laura McCaffrey knocked on the door as she opened it, stepping inside with a paper bag. "Thanks for the truck. I brought a gallon of milk and a nice log of goat cheese for the gas—Dinah?"

Alex, the second twin, jumped up to take the bag from her. But Laura just stood there, staring at Dinah. And then she rushed to hug her.

Dinah held herself steady, even though seeing all these people again made her want to sit down and cry, these people who had known her mother and brother and had come in and out of her house as if it was their own. They were a kind of home themselves, one she hadn't been able to articulate.

The woman's soft, perfumy arms went around her. Mrs. McCaffrey's peachy-white skin was grayer, her hair more brittle and fly-away, than when she'd last seen her. "Dinah, darling," she kept saying. And then she pulled back and shook her a little. "What have you done?"

Dinah stepped back from her. "It's a lot to explain. Are you and John alright?"

"Yes, yes we are—but—you, there were posters all over town. What did you do?" She dropped down into a chair by Mrs. Franklin.

How was that her question? "My family was killed." Dinah looked her in the eyes until the woman looked away.

Silence fell. Laura fidgeted. "You just can't fight fire with fire. There are rumors, you know. We've heard what you're doing, and I understand the pain you must be in, dear. But your mother was so kind, how do you think she'd feel about violence in her name?"

Dinah slowly turned toward her. "What do you suggest? Should we organize a meeting and nicely ask him to not kill us anymore?"

Laura sputtered. "That's quite rude, young lady. Something must be done, but we have a sheriff for a reason. If we pressured him to do his job, we might see improvement."

"Gabriel Gates pays his salary, you know that," Mrs. Franklin said. She glanced at Mrs. McCaffrey, then let out a heavy sigh. "I can't even imagine, Dinah. You're living my worst fear and you're so young."

Was anyone ever old enough for this?

The people she trusted most in the world were too young for the lives they lived.

Laura wiped her sweaty face with her hand. "Um, Chrissa, honey, there was a—a problem with John's prescription. Can I use your tablet to send a note to the doctor? One day we'll get a house computer, but with this spring's goats being so sickly we just haven't had the money—"

Chrissa handed her the tablet. "It's not going to get better unless we change something."

Laura pursed her lips while she typed away on the tablet.

The twins nodded. "He's like mold. Just keeps creeping forward," Alex said.

Laura slid the tablet onto the table, shoved her chair back, and stood up. "We were doing alright here, and this will make things worse. A terrible accident happening to your family doesn't mean everyone else should pay for it. My own nephew works on Mr. Gates's ranch—he wouldn't work for that man if he's as terrible as you say he is. We need to get someone in St. George's town council to represent us, who can work for better circumstances for the farm families. We can attend the meetings, too, and calmly, without hurting anyone, argue against the fees and push for lower interest rates and water prices, but it simply may be a slow process."

Dinah's mouth fell open. A decade ago, maybe that would have worked. But now, it was just ignorance.

"Band-Aids won't help a broken bone," Mrs. Franklin said.

"Mrs. McCaffrey." Chrissa stood up slowly, holding her tablet. "What was that number you messaged?"

Laura went pale. "The doctor—he wasn't in town today, but he had the pills on hold at the general store—"

"That's not the doctor's number," Chrissa said.

Laura's white face flashed pink. "Dinah brutalized that man! She broke the law. We can't stand by that."

Dinah backed a step toward Johnny. "You turned me in?"

Everyone went still.

"I didn't turn anyone in. I just let the authorities know she was here. If she didn't do anything wrong, they'll let her go."

For the first time since coming into the house, Johnny moved away from the door. He strode toward Laura McCaffrey. "What number was it? Where did you get it?"

She backed away, keeping the table between her and him. "From the flyers. It was from those flyers with her photo."

Johnny immediately headed for the door. "Come on."

She'd known this woman for every day of her life. "That wasn't the sheriff's number, Laura, that was a bounty hunter tip line."

Laura's chin went up. "They're appointed deputies, aren't they? The flyer said so."

"Dinah," Johnny said softly. "Your dad's here."

"Why did you do this, Laura?" Mr. Franklin demanded. "You talk about violence not being the answer?"

"We need the money," she yelled. "John's heart—" Her voice, crying now, followed Dinah out of the door.

Her dad, in the driveway, backlit by winter sunlight. He closed his truck door. "Dinah, they said you insisted on talking to the neighbors. I couldn't let you be out here alone—" She didn't have the time for this. Any moment, they'd be here. "So you decided to protect me *now*?"

Johnny cranked the motorcycle to life.

"I'm here because I realized I could do something about this." His face had gone gray since he'd left their farm. "What will it take for you to believe me?"

"I'll believe you when you die for it." Dinah slid onto the broad leather seat behind Johnny.

Mrs. Franklin ran out of the house. "Go, go, there's vehicles coming up the back road. We'll delay them." She grabbed Dinah's arm. "We'll be at your home tomorrow. He's not messing with Charlotte County again."

Her father ran for his truck. "I'll try to lead some of them in another direction."

"No. Stay here," Dinah said. "Help them."

Johnny gunned the engine and the bike leaped forward. She jerked against him with the force as they whipped down the road.

If they pulled onto the highway, anyone who saw them traveling so fast would guess who she was. They had to stay on the back roads, but this one didn't cross any others for a few miles. Short of pulling off into the pasture and hiding, which they didn't have time for, their only option was to outrun them.

Johnny shouted. His swearing was torn away by the wind, but she knew what he'd said because she'd been thinking it, too. She twisted around.

Three motorcycles rode in formation behind them. A hundred yards away, maybe less.

The engine surged when Johnny cranked the throttle and the bike shot forward. Dinah gripped his waist and clenched the leather seat between her knees.

The tires on this bike were broader with deeper tread than his little motorbike. That would have to be enough for going this fast on the snow. Wind stung her face and hands. Johnny was taking the worst of the wind, even with his leather jacket.

Highway 65 was right ahead, the only turn on this road for miles. It lay wide and open, the forest cleared back dozens of yards on each side and leveled out for the fleets of massive farm equipment. A perfect, polished scar running through the mountains.

"Hold on," Johnny yelled.

He slowed just enough to not roll the bike as he turned onto the highway, but it still slid as they hit the icy, uneven edge of the asphalt.

He'd chosen the highway for speed, because right now they were going down either way.

Dinah buried her head between his shoulder blades and tried to breathe through the whirlwind around them.

The whine of the engines behind grew closer. The three bikes spread out in a wide triangle covering both lanes of the highway. The motorcycle fishtailed a little under her, and Johnny swore again.

They'd never be able to catch them if Johnny was riding by himself, but having a passenger made the bike harder to handle and a lot more dangerous in a chase.

Johnny glanced down at the small mirror on his handlebars. He shook his head.

Have mercy on yourself, Kara had said.

They'd told her not to go. Kara had begged her. Johnny had, too. They'd known it was too much to risk, and she simply hadn't cared.

A shot echoed and snow and dirt puffed into the air ahead of them. She twisted around. Snow scattered again. One of them had a pistol.

Bounty hunters were firing at her, at Johnny, not because of Laura McCaffrey's warped idea of nonviolent niceness or Gabriel Gates's power-grab, but because Dinah Caldwell had a death wish.

Try forgiving yourself for that, Kara.

A crossroads appeared ahead, leading up into the mountains. Johnny braked. Dinah tightened her grip when he turned onto the gravel road.

Gravel sprayed away from the tires. The bike fishtailed again, but he didn't slow down. The road dipped down a hill and around a curve. The mountain pitched away below the road.

In the tiny side mirror, she could see Johnny's jaw set hard, teeth gritted.

The three men lost time braking for the turn, and they were

having trouble gaining it back. Johnny kept away from the edge of the road, switching back and forth from right to left as the road swung around the mountain and the drop-offs and rock walls changed sides. The bikers, though, had to ride single file or run close to the shoulder.

That's why Johnny had turned onto the gravel road. He was trying to run these bikers over the edge.

The road tilted up, and Johnny downshifted. The men had stopping firing, only able to have one man in front now and all of them probably wanting both their hands on the bike, but they were getting desperate. One of the bikes inched closer.

"Hold tight," Johnny yelled. "Curve ahead."

He must know this road, because all she could see was the crest of the hill.

These men wanted her, not Johnny. He could get away if she gave herself up.

A crack split the air. The middle bike shot straight up into the sky and came down on its side, the driver screaming. He must have hit something.

The last motorcycle slowed for a moment when he passed the crashed bike, but the man in front didn't even look back.

This was it. Another minute and the frontrunner would force them off the road.

She'd been utterly wrong, fatally wrong about what she could do. About what all of this was worth.

If she gave herself up, Gates would use her as leverage against the bootleggers and her neighbors and Johnny. She wouldn't let him use her that way.

If she died right here instead, he wouldn't be able to do any of that.

They'd keep going without her. Kwamé, Lissa, Akosua, and Burns would keep to the plan and Kara's family would, too. They didn't need her in order to finish this. It didn't have to be her. Not if this was the cost.

The hill pitched downward, and Johnny slowed. He ducked automatically when a gunshot split the rock above their heads.

The road curved right at the bottom of the hill, and Johnny kept to the outside, even though the drop was hundreds of feet. They skidded on loose gravel and Dinah looked over the edge.

If she jumped, she'd be dead when she hit the bottom. The bounty hunters would go after her body and Johnny could keep going.

Her own death didn't frighten her. She wasn't eager for it, and she wasn't happy or even sad that it was coming. Death simply felt familiar.

Dinah filled her lungs with cold air. Slow and certain.

She loosened her arms from around Johnny's waist as they rounded the curve.

Now. It had to be now.

When he felt her move, Johnny stiffened. He let go of the handlebars with his left hand. He clenched her knee in an iron grip.

Dinah stayed on the bike. The gloved hand pressing her knee close into his own leg was enough that her chance was over before she knew what to do.

The motorbikes were close now, a dozen yards behind them, going down the hill much faster than Johnny had. They clung to the inside of the road on the left, protected by the cliff wall instead of the open right, and the closest man accelerated at the bottom of the hill, trying to cut them off.

But the road swung into an s-curve, and suddenly Johnny and Dinah were protected by the rock wall and the drop stretched in front of the men behind them. Whether the first biker couldn't slow down in time or he hit black ice, she couldn't tell, but he was gone in less than a second. His bike just kept sliding and disappeared over the edge.

The final bounty hunter slowed to a stop. He paused there in the road, his feet steady on the snow beneath him. Johnny braked, too, slowing down to a crawl. The man raised his hand in a wave, then turned his bike around.

Johnny kept going, but much slower now. Dinah's hands hurt from gripping him so hard; she'd probably bruised his ribs. She loosened her grip, but he shook his head.

"Don't," he said. ·

The road came down again and crossed the highway, then climbed back up into the hills. Now she knew where they were; this was the road to the cave.

Johnny went past the road to his cave and looped around, in case anyone was following them farther back.

*That girl is gonna get you killed, Johnny boy.*

She hadn't wanted to believe that. Acceptance of her own impending death had seemed like what she owed Warren and her mother. They had faced it, and she had to, too.

But it couldn't be right, because it had nearly killed Johnny. If one of those men had gotten a lucky shot, right now she'd be screaming over his body in the snow.

They rolled into the cave with the still, and Dinah slid off. Johnny took the bike farther back and she waited for him, sitting on the cold ground and not even caring that the snow melted into her clothing.

Johnny didn't say a word as he walked toward her, but when she was within arm's reach, he pulled her up and crushed her to him. He buried his face in her shoulder, his breathing harsh.

"You're a good rider," she said.

"You tried to jump off." He backed away from her a step and swallowed hard.

Dinah looked past him into the shapeless dark of the cave. "I thought it might save you."

She waited for him to say anything, but instead he watched as a squirrel leaped, chattering from a maple to a walnut tree. Dinah looked up to the treetops, at the fading afternoon sunlight. Black-haw and dogwood and evergreens knitted together by wild rose and ivy, spilling down this mountain and up the next, a dense sea of green and gray. The vastness of the forest felt calm, a barrier for everything she was hiding from to crash against.

"Why didn't you jump, then?" Johnny asked.

A slip of black and silver beyond him collected into Wolf, lying in the depression made by the rising roots of a huge old tree. She was mostly surrounded by the underbrush, but Dinah could still see her.

In these woods, life was stitched into every bit of soil, every fiber, every dappled spot of sunlight dripping down to the forest floor. But it was full of death, too, the rot and decay and starvation that made a sea of life like this feel so static and unchanging. Predators. Prey. Cycles.

She wanted to be more than that.

"I don't know." His hand on her leg. He'd made her pause, but he hadn't made her decision. She'd decided not to, and she'd decided so quickly she didn't even know why.

"That's your whole thing, isn't it." He leaned back against the rocks. "You just don't plan on living."

Surely he'd known that already. Dinah looked up into his light eyes, shadowed by his dark hair and the angles of his face. Watching him realize it was awful, but she didn't break eye contact. "No matter how carefully we plan, at some point someone is going to have to take the risk to get the shot or get close enough to kill him, and it should be me."

Johnny yanked a tiny sapling out from a cleft in the rocks. His face had gone white and it made the hollows on his face sharper. "Explain to me why it should be you."

He already knew why. She was sorry, she was so sorry, but to stay alive, she'd have to be able to live with what had happened, and she couldn't. "Have Cole come stay with you up here. Or go live in my house. You can have it. It's yours, after."

He looked sick. "I don't want your house."

Her joints and face ached with the cold, but walking toward his home would take some measure of letting this go, and Johnny was rooted to the ground.

"What do you want, then?"

He gave her a dirty look. He'd tried to tell her last night, and she'd shut him down.

Johnny flicked the little sapling away. "You don't want to hear what I want."

She bent to pick up the twig. "It's not that I don't want it."

He yanked his gloves off and shoved them in his pockets with frustrated movements, like he needed something to do. "I don't get it, Dinah, I just don't get it. You're so angry at your dad for abandoning your family, but you're so ready to abandon us that half an hour ago you nearly jumped off a cliff. You won't even talk to your dad after what he did, which, yeah—but you expect me to be fine with you abandoning me?"

His words latched onto a vein inside her. She shook her head and peeled a tiny strip of soft bark off the twig. "No. You can be angry."

What had happened to them, that he felt this way? What had happened to them, that she would even for a moment consider changing everything for him?

"I can't do this anymore," he said.

She lifted her head. "I'm trying to *not* abandon my family. If they're gone, and you're here, no matter what I do I'm failing someone."

People didn't get over losing their family. They moved on, maybe, tried to black it out, forget. Erased that chapter of their lives.

And she could not do that to her mother and Warren.

"That man has already taken so much from you. You're just going to let him kill you, too?"

"If you think I have a choice, then you don't get it. What am I going to do? Move back into my dead family's house and live there alone? Stay here depending on you for the rest of my life? Go be homeless and alone in the city while I try to find a job without a high school diploma and no job training?" She was rootless, cut loose like grass left to dry out and blow away. "I can't live like this. I can't get Warren's face out of my head. Every kid I see looks like him. I can't stop dreaming about Mom. I'm so tired of trying. I can't try every day, for the rest of my life."

It was selfish of him to ask her to live with this for thirty, forty, fifty more years. She didn't have that many years left in her.

Johnny turned away and ran his hands through his hair. His boot crunched something, and he picked up an iced-over pine cone. He pulled his arm back and threw it hard into the trees. Wolf bolted from the underbrush and disappeared.

He sighed and watched her go. "I always insisted I was fine up here, but I wasn't, and you convinced me I could change things. That maybe I didn't destroy everyone I touched. So I started trying. But I can't handle this anymore. What if Cole gets hurt because of us? What if me picking the wrong girl again gets my own brother killed, destroys my job, gets Lissa and Akosua or Burns and Kwamé killed or thrown in prison? I never should have gotten involved. You think you failed your family, but they were lucky to have you. You were exactly what they needed. What you're doing right now is failing them. And everyone else. I can't do this with you anymore."

"You . . . what?" The twig fell out of her hands and landed in the snow.

He kicked it off the path. "I have to go talk to my dads. You were right about that. I have to make things okay between us and tell them what's happening with Cole. And I have to hope Cole is there and beg him to come stay with me instead. Because you nearly killed me today, too. If you had jumped, you would have unbalanced the bike enough to send both of us over the cliff."

His hand on her leg. Keeping them both alive.

"You should stay with Lissa and Akosua. Or Kwamé. Or hell, go live with Kara. She's obviously way more into you than you think she is. Just do what you're going to do." He pulled the keys to his little motorbike out of his coat pocket and tossed them to her. "It's yours. No idea when I'll be back, but you should have several hours to pack up. I'm sure I'll see you at least once more."

Johnny walked back into the cave, and the rock reverberated with the engine of the motorcycle. He rolled out onto the path and eased it slowly over the snow and ice, his helmet preventing her from seeing his face.

And then he was gone. The woods fell silent, his presence fading with the disappearing rumble of the motorcycle.

Her hand clenched around the jagged metal of the keys.

She sank down into the rocks and snow. Tipped her head back onto the stone wall.

He thought he destroyed everyone he touched? He'd locked himself away up here and refused to allow himself to help anyone, even though he couldn't stop himself. He built things, he took care of people, he gave himself to everyone who needed him.

The wrong girl. He'd called her that a few times now.

Maybe she was the wrong girl. Everything about her was wrong.

*I've wanted to be more like you since we were six years old.*

Kara. In another life, the girl she lived with until she was old and gray, and their kids and Warren's kids grew up running through the woods together and whittling little birds out of oak and learning to play guitar on her front porch.

In this life, the girl who loved her more than she deserved to be loved.

The slush and ice on the path bit through her jeans. Her chest hurt so badly every muscle around her lungs was screaming, so she screamed, too.

She screamed until her throat was as raw as her lungs and the cliffs around her carried her voice away.

When she couldn't make another sound, she leaned back onto the cliffside and let the snow soak the rest of her clothing.

Her hands scraped something stiff in her jacket pocket. She

pulled the photo she'd taken from her father out of her coat. All of them, in a moment that had been real, before they'd all been stolen away from themselves.

Her father. Gabriel Gates. Her entire life right now was in reaction to those two men.

They weren't controlling her, maybe, but they were the reason for everything she had done.

They were why she'd nearly killed herself and Johnny.

They were why she was here on the path, alone, instead of beside the people she wanted more than anything else left on this earth.

*You deserve to make choices free of him.*

Kara, again.

Those men had lived inside her head for long enough. They would not make one single other choice for her. She wouldn't be a reaction for one more day.

Her grip was crushing the photo at its edge. She let go of it, smoothed it out on her legs. She wanted to tear her father out of this photo.

She stared into her own eyes, her younger eyes. Johnny had said that girl was exactly who her family had needed. That they'd been lucky to have her.

What if that girl had never needed to take her father's place.

What if her mother and Warren had thought she was enough all on her own.

She was her own part of this family, this twenty-five percent of who the four of them were. She couldn't be anyone else's part, but she could be her own—and if the rest of them needed her, then she had to be stronger and truer.

Her mother had wanted Dinah to be her daughter. Warren

had wanted her to be his sister. She'd known this. Her father's wrongs had never been hers to set right.

Her job in her family had always been to be as strong and as true and as kind and as brave as she could be.

And if she was not that, only then was she failing her family.

She hadn't abandoned them before, and she hadn't failed them. She wouldn't now, either.

She could have taken the jump. But she hadn't.

Because her father and Gabriel Gates, her grief, and her guilt did not own her. She still, in some small measure, belonged to herself.

Only when she'd lost Johnny had she realized she still wanted something out of her life. That she still could want things, good things.

She just hadn't known that in time to tell him.

Dinah wiped her face. Her ice-cold hands felt so good on her hot skin that she pressed her fingers against her eyes.

Her father might have let his own weakness have the final say in breaking them apart, but that was his problem now. She wasn't going to let what he did consume her whole life.

She had always fought for her family. She could keep doing that.

Dinah grabbed the keys she'd dropped in the snow and stood up.

Johnny wanted her gone by the time he came back.

But screw that. She had things to say to him, and she wasn't going to start letting him tell her what to do now.

Inside the cave, she peeled off her soaked clothing and rubbed her skin red with a towel. Dry pajamas warmed her enough that she could settle her brain. She slid the photo into a clear plastic bag to keep it safe, and she pulled out Johnny's little utility knife from the cabinet to do what she'd thought of while she'd hid behind Kara's steps.

If she was going to live, she needed more options.

Using his screwdriver, she opened the case of the knife and lifted out the razor blade. It was about an inch and a half long, so it would fit just fine. She laid her one clean bra across her lap. She carefully slit through one layer of fabric on the inside bottom edge of the left cup, right over the underwire. She reinforced the pocket she'd made in her bra with duct tape, slipped the blade inside, then used the sewing kit from her backpack to loosely stitch it up.

The rest of the afternoon and long into the night, she waited for Johnny.

# EIGHTEEN

EVEN WRAPPED UP IN THE BLANKET FROM THE BED, SHE couldn't get warm in the sixty-degree cave. Waiting for Johnny kept her nervous and awake long after she hit exhaustion. She'd tried to think of what to say, had tried a new version every hour, but they all sounded like excuses or desperation or half-truths.

Johnny had accepted her as she was. He'd met her at every step with what she'd needed right then. But Kara—Kara had always seen her in another way. As the best parts of herself. As Dinah, without the guilt and atonement. As Dinah, free and fearless.

That more than anything made her pull the texter out of her coat pocket. She opened a message to Kara.

She didn't know what to tell Johnny, and she didn't know what to tell Kara, either. But she typed too many things into the little digital screen anyway. She typed everything.

I almost killed us on the ride home. We got away but I can't do this anymore. Something has to change.

I'm sorry I left you the way I did today. I know you don't blame me for all this and I'm working on not blaming myself for what's done. I didn't want to leave you the day it happened or today, either.

Looking at you this morning hurt because I can't see you and not see Mom and Warren. I wish you were here and I didn't have to type all this. You said you would have thought about you and me, and I keep wondering what you meant. No matter what happens tomorrow—

She didn't even know what else to write. How to finish that sentence. She couldn't promise to never leave her again, not with tomorrow coming. She couldn't say she loved her, because she had no idea which love it would mean and what that meant with Johnny and how to be only her friend. Even though there was no *only* about a friend.

She was finally trying to let go of what she wanted with Kara, but it might take a while for that choice to settle.

And there was no way to say all of these things to her, not without accidentally asking for much more than she could.

So she sent the message how it was. Unfinished. Difficult to parse. Disjointed and scattered with contradictory things.

The screen stayed silent. No reply. No buzz of a response. The cave stayed quiet, too.

When the door creaked open in the early morning and boots echoed in the tunnel, she unwrapped herself from the blanket and stood up.

Johnny, frosted with sleet and his shoulders hunched, stopped at the edge of the room.

"Are you okay?" she asked.

He eyed her warily, as if she was Wolf and might bite him.

"I know you wanted me gone by now but please listen." She

took three steps toward him but he immediately went rigid, so she stopped where she was. All her planning had been useless, because now that she saw his wet coat and cold skin, the dark slashes of his eyebrows and the slight arch from his once-broken nose, she knew exactly what she wanted to say. "I'm not leaving you. You were right. I made terrible decisions and I didn't have the right to risk your life with any of them. I'm so sorry. I hate that I hurt you."

Something was different about him. Even slouched and exhausted, he seemed different somehow. Johnny peeled off his gloves and coat and dropped them in a soggy pile. "Hurting me wasn't the issue."

He was only partially right about that. "I'm sorry."

"You don't have to be sorry. It's your life."

And she'd almost lost it. "I don't want to be just a reaction."

His gaze shifted toward her. "What does that mean?"

All she had left of herself was whatever tiny part had held on when Johnny's hand had touched her knee. The part of her that had come home and sewn a razor blade into her bra. She closed her eyes. "I thought I had chosen all these things, but I was just a domino Gates tipped over. And I can't be that. I can't let him decide who I am and what happens to me."

Relief softened the lines in his face. "Look, I was horrible to you. I can't believe I compared you to your dad—it was totally unfair and not the same thing at all. It's only been two weeks since you lost them. I pushed you way too hard. Grief takes time. I just don't want you to die before you get that time."

She crossed the space between them. "Kara said something about forgiving myself. I think I've been blaming myself for years for not being better at making up for what those men have done. I can't keep trying to pay for their sins. I feel like I'm suffocating. I don't know how to stop being a reaction to Gates, but I have to figure it out. He cannot have me."

His cold hand touched her arm. "Not everything was a reaction. Some things were your choice." His tone was asking. Hoping.

She gripped his hand. A few things had kept her tied to herself. A few things had been so right and so close to her center they'd cut through everything else.

Like trying to live up to who Kara believed she was. Like this lanky boy with his sleet-crusted hair and cold skin. "How do you normally warm up out here?"

"The hot spring."

"Then let's do that." Whatever was left to say, they could say when he'd thawed out.

Johnny raised an eyebrow. "No, not like put my feet in the stream. I go swimming in the deep end. And I don't have a swimsuit."

She didn't have a swimsuit either, but hot water sounded so good she could almost feel it. "Let's go anyway." The stunned look on his face almost made her smile. "Unless you still want me to leave."

She'd started to step away from him, but he yanked her back so she bumped into his chest. "Don't leave. I just couldn't handle you giving up like that. I regretted telling you to go as soon as I got to town. My plan was to come back here and then immediately start looking for you so I could tell you I understood and wanted you to stay. No matter what."

Dinah stiffened against him. He was trying to meet her eyes, but she had to turn away at first because she could not look into that kind of acceptance and stay who she was.

She closed her eyes for a second, and then met his.

There, that's what was different about him. The creases around his eyes had let up. The line between his eyebrows, always making his eyes seem tight and tired, had softened. He looked . . . younger.

She stepped back and opened the door to the tunnel. "Coming?" She headed for the spring before he answered.

This might be the one thing she could not do, but she had to try. If she was going to live, she had to at least try.

It wasn't even a choice, because Johnny simply was.

By the time he caught up, she was lighting the lantern by the water. He'd grabbed towels and she followed him down through the cavern to the basin where the water collected into a deep pool. Steam curled up until it dissipated near the ceiling.

Johnny kept glancing at her, but she simply had no idea how to tell him yes. That whatever he wanted, she wanted it, too. That *like* was too small and she wasn't sure if they were too brittle for more than that, but he was already part of her, and anything less was a lie.

"I'll turn around so you can get in first," he said. He turned around, and her pants and shirt rustled as she yanked them off. Her underwear and her bra would do as a swimsuit. Water rippled around her feet as she walked in.

"It gets deep fast," he said.

"I'm wading out." Her voice echoed toward him over the water.

He peeked hesitantly at the pile of clothes over his shoulder. Dinah laughed, shoulder-deep in the hot water. "You can turn around. How long do you think it takes?"

He turned all the way around, grinning. "Warmer now?"

"It was for you, not me." All he'd be able to see was the black bra straps on her shoulders, but still. Her face would be a little warm even without the hot spring.

"Hey, I turned around for you," he said. "Are you waiting for a show?"

Her eyebrows went up, but she didn't move. He reached over his head and grabbed his shirt by the back and shucked it off in one motion.

Feeling her skin turn bright red, she ducked under the surface. Seconds later, something plunged into the water near her.

She swam away from him, but he went after her. Minerals clouded everything, and she didn't want to open her eyes in this stuff, so she surfaced. He was treading water, looking around. She touched his shoulders from behind, slid her arms around his neck. "Hey," she said.

Johnny turned around. "Hey." His hair was dark with water. He pulled her up against him, his hands on her bare back.

She pulled him a little closer. "How did seeing your dads go?"

He looked somewhere past her. "Cole was there. I just—I wish I could change it all. Everything I could have done and didn't. I was so hard on him when we were growing up. And my dad and stepdad really needed me back then. I could have done so much more. I don't know how I didn't see it."

Dinah lifted her hand to brush his wet hair off his forehead. "You were a kid."

His skin glowed where the light from the oil lamp landed, darker where his muscle and bone curved away from the light. "I still could have done something."

"I know," she said. Of all people, she knew. The wound wasn't really about what they could or couldn't have done. It was about feeling like their love alone should have been enough to save their families, to force the world into spinning the right direction, and it hadn't been.

"I mean, I tried." He pulled back from her, the water washing between them. "But trying won't fix what I should have done years ago when this started." His face hardened. "Cole barely knows me anymore. Dad has given up on parenting him and Adam is just desperate to give Dad every chance he can to live. I should have been there. But that man threw me out of town. Why didn't he just break my arm instead of my nose and tell me to stay away from his daughter? Why did he have to dump me in the woods like a stray dog and ruin my life?"

"I'm sorry," she whispered.

He tipped his chin down and rested it in her hair. "I told them what Gates is doing to Cole. How he gave him that gun. They tried to convince Cole to move to St. Louis with them, but he ran out of the house and disappeared. They leave tomorrow. Today, technically."

Johnny shrugged, but his eyes told her what a lie that shrug was. "I'm glad I went, though. Before Cole left I gave him one of the texters. I hope he's not mad enough to throw it away. And I got to really talk to my parents about where they will be and this clinical trial and stuff."

"I'm glad you did," she said.

The words floated on the water between them, and they listened to the sounds of the cave, of echoing drips and magnified whispering of water against rock.

"What did they say?" Dinah asked.

Johnny drew a hesitant breath, sending the water rippling. "Adam said I never ruined anything. Dad said—he said the hard part of the last several years was just me being gone. They said they have good lives and they're hopeful about the cancer trial and that they're proud to be my dads."

He wasn't seeing her right now. He was back there with them, standing in a snow-crusted backyard. His voice sounded thick. "I didn't know they thought they'd had a good life."

Maybe some love wasn't all that brittle.

She touched his forearm. "Tell me what you wanted to say yesterday."

He pulled the tie from the end of her braid and worked his fingers through her hair, separating the strands until they hung loose. "That's not a good idea."

Slowly, lightly, he ran the long strands through his fingers, brushed her bangs away from her eyes, traced her eyebrow with his thumb.

"Okay. Then I'll do it," she said. If she was being her own self and not taking on every wrong to right, then this was what she wanted. "I want you. Whatever we have time for that to mean. Even if it's years."

She pulled him hard up against her and lifted herself in the water, arms around his neck, so they were eye-to-eye. But he pulled back, watching her with an expression so open she could tell he didn't believe her. His chest rose and fell in the dark water.

Her hands slid into his hair and her fingers threaded through it. Her bare leg brushed his under the surface. "You don't have to believe me. But I hope you can."

No matter what he said about how good his parents were, he'd had needs they hadn't met. Maybe they hadn't been able to. But it still left marks, just like his brother's rejection did. And the way he'd been forced to leave everything he loved and cut away all his ties made it even harder for him to tie himself to anything else.

His hands came up, feeling her skin and ribs and the muscles in her arms and shoulders. "I don't understand why," he said.

Why him. Why this. She could feel why, could feel it stitching itself to her muscles and tendons more each day. Could sense its shape and durability, and the little cracks that could still fracture it. But to put it into words for him, when it wasn't even formed yet?

She tried to say something, but then couldn't.

"What?" he asked.

"Nothing."

"Something."

"I love you," she said. "That's why."

It took him a minute to respond. "Yeah?"

"Yeah."

Being this alone was a language barrier only experience could cross. Even with his family, Johnny had still been alone. Still been asked for more than he'd been given. Still paid the tremendously high cost of loving other people.

She had, too. And they would keep paying that cost.

Sometimes—most times, this time—it was worth it.

"I didn't think you'd ever want me that way. That you'd ever let yourself think about it." Johnny slid his hands under her thighs to hold her up, her legs around his waist in the water. "When this is over, we can go somewhere, together."

He couldn't mean that. "You live up here."

"It's just a cave."

His work was up here. A job meant life. Food. Heat. He'd spent two years putting everything he had into making a second home. "You'd regret leaving, eventually."

His grip tightened on her legs. "Let me decide what I'd regret."

He was right. That was his to give. "I'm sorry. I've needed a lot from you."

Johnny let go of her legs and slowly lowered her down until her toes found the bottom. He touched the ends of her hair hanging over her shoulder. "Don't apologize. I'd stopped wanting things before I met you. Now I can't stop."

Without roots, without being wanted and needed, people just floated away. After she was done with her revenge, drifting would be all that was left, and that was pretty close to dying anyway.

But this—this was being alive, and something inside her was desperate for it.

"I'm serious." The color showed high in his face even in the dim light. "I want to be your family, Dinah. Last night, I was going to tell you that I didn't know people as loyal and determined and kind as you existed, and if I could ever earn any of that, I'd . . . I don't even know what I'd do."

Dinah reached up, threaded her fingers through his hair, and kissed him. She'd never kissed him like this, she'd never kissed anyone like that. Her hand went to his neck, a finger over his artery, where she could feel the thump of his pulse under his skin.

Nothing had ever convinced her that her life was still hers like her mouth on his. His heartbeat made her want to feel her own. Watch it send red all through her, until she could stand up again.

He kissed her back so hard she stumbled a little on the uneven bottom of the pool. The sudden break in the moment made him laugh. "Should we get out of the water?" he asked.

Dinah nodded, not because she was afraid she'd slip, or even because she was warm enough. She wanted to leave the water because for once and finally, this was good.

They waded out, the receding water revealing his boxers, light gray and clinging to his hips and thighs. He wrapped a towel around his waist immediately and didn't glance back at her until he tossed her one. But then he paused, staring at her body, her black bra and purple underwear.

It would be so much less nerve-racking to wrap herself up in the towel and go back up the tunnels. But water drops rolled down his shoulder, clinging to the curves of his skin, and he was smiling at her. This burning under her own skin was aliveness, and she wasn't leaving.

She flicked water at Johnny as she wrung out her hair.

"Rude." He snatched her towel and snapped it at her.

She grabbed her towel back, but her fingers caught the one wrapped around his waist, too, and she yanked both of them away.

And then it was obvious why he'd wrapped the towel around himself so quickly. "Oh my god, I'm sorry." And then she couldn't stop herself from laughing.

She could see how embarrassed he was from the set of his shoulders, and she wished she could stop laughing, but it must be nerves, because she couldn't.

This would not do much to prove that she wanted his trust. Biting her tongue to keep her mouth shut, she handed him back his towel and then spread hers out on the rock to sit down. "Here. But you don't have to cover yourself up. It's fine."

He stood there hesitating for a moment, then shook out his towel and sat down beside her. Farther away than she'd hoped. "You say that, but you're the one laughing."

"I'm so sorry." Dinah covered her face with her hands. "It's not because it's funny, I think it's just nerves." She took a deep breath and lifted her head. Watched only his face.

"Well, it's delightful," he said dryly. "Every guy's dream."

She'd thought he would have moved closer to her, but he was staying in his spot.

He'd work to earn whatever he could, but he wasn't going to ask for anything more, and he definitely wasn't going to take a risk on something so breakable.

And that thought was not one she could laugh about. "No, really, it's okay—how can I make it even?"

He sighed dramatically and laid back on the towel. "I'm afraid you can't. It's lasting damage."

"I know you're joking, but it's important to me that you know once I'm in, I'm all in."

He exhaled hard, and then didn't breathe for a moment. "But how many things can you be all in for?"

She finger-combed the ends of her hair so that her hands would have something to do. "What do you mean?"

"Say the moment you were talking about comes. Someone has to sacrifice themselves to get the job done. Do you do it? How can you be all in for that and for . . . this?" He gestured vaguely to her and then to himself, like he didn't have a term for what was happening. Or more likely, didn't want to risk using the wrong one.

"If you had to pick one," he insisted.

And here was the part that could end them. "You know I'd take that chance. He murdered my family, Johnny, I would have to kill him." She reached over to touch his jaw, turned his face toward her with a finger. "But. I will do everything I can to make sure I don't have to risk that. I want to live my life, and you can trust me about that. It's a terrible thing to ask, but I need you to accept that I'm not going to give up, and I might not live."

He turned his face toward the ceiling. After almost a minute of staring into the dark, he said softly, "I'm trying."

Even that was enough for her, right now.

She touched his hand, squeezed it hard. "I can deal with that."

He pulled her down by her hand and kissed her so fiercely she stopped thinking for a moment.

It was so much harder than she'd thought, to want these things. To be this vulnerable with someone. Even when she could tell from how he watched her that he wanted her as badly as she wanted him.

She leaned over him from where she sat. She almost changed her mind, but then she reached back and unsnapped her bra. She pulled it off and tossed it over by her clothes. "How's that? Are we even for me laughing now?" It wasn't about being even. It was about sharing the risk.

Johnny glanced away, almost like he wasn't sure he was allowed to look at her.

"Sorry. Was that weird?" Because to her, it didn't feel strange at all.

He looked back at her. "No, no, it's not weird." His glance flicked down her body, then back up to her face. His erection was still hard, and his eyes were so serious. It was both unsettling and entirely thrilling to know the effect she had on him.

"Why do you look like that?" She liked it better when he was smiling, like he had been while she laughed at him.

"You should try it sometime," he said. "Just try being a non-gay guy and having a girl like you dripping wet and—and naked, right next to you. See if you can avoid the boner."

"Is that how you identify?" she asked. "Non-gay?"

"My dads are very disappointed." His glance flicked down from her face every other second like he couldn't help it.

She knew the feeling—Kara had changed in front of her so

many times or bent over in low-cut shirts often enough to give her trouble sleeping.

Clearly she was going to have to teach this guy how to make a move after an invitation.

"Well." She leaned away from him a little. "We really must be different. Because I am a girl who doesn't discriminate between genders, and I can still say that having you stretched out like this with all your muscles wet and that farmer's tan does absolutely nothing to me."

His hand shot out and grabbed her knee to yank her toward him. She shrieked and had to catch herself so she didn't fall backward. His hand tickled all the way up her bare side, and she couldn't quit laughing even long enough to breathe.

"You're a monster." He rolled on top of her, hands crawling under her ribs and giving her muscle spasms. She kicked, tried to catch him with her elbow, but he had her solidly pinned. Her head smacked backward and hit the towel-covered rock floor.

"Ow ow damn it." She laughed. "Shit, ow."

Johnny braced himself above her on his hands. "That sounded like it hurt, so I do feel a little bad for you. But also, you are cruel." He shifted off her and propped himself up on his side. "Is your head okay?"

There was so much she wanted to tell him, but she didn't know how it was supposed to happen or what words to say it with. So she rolled on top of him and sat up. She wiped a water drop off his forehead and brushed her thumb over his cheekbone.

He lowered his hands to her thighs, and then his grip tightened, like he was trying not to move.

"Dinah." His voice sounded hoarse. "What do you want?"

Could she want everything?

"Us," she said.

She could tell what he wanted, too, because he was breathing like that, and his skin was hot under her hands, and his eyes had that look she'd seen from him before.

And then his hand touched her face. Johnny pulled her down and kissed her, and she could feel his shoulders and hands relax a little. Her own body, though, was utterly betraying her. She felt strung tighter than her old guitar strings.

*Want* wasn't so simple. Not for her. This kind of want went so much deeper than desire. *Want* was a need deep enough it would change her cells and her marrow. Whenever her life was over, a doctor's autopsy would show what she, Dinah Caldwell, had wanted. *This muscle, that callus, even these laugh lines,* the doctor would say. *See these scars right here? These are from the things she wanted.*

So much of her skin touching so much of his left her unable to think anymore. Kissing him seemed endless, and every time he moved, it tuned her more toward his pulse, his large hands, the raspy texture of his face from going too long without shaving.

If she was going to live, she was going to use her whole body for it.

She found the hollow of his hip just under the band of his boxers, her hands following the heat spreading over his skin. He got her hint and shucked off his boxers, and this time she didn't laugh. She slipped off her underwear.

He snagged his pants and pulled them over, yanked out his wallet. "I have a condom."

She'd seen condoms before—in sixth grade Jeremy Klein had found an unopened one in the road and had brought it to school to show everyone. He'd used it like a rubber band to launch pieces of crust from his sandwich at people across the lunchroom.

Johnny unwrapped the condom and rolled it onto himself. It took him a second to get it to unroll correctly. "Sorry. Um. I haven't really done this before."

Oh. That did help a little. "Me, either." She touched his jaw, traced a finger along the sharp line. "There's probably no good way to make it less weird?"

He laughed, and that helped even more. Maybe it was normal to laugh during sex. She wanted it to be.

She felt the dark fringe of his eyelashes with her thumb. His hands brushed down her stomach. Tightened over her hips. She kissed him again, kissed him for a long time.

"Can I?" he whispered, touching her thigh. She pulled his hand between her legs. Maybe he'd said he was nervous, but it didn't seem like it now. His fingers were so different from her own. She'd thought she wanted him before, but this was like every cell in her body was learning a new language.

Letting someone else have this much of her was so unexpected. She briefly wondered if she was what he'd expected, if he had any thoughts about her breasts or the white scar on her thigh from stick-fighting with Kara seven years ago. But he was so beautiful, and he was letting her have all of him, too.

He buried his head in her shoulder when her hand closed around his erection. She wasn't sure what motion to use, and it was surprisingly warm. But he sucked in a sharp breath when she moved her hand up and down, so she kept doing that. Maybe he thought she was terrible at it, though, because it was hard to remember to keep doing it with his hand making those small, steady circles between her legs.

"Is it okay?" he whispered. "Should I . . ."

She slipped one of her legs between his. "Keep going."

His hand stilled, pulled away. "But is it not—"

"No." She gripped his wrist and pulled his hand back against her. "It's good. Keep going."

A slow smile slid over his face. "I like that."

Why was he talking so much? "You like what?"

"When you make me do stuff." He slid his index finger inside her. She went rigid in surprise, but his thumb kept making those circles, and she slowly relaxed. It was weird. Weird good, but still weird.

His teeth found the skin of her neck. It should be strange to ask him to bite harder, what kind of person wanted to be bitten, but the words fell out of her anyway. He made a sound that was half a laugh and half a groan, and that was the best sound. He sank his teeth into her shoulder so hard little bursts of pain ran up and down her neck, and they somehow drowned out everything else.

She pushed on his chest and flipped him over on his back. She settled on top of him again. His hands were too distracting, so she pinned them over his head, his biceps bunching.

She moved back on him, pushed him into her. He flexed his hips underneath her as she moved, and it suddenly hurt. "Ow. Wait." Maybe she shouldn't have done it that way.

He held still, and it burned so badly that for a second she wondered if they could just go back to hands and never do anything else. There was no real need for a penis, probably.

"What should I do?" he asked.

She couldn't figure out how to answer him. Maybe she was doing this wrong. But he watched her for a second before pulling one of his hands out of her grip and lowering his arm. He slid his fingers between her legs again, moved them carefully, and slowly the pain began to change. The burning eased, built toward something else.

This was better. And it got much better when she could move again. It took a bit to find a good rhythm with him, but once she did, he tipped his head back on the towel-covered cave floor. His neck was all stretched out, the connecting muscles standing out of his shoulders. Where he'd bitten her still burned with a soft heat, and she was alive, so she leaned down and sucked the point between his neck and shoulder into her mouth. His hand scratched up her spine, so she bit down. His heartbeat raced against her chest and he kept moving inside her, so she bit harder. The sparks spiraling across her nerves turned into heat she could feel in her thighs, her stomach, her hands. The points of her teeth weren't breaking his skin, but she almost wished they could. As if she could fuse him to her, consume him in some way that wouldn't hurt him.

"That—that's gonna leave a mark," he said.

Good. She wanted people to see it. Right as she let go of his skin, she came. It was different with someone else. It was new, it was theirs. She moved her lips to his jaw, then to his mouth, and it felt like it had been a long time since she kissed him last.

His hands found her thighs and his fingertips dug in. She sat up a little so she could see him better, and he must have thought her breasts were alright, because he let go of her leg to grab her there. He turned rigid underneath her for a moment, and then slowly relaxed. He loosened his grip, stroked his thumb gently over the red fingerprints on her breast, then flung his arm over his face. His chest was heaving.

Dinah shifted off him. It was weird, moving away from him,

but it was also a little weird being close to him, right after, with a clearer head. She'd bitten him so hard. "You okay?"

"Yeah, just . . . I forgot to breathe there for a bit."

She propped herself up on her side. "Is that good?"

"Definitely good." He tipped his head to the side to see her. "I mean, I think?"

She collapsed on the towel beside him. "Yes."

He touched her hand hesitantly. "I didn't hurt you, did I?"

Dinah shook her head. "Only in good ways. Pretty sure I bruised you, though." She touched the spreading red mark on his neck with a fingertip.

His hand went to the spot. "I knew you couldn't resist me."

She rolled her eyes. "You knew no such thing."

The smile slid off his face. "No, I didn't."

They didn't say anything else, just lay there listening to the water for a while. Eventually Dinah got up and jumped back into the pool to rinse off, and Johnny followed her. She floated on the opaque water, listening to the quiet splashes as Johnny swam. Her eyes dilated in the darkness, trying to adjust, but she could still barely see. It took a lot of trust in herself and physics to believe that she wouldn't sink to the bottom out here on the edges of the lamplight, in the dark and the rocks. And it took some balance, and knowing where her center was, being aware of her muscles and lungs.

Hope was a violent thing, and she wasn't going to let it go.

# NINETEEN

ONCE SHE'D WOKEN UP IN THE BED BESIDE HIM, DINAH couldn't stop watching his face. It was morning and she should be getting ready to go to Kwamé's, but she didn't want to wake Johnny and she didn't want to roll over to get up.

She probably couldn't make the world a better place, no matter what she did. But she would not stop until she'd made their own world better.

His eyes drifted open. He watched her for a moment before saying anything. "Are you okay?"

"I hate that I can't, you know, find a cure for this."

Johnny's thumb came up, brushed her chin. "You're the cure."

"I'm not."

"You are. You and Lissa and Kwamé and Burns and Kara."

She couldn't sort through what he meant while he was looking at her like that. "I thought you believed life was just cycles of power or whatever."

He sat up a little. Brushed his sleep-ruffled hair away from his eyes. "I guess you're changing my mind."

She hadn't changed anything yet. Dinah sat up but immediately realized she was braless, just wearing a t-shirt and underwear. Maybe it didn't matter. She glanced at him, then got up anyway and filled the tea kettle.

Johnny immediately groaned when he stretched his back.

She was stiff, too. "I don't know why we did all that down on the rocks when there's a perfectly good bed up here." As soon as the words left her mouth, heat climbed in her face.

"Good point. Next time, we'll use the bed." He stood up with a smirk, shirtless. A large purple-pricked bruise marked the point between his neck and his right shoulder.

She'd done that to him. It would take days to fade.

Good.

But he was misinterpreting her stare. His stance had turned stiff. He crossed the tiny room to her. "It doesn't have to be this fast."

She set the tea kettle down on the little plywood counter. Her finger outlined the hickey on his neck. He was watching her hand, so she touched his jaw and tipped his face up until he made eye contact with her. "I'm not good with slow."

He smiled.

She moved her thumb from his chin to his lower lip, testing the skin there.

He lightly bit her thumb. "We need to get to Kwamé's. It's Wednesday."

Today, the web Gates had been weaving had closed on all of them.

The bootleggers were in open defiance of county law now. And today the last weapons shipment was coming in on the combines from down south. Once they picked it up, they'd head to her house. To wait for Gates.

Right now Johnny was standing in front of her, alive and in her hands, and once they left this cave, she wouldn't be able to guarantee he would stay whole.

His lips brushed her thumb when he spoke. "You're not the wrong girl. I'm sorry I said that. You're the right girl. You know that, yes?"

Her hand slowly fell to her side.

"Last night, you said I had to be okay with you maybe not surviving." His hands moved up to her shoulders and his grip tightened. "But you're forgetting that wherever you go, I'm going to be there, too. I won't let him have you."

Her sigh was slow and heavy. All she could do was cover his hand with her own and squeeze it. Press their skin and muscle and bones together until he felt like her own self.

They drank their tea quietly, and this was the kind of quiet she liked.

Kara. She hadn't responded to Dinah's message yet. The texter had stayed silent all night, and there was no message waiting for her this morning.

Something could be wrong. Or. Maybe Kara had read between the lines, figured out what Dinah hadn't been able to articulate, and there was simply no response to give.

That was okay. It had been her worst fear once, but it was okay.

She'd thought last night might have changed how she felt this morning. But it hadn't. She was all in for Johnny. She was all in for her own self. But it would probably take some time for her to change how she thought about Kara. Years couldn't be undone in a few days.

Knives. A gun on her belt today. A button-up shirt. She'd stress-dreamed that she'd forgotten to wear a button-up and everything had gone wrong. They packed quietly and didn't say a word on the bike. Her boots struck the dried grass and dirt of Kwamé's yard when she swung off, and she shoved away everything that was not today.

They'd passed Jay Kang posted as a lookout at the last turn before Kwamé's house, and Kwamé's brother Kobe was up in the pines at the edge of the yard with his rifle.

The porch was stacked full of crates and boxes—ropes, flashlights, lanterns, water bottles, shotgun shells, rounds for the rifles. Akosua sat on the steps, sharpening a crate of knives. Most of them too small or too cheap to be used more than once. But they were still something.

Akosua nodded to a box behind her. "Your stuff came in yesterday. Lissa and I picked it up."

"Thanks." Johnny took the porch steps two at a time and knelt by the box.

Dinah followed him. She'd looked over the small, sealed cartons inside as he explained each one. Magnesium and aluminum, because they hadn't been able to find enough of either one on its own. Some kind of oxidizer. Ammonium perchlorate. The pieces of pipe.

Johnny had made a few similar things for Gates, he'd said, to clear squatters out of abandoned buildings, as intimidation for late payments, to enforce evictions for foreclosures. Loss of balance, a few seconds of blindness and hearing loss, vomiting and disorientation. But no fatal wounds.

They took the box out into the woods, beyond the damage radius of everyone working near the house. He handed her earplugs and slid in his own. Just in case. "Keep these with you," he said. "We won't have much warning before we need them."

For each grenade, he shoved the thin aluminum pipe inside a length of steel, packed in the chemicals, and laid the fuse. The pyrotechnic compound would consume the aluminum instead of throwing it as shrapnel. The cut-outs in the steel pipe would let out the flash and sound.

"These will actually work?" Dinah asked. "If they don't, we have a problem."

He nodded. "You are looking at five stun grenades, effective range maybe ten feet. There's a burn risk, but it will mostly disorient. They'll give us five seconds, max." He cleaned up the packaging around them in the pine needles. "I say that, but the first time I made these, one went off accidentally and I couldn't see for hours and lost my hearing for two days. Puked four times. So."

They wrapped the stun grenades in rags then packed them away carefully in the crate. As they worked, the gray sky turned to snow flurries.

Hooves clipped on the dirt road. Maisy, huffing and puffing in the cold. Kara. Here. Miles from home.

Dinah shoved the bag she was carrying at Johnny. She ran over to Kara as she swung down from Maisy. "What is it? What's wrong?"

Kara's wild curls had escaped her ponytail. She looked fine. She looked better than fine, she looked excited and certain and clear-eyed.

Kara touched Dinah's hands, gripped them for a second. "Nothing's wrong. Well, nothing new anyway. I got Lissa's group message that you were meeting here to finish getting ready. My parents will come to your house after Gates is secure and they have the all-clear. All the kids are in the Franklins' basement, just in case."

After, they'd head to town. Too many people at her house before that point, and it would give away the ambush.

Her skin was left warm from Kara's hands. Dinah couldn't stop herself. "So—you got my message?"

Kara nodded. She tied Maisy to a low branch of a tree. "Sorry I didn't reply."

"It's okay." And it was. It had to be. Dinah turned back to Johnny, but his face stopped her. He was staring so hard at Kara that Dinah turned back around to see why.

Kara wiped her face clean of any expression. Then she lifted her eyebrows a bit. Smiled.

Dinah glanced from Johnny to Kara and back again. She'd missed something. And neither of these people were going to say anything.

Fine. They could be like that.

Dinah walked toward the house. "We have work to do."

The last shipment would come in the same way the bootleggers shipped their moonshine out of the county—stashed on Tyson-Deere or Amazon's fleets of self-driving combines, planters, hay rakes, or grain trucks coming through on the highway. Snaking through the Ozarks, Highway 65 ran all the way from Louisiana to Minnesota, one of the few highways left intact that crossed over half of Amazon's statewide farms. It was now mostly used for traveling farm equipment. That's why the black-market shipping trade had picked that route, too, apparently. Access to areas without much access. The computers guided the fleets of automatic equipment from one vast farm to another, managing hundreds of machines at a time. The cameras on the machines would only trip and alert the engineers who monitored the computers if something blocked the road or damaged the equipment. Then they'd call whatever mechanic was closest to the fleet, who would go fix it manually.

Of course, mistakes happened. Sometimes deliveries or pickups would trigger the cameras. But most of the engineers, Burns said, lived on sparsely supplied farm outposts, only a few per state. The nearest city might be six or eight hours away, if they even had a vehicle to get there. Amazon stocked their little farm outposts with "essentials" for the mechanics, agricultural specialists, and engineers to purchase, but it was little variety and shipping anything else across millions of acres of farmland was prohibitive. So the engineers relied on these black-market deliveries, too.

Kwamé had laughed. "Who do you think buys half our moonshine?"

So, the bootleggers were careful and everyone else looked the other way. Which was how they could order in five hundred capsaicin capsules for use in the 12-gauge shotguns. The shotguns had come modified for the less-lethal rounds and turned into riot guns for crowd control. That way, Cole and Mrs. McCaffrey's nephew and Burns's brother-in-law and all the rest of their families who worked for that man wouldn't end up dead if they decided they had to fight for their jobs.

Kara pitched in right beside her and Johnny, filling the trucks with gas, checking tires, making sure the batteries on every texter and radio were charged. Small failures could be the reason they lost everything. But no matter what Kara was doing, Dinah could feel her attention, her awareness of where Dinah was and what she was doing.

Johnny brought them both lunch, and they sat on the porch

and ate with everyone else. She sat between him and Kara to eat, and it felt so normal she didn't know what to do about it. Kara wasn't watching him the way she was watching Dinah, but she wasn't ignoring him or tense around him, either. She sharpened knives with him and Akosua, thanked him for lunch, laughed when he made a joke. It felt good, this normalcy in the moments before everything would change.

Her father insisted on coming to get the capsaicin capsules. He climbed into Burns's truck with Kwamé, so Johnny and Dinah crammed into Lissa's. Kara and everyone else stayed behind, cleaning and loading the guns, making food to last such a large group, and gathering the last of the ammunition and supplies.

The ride to the pick-up point was quiet. This was the last thing before Dinah and these people who had become her friends would drive to her home, take Alan Fry and anyone else there by surprise, and hide in the house until Gates arrived to check on the pump house.

Tonight, Gates would cease to be a free man.

Lissa and Burns parked in the cover of the trees, back from the road. Dinah and Johnny unloaded his motorcycle from Lissa's truck, and Kwamé climbed onto the back of it with Johnny. Then they waited.

Dinah crouched farther back in the trees with the others. Lissa and Burns had their rifles up, covering Johnny. Since the business license law had gone into effect today, no one was taking any chances. This had nothing to do with moonshining, but Anders and Gates wouldn't need much of a reason.

It was all she could do to ignore her father behind her. She could hear him breathing, and she didn't want to. But she wasn't here to make up for what he'd done. She was here to smash Gates's world to pieces.

The low, churning growl of the combines spilled down the road. It was a moment before she could see the train of hulking green machines crawling over the hill to the south. The massive headers spread across all four lanes and the median and still spilled onto the cleared grassy shoulders on each side. They were tiered, almost like square cakes, with a giant arm coming out of the top. A platform just big enough for walking that circled each tier, ladders leading up.

Johnny, Kwamé riding two-up with him, pulled forward, out of the trees. The highway was clear to their north and south, just the combines pulling alongside their hiding spot in the woods. Dinah tensed anyway, pulling her jacket tighter to keep the wind from seeping through the gaps in her button-up shirt. She should zip it, but having it zipped restricted her access to her knife and the pistol on her belt.

The package was on the third combine, inside one of the doors that marked the giant metal tiers. Johnny pulled ahead of the first harvester, then slowed down until he matched pace with the third. He could get close with the motorcycle, riding slightly behind the wide header, so that Kwamé could grab a handhold and pull himself up onto the machine. His long legs helped, and the bike only wobbled a bit as he shifted his weight and climbed up the ladder to the first level eight feet in the air.

Kwamé entered a code for the door and pulled out a large backpack. And then someone appeared around the corner of the walkway, a revolver leveled at Kwamé.

"Shit," Lissa said.

Figures with rifles, too far away for Dinah to identify faces, rounded the corners of the combines ahead and aimed at Kwamé and Johnny.

Kwamé froze where he was. Slowly raised his hands away from his body. Johnny held the bike steady, riding alongside the combine. Waiting.

"Don't fire," Burns said. "They'll both be done for if we do."

The figures climbed down from the tiers. Walked carefully out across the headers of the big harvesters. They jumped to the ground, rifles trained on the woods, untouchable because of the man with his revolver trained on Kwamé and Johnny.

She couldn't do a thing but sit there and watch it happen.

The man directed Kwamé off the combine and onto Johnny's motorcycle. Half the men on the ground turned their rifles onto Johnny again. The man on the combine signaled for Johnny to pull over. And Johnny couldn't simply open the throttle and disappear down the road—he was already speeding toward the men who had climbed off the combines ahead. Guns ahead and behind him.

The winding train of combines was passing them now, heading for the Missouri fields.

He slowed to a crawl. Brought the bike to a halt. The man climbed out onto the header and jumped down to the highway. Stepped out of the way of the passing combines.

Sheriff Anders. All three of his deputies. Plus Shaw and Adwell.

Gates knew. He'd known about their ambush and had decided to strike early. How had he found out? Why wasn't he here himself?

All these men had to do was ride the train of combines until they'd shown up.

Shaw and Adwell told Johnny and Kwamé to get off the

motorcycle. Took Johnny's Glock and Kwamé's pistol. Pulled the backpack off him and opened it.

"Drop your guns and get out here," Anders called. They weren't far enough back into the trees for him to not see them. Passersby wouldn't have seen them, but someone who knew they were there would.

"We have to do it," Lissa said. "Stay here, Dinah. We don't need him seeing you."

Burns, her father, and Lissa all lowered their guns and stepped out of the woods.

"The girl, too." Anders sighted down the barrel at her. "I can see her."

This should have been simple. Get the rounds for the riot guns, go to Kwamé's, load up, take back her home. Ambush Gates. By tonight it would have been done.

The riot guns were supposed to save lives. They were a way to plan carefully, to not rush headlong into revenge. And that was why she'd been caught?

Anders fired. The tree over her head shuddered and dropped leaves. "Now," he said.

Dinah stood up from her crouch. She walked out of the trees, hands up.

Johnny's eyes followed her. She glanced at him, fear and shock on his face. Lissa, Burns, and Kwamé were stoic as ever. Her dad was pale and sweating, hands high over his head like he hadn't been able to wait to surrender.

Fine. He could surrender. Because she wasn't going to let this happen their way.

These people were her neighbors now, too.

"Everyone on your knees," Anders said.

They dropped to their knees. Her kneecaps smacked into the asphalt. That would bruise, but she'd never expected for today to end with a bruise high on her list of problems.

The deputies, Shaw, and Adwell closed in around them. Shaw dropped the backpack he'd taken from Kwamé on the ground, a stocking cap pulled over his bald head against the cold. "This is just nonlethal ammunition. Some kind of powder inside plastic rounds. But nothing to do with moonshining."

"Damn it." Anders kicked Burns's knee. "I was hoping to bring all y'all in. But it ain't breaking no law to have toy bullets."

Dinah risked a glance at Johnny. This was just a trap because of the license law?

So Gates didn't know about the plan for tonight. This was only business as usual.

Johnny flexed his fingers. He was fraying, desperate to do something. She shook her head at him.

"We'll get you fair and square before long," Anders said. "I can wait for a nice, clean arrest. But I came here to arrest somebody, so let's make it you." He kicked Dinah's leg.

Her dad jerked forward. Adwell moved the barrel of his gun toward him. "Easy, old man."

"You, I can arrest no problem." Sheriff Anders hooked an arm through hers and hauled her to her feet. "You stabbed Alan Fry and sent a death threat to the county's biggest employer."

"Dinah," Johnny said. Shaw's gun swung toward him, his hulking frame surprisingly quick.

Dinah met his eyes, but there was nothing she could do. There was nothing he could do. Sheriff Anders zip-tied her wrists together and spoke into his radio.

No one moved. No one said a word. The only sound was the

fading growl of the combine train, snaking away toward Missouri.

A police car crested the hill to the south, lights flashing. It had been waiting somewhere. Of course it had. The car pulled up beside them, slapping the snow-frosted trunks in flashing red and blue. The colors washed over her jacket.

A uniformed deputy stepped out of the car and opened the back door.

If the others tried to rescue her, they'd be attacking a police officer and that would be all Sheriff Anders would need to arrest every one of them and probably kill somebody. He was probably hoping they would. And that would mean nothing happened tonight.

Even if she was in jail, the plan still had to keep going.

Anders shoved her toward the police car, a smirk on his face. The deputy in uniform forced her head down as she fell into the back seat. Sheriff Anders and the deputy climbed into the front, the doors locked, and the car pulled away.

Out the rear windshield, Johnny and the others remained on their knees at gunpoint. No one moved. The image stayed breathless, like it had been painted still by the flashing red and blue, until the car crested the hill toward town and the mountains wiped them away.

# TWENTY

THE POLICE CAR SLOWED DOWN LONG BEFORE THEY REACHED town. They shouldn't be stopping on the shoulder of the road like this. Except that a small blue car was churning the thin snow into slush down a side road, heading right for them. It stopped beside the police car.

Shaw stepped out of the blue car. Russet beard, heavy lines on his face, a thick jacket that hung on him like it was weighted with things that were bad news for her.

But she'd been arrested. No one had read her any rights, but Anders was taking her to the county jail. And Shaw had been behind them, with the others. He must have left immediately. Why? Why was he here?

Her door jerked open. Dinah scrambled away from the hands, but all three men grabbed her legs and hauled her out even as she kicked hands, legs, knees, whatever she could reach. She screamed as loudly as she could, the sound coming out like her lungs were shredding. Sheriff Anders backhanded her so hard she heard her jaw pop. Blood flooded into her mouth.

Shaw pinned her feet together and the deputy zip-tied them as easily as Anders had tied her hands a few minutes ago. All three men searched her, stripped off her boots, took her knives out of them, pulled the knife out of her belt, even took the belt itself. They cut her jacket off her since they couldn't get it off over her hands. They even searched her hair, took her ponytail holder.

She spit blood onto the road. "Give me back my boots."

Shaw laughed. "You won't need them, girlie. Word of advice: The rich think they're right because they have money. The poor think they've been wronged because they don't. There is no right or wrong, just money, the people who have it, and the people who don't. Stop trying to change that."

He and Sheriff Anders picked her up by the arms and legs. Dinah kicked, but it did nothing in their grip. The deputy popped the trunk of the blue car. The men dumped her inside.

The trunk slammed shut.

She could barely move. It was so dark she couldn't see anything—no shape or form to the space around her. Dinah rolled onto her back even though it crushed her hands. She pulled her knees up to her chest and tried to kick the trunk lid open. But the trunk was too shallow for her to get enough leverage.

Her knees were the only part of her body she could move. Rolling onto her side, she tried to feel around for something sharp with her legs. As far as she could tell, though, the trunk was empty. She couldn't even get at the little blade sewn into her bra. She fumbled at the fraying carpet edge with her feet until it peeled back from the left taillight. Kicking both her feet at once, she shattered the light and a beam of sun filtered into the truck. She scooted around so she could at least see out, but there were no hitchhikers or cars or anyone around to see or hear her. And she couldn't even stick a hand through the hole to wave, because her hands were tied behind her back.

It shouldn't have been this easy to crush her. With all her fury, all her revenge and all her dead certainty that she would kill Gabriel Gates, she'd been so easy to crush. One gun pointed at her, and here she was tied up and helpless, and all she could think was that she wanted her mom to tell her what to do.

Her chest tightened so much it felt hard to breathe. But it couldn't be hard to breathe, because she was pulling in air twice as fast as normal. She could feel her heartbeat underneath the plastic cinching her wrists together.

Panicking. That's what this was. Don't panic. That's what her mom would say.

That was like telling someone who couldn't swim not to drown.

Dinah pressed her face into the carpet of the trunk and screamed until she went hoarse and her voice choked with tears.

Salt spilled between her lips. The trunk carpet smelled bitterly like motor oil. Her arms were going stiff and her feet were falling asleep.

Her thoughts started to slow. Okay. Catalog what she was feeling. That might help. She had to stop panicking. Whatever happened next would be her chance, and if she was panicking she wouldn't be able to take it.

Carpet burn stung her face. The earplugs Johnny had given her for the stun grenades pressed into her thigh, soft little points in her pocket. Her bra strap was falling down her shoulder and she couldn't fix it. Her button-up shirt had gotten twisted sideways underneath her.

Her feet were cold. Why hadn't they just let her have her damned boots back?

There. Better. A full, slow breath.

The slick whine of the tires on pavement changed to the crunch of gravel. The car slowed. Rocks pinged into the metal underneath her.

She breathed deeply, made herself picture her mother. The lines around her eyes, the foam of wavy brown hair usually tied up in a sensible knot. The wrinkles in her hands. Sturdy sweaters and a mind that knew exactly how much a pound of butter was without measuring. The mind and heart that had created a system to keep all her neighbors from starving, that had created something from nothing, to care for the people she loved.

And that was what Dinah would do.

Dogs started barking even before the car parked. The car doors slammed. The trunk jerked open. White light blinded her for a moment until her eyes adjusted to daylight again.

Shaw picked her up like she was a baby and carried her, kicking, around a building.

They were behind some plain brown houses. Small ones. Hounds trotted along beside them. Shaw kicked at one when it got too close.

Open pasture spread acres back, fencing crowding the landscape. Cattle and horses grazed the frosted grass along the fence rows.

The only place this could be was Gates's ranch.

Johnny and the others would think she was in town. At the county jail. Not here.

Shaw kicked open the door to one of the little brown bunkhouses and dropped her into a kitchen chair. A great bear of a man, he watched her for a second, shook his head, and left.

This mercenary had nothing to do with her home, her neighbors, her county. The money Gates had slowly filtered away from all of them had gone to hire this man, using their own resources against them.

As far as she could see, Gates wasn't in the house. Shaw had dropped her in the middle of the tiny, utilitarian kitchen, by a narrow table. Doors to the left and right of the kitchen probably led to bedrooms. One open window sat square in the middle of the back wall and a weak fluorescent light hung overhead.

At least she could stretch her legs out straight. Her knees were stiff enough they hurt.

Think, Dinah.

The table legs. They were square. She scooted her chair closer and pushed the zip-tie on her ankles up against the table leg. The square edge scraped the plastic of the zip-tie, but the table was too light, and it slid away from her. She curled her feet around the leg to hold it in place. That worked a little. She scraped the tie against the edge as fast as she could. Eventually, it would have to weaken.

Something tapped the open window. She paused. The tap on the screen came again.

"Dinah?"

"Cole," she whispered. Relief flooded her.

"I can't get to the door without someone seeing me," he said. "Can you hear me?"

"Yeah," she said. "Do you still have that texter Johnny gave you?"

A long pause. "Yes."

Thank God. "Text Johnny. Find out if he's okay. Last I saw

Sheriff Anders and Adwell had guns on him and everyone else."

"They wouldn't hurt them." She could hear the disbelief, the edge of questioning, in his voice.

She did not have time for challenging this kid's loyalty. "Cole, if you care about your brother, just do it."

If Johnny could respond, he would. And if he didn't, if he couldn't, then what she did next was going to be very different.

Cole's heavy exhale traveled through the window. "He says they're okay. Anders and everyone else left as soon as Shaw did and let them go."

The cramp in her gut eased. She closed her eyes for a moment, and then picked up her feet again and kept grinding the plastic tie against the table leg. "Tell him I'm here and okay. And to go ahead with the plan. Say exactly that."

Suspicion clouded Cole's voice. "What plan?"

"Please just tell him. It's the only way to fix things."

"I'm not telling him to go ahead with any plan unless I know what it is."

"Damn it, Cole. If you ruin this, we could all die."

"So tell me."

If she couldn't get Cole to text Johnny, the whole plan could fall apart. If they were heading here or to town to rescue her, they'd lose their chance at Gates.

Cole worked for the man, but she'd have to bet on the fact that Cole cared about his brother. That Cole knew, he had to know, that Gates was a threat.

Dinah took a controlled breath. "You know Gates is trying to kill us. He has to go. He's killed people before."

"So you're going to murder him?" The disbelief hung heavy in his voice.

"No. A few of us are going to wait at my house till he comes by, to limit who gets hurt. We're going to hold him for trial."

That wasn't all. But it was true, and right now, Cole didn't need to know the rest.

Something thumped against the wall, like he'd punched it. "This is your fault," he hissed.

"Mine?" she almost yelled.

"You and Johnny are so brainwashed. If you wanted to save lives, you'd let Mr. Gates keep building his businesses. He employs almost two hundred people! Why shouldn't he be allowed to make money? If it was me buying everyone's crappy businesses and turning them around, would you murder me, too? Is there some point of success that means you have to give up all the money you've earned or die?"

"It's not the money, Cole, it's how he's getting it. He's stolen it, and he's starving people. It's not success, it's selfishness and greed."

"That's just people talking shit because they don't like him. He built all this himself. He pulled himself up by his bootstraps and he earned it."

Dinah snorted so hard it hurt her throat. She'd done a number on it with all the screaming. "That's how *you* would earn this money. That's how you would run those businesses. It's not how he did it."

Something thumped against the wall again. "Maybe you deserve to sit in there."

She spit blood out of her mouth. "Cole."

No answer.

"Cole!"

Nothing.

She hadn't wanted to blame him before—he was desperate, he was afraid, he was a kid. He was alone. But this, she absolutely would blame him for.

She kept grinding the clear plastic tie on the kitchen table. It was starting to show a white spot where the plastic was straining, so eventually it should work. Then she'd just have to get her hands free.

But then she heard boots. She stopped, set her feet down. Hung her head. If he thought she was trying anything, he'd put her somewhere harder to escape. With the blood from when Sheriff Anders hit her smearing her face, she looked pathetic. Might as well use it.

It wasn't Shaw returning for her, though. It was a skeleton in a suit, the sleeves a little too long. Neatly trimmed brown hair, leathery tanned skin. He looked very normal, very average.

Anger simmered underneath his movements. Gabriel Gates dragged a chair out from under the table. It scraped loudly along the floor as he pulled it over, close to her. He sat down.

"You and I have gotten off to a bad start," he said.

Give the man an award. She wasn't going to acknowledge that.

"What we've got here is a clash between what you want and what I want. I'm going to win the argument, because I am the one who can back up my threats. But before I do that, I want you to understand what you've done. None of this needed to happen."

She couldn't not look up at him.

If she could get at the razor blade sewn into her bra, this would be over.

He leaned forward, braced his forearms on his knees. Clasped his hands together. "I admit I hit your mother. She was angry that I was foreclosing, and the situation got out of hand. It wouldn't have been fatal if she hadn't moved. It wouldn't have broken her neck."

Dinah forced her anger down, let it curl into a ball inside her.

"But the kid, that wasn't even an accident. You're blaming me for a thing that just happened. All I did was send my people after you two. I wanted you brought in so we could have a chat. Figure out what to do with two homeless orphans. That's all."

Just kidnap them and drag them to their mother's killer. No reason to be upset.

"It's not my fault you both ran away. You chose to run when your brother had asthma," he said. "I had no idea he was sick. You can't blame me for that."

She kept her mouth shut. To even open her mouth right now would give those words ground.

"This is the problem with you people. In this country, a man with the will and the smarts can build his own empire. He can be king of whatever he owns. That's the whole point, isn't it? It has nothing to do with any of you—I don't bear anyone ill will. This is just how freedom works. Some people get the short end of the stick. It's always been that way. Life can't ever be truly fair, do you understand that? And you people can't keep punishing me for that."

Dinah stared at the floor. At the weakened white spot on the zip-tie. Banging and pounding started up outside, the scream of drills on metal. "So you're saying the problem is that we're mad. We should just let it happen, not get upset, and things will be fine. Because this is freedom?"

"I never said things would be fine. I just now said life wasn't fair."

So lie there and wait for it to be over. Accept what he wanted and don't make it harder for him by getting angry.

Gates grabbed her jaw and pulled her head up, forced her to look at him. His fingers pressed into the swelling bruise where Anders had hit her. "I wasn't even angry when you tried to kill me in your house. If you hadn't insisted on getting in my way and challenging me in public, I would have forgotten all about you."

Him forgetting about her was something she would never let happen.

A truck's engine revved, drowning out the banging.

His grip on her jaw tightened. "What do you have to say about that, girl?"

Using her gender like an insult wasn't going to work out well for him.

He shook her. "Answer me."

"You're never gonna get the chance to forget about me," Dinah said. Every bit of her was afraid right now, but that had stopped mattering some time ago. Fear wasn't making her decisions anymore.

Gates let go of her. He eased back in his chair. "Unfortunately, you're right. I just had a chat with Cole. He was really upset. He told me you and your friends have some kind of ambush planned. That it's only a few of you. And that you really wanted him to send a message to his brother."

Cole, no.

Gates pulled the texter out of his pocket. "I decided if you wanted it that badly, I should let you have what you wanted, for once. So I sent your message." He held it up for her to see the screen.

Dinah is here and okay. She says go ahead with the plan.

No no no. Please God, no.

Johnny had replied: On it. Give us a heads up when he leaves.

And Gates had responded: Will do.

"You know what's funny? I wasn't even going to go out there today," Gates said. "I wasn't going to check on the pump house again. It's pretty much ready to go. I had other things I needed to do here." He stood up slowly. "But apparently I've got mountain hicks and some kids who want me dead waiting, and now I've got to take care of that, too."

The scream of the drills outside cut out.

Gates leaned down until he was in her face. "You told Alan Fry to tell me that you were my angel of death. But I've read my Bible too, and you know what? The angel of death is not a teenage girl."

He straightened and walked toward the door. "I'm going to deal with you later. For now, you can know that your friends are dying while you sit here." He slammed the door and the lock turned.

It was not comforting that his bunkhouses locked from the outside. What the hell did he use them for, besides giving his ranch hands a place to sleep? Cole had said he was living in one of these now.

Scraping and slamming picked up again outside, like trucks being loaded.

"Dinah."

The scratchy voice through the window again.

"What have you done?" Dinah whispered.

"I don't know. I'm sorry." She could hear the strain, his voice tripped by tears. "He's going to kill Johnny. He's going to kill everyone. I didn't think he would. I warned him so he wouldn't go out there. He took my texter before I could tell Johnny. And he's screwed big steel plates to the trucks and he says I have to go with him."

"Don't go," she said. "Help me get out of here. I'll take you with me."

"I can't. He's right out front. He'll see me. And we're leaving now. Maybe if I go, I can get my texter back and warn Johnny."

She squeezed her eyes shut in frustration. "Do not go with him."

"I have to," he whispered. "But I got the keys to the blue car. It's still parked back here. I put them under the mat for you. If you can get free, head for the car. He's got the dogs guarding the door of the bunkhouse and they will bark their heads off if you open it. Go out the window. Run away. It's your only chance."

Engines revved out front, and Cole was gone.

The trucks surged out of the driveway. Quiet fell over the bunkhouse. She could hear the refrigerator running, and the sound of a dog snuffling near the door. That was it.

She was not waiting for that man to come back for her. Dinah pulled the table close again and scraped the tie binding her ankles up and down it as fast as she could.

The zip-tie broke. Dinah stood up. Something metal and sharp had to be in here somewhere. The doorframes were too rounded. No knives she could see. She opened the drawers with her hands tied behind her back, twisting to look over her shoulder, until she found an old steak knife. It took her a second to pick it up without being able to see what she was doing. It had a thick wooden handle, though, so she could get a good grip on it. Her hands were tied one wrist on top of the other, and the only way to get the blade behind the zip-tie was to fish around with the tip of the knife against her own skin until it caught the tie. She let the knife fall through her hand a bit until she had a grip on the blade itself, then wiggled the blade up between her wrists. The blade scraped her skin every time she moved it. The tip stabbed the base of her thumb.

Not dropping it was harder than she expected. It felt like her muscles were working backward, all her coordination messed up by the position of her hands. The tip of the knife finally caught the tie. She sawed back and forth, the teeth biting into the plastic. It was dull and mostly only dragged the tie around.

She gripped the blade tighter. The teeth bit into her fingers. She sawed again. This time she could hear the plastic fraying. She pulled her hands farther apart to tighten the band and kept sawing. The knife snapped the plastic.

Her hands were free.

She stretched her arms, worked the blood back into her shoulders.

Someone was probably still in the main house. Burns's brother-in-law, the cook. Another errand boy or someone.

Seconds mattered. Her house wasn't far by vehicle. She used the knife to cut the screen out of the window. Slid the glass all the way up. Pulled the table over and climbed up on it.

This window was far too small for a man to climb out of. But it was plenty big enough for a teenage girl to crawl through, if she slid one shoulder out first and wormed her way through.

Dinah dropped to the ground and ran to the car. Right now, speed was more important than being sneaky.

The keys were under the mat like Cole had said. At least he'd done that.

And in the back, her boots, gun, belt, knives, and everything were dumped on the floor, right where Shaw had thrown them. No texter. She couldn't find it anywhere. She threw everything onto the front seat and slammed the door.

The car was not self-driving. No big computer display, just some dials on the dashboard that showed speed and the level of the gas tank, and a lane-guide system in a little panel by the radio. Actual manual metal keys you had to insert into the ignition. Thank god, because she'd never used a self-driving car and she had no idea how to convince them to drive off-road.

Dinah cranked the car to life and tore through the yard. She hit the gravel doing fifty miles per hour and didn't slow down even though the car swam and fishtailed.

When she reached the highway, she set the cruise to seventy and reached to grab her boots. The car's lane guidance panel flashed and pinged at her every time she crossed the yellow line. She took up both lanes to keep from careening into the ditch while she pulled on her left boot, steering with just her pinkie finger. Then her right boot. The lane guide blared its little siren constantly and she didn't have time to figure out how to turn it off. She had both boots on by the time she reached the giant curve toward town. But instead of taking the road through town, she slowed down enough to bounce through the shallow ditch into a field. The lane guide screamed. She punched it but it kept on blaring.

The hay had been harvested already, and the dry ground held the car just fine as she jammed the accelerator to the floorboard. This field would spit her out on the other side of town. She had to take a detour around a stand of oaks, but it was still faster.

Dinah hit the blacktop again and floored it.

She could not be too late. She would not be too late. Another shortcut through an empty cornfield, the tires shredding the stubby stalks and skidding in the ruts.

Come up behind Kara's, so she could get to her place from the other direction. A mile and a half longer, but she couldn't risk passing Gates on the way.

She nearly ran right over a body in the road. Dinah braked and swerved so hard the car spun sideways. She corrected too sharply and swung the other way before evening out. She hadn't hit whoever it was. But the blood on the pavement told her it was too late to stop. And she could not stop, no matter what.

She looked in the rearview mirror. Less than two miles from her house. One of the lookouts they'd posted, that's who that was.

Someone had died today already.

Dinah pounded the steering wheel with her fist. She screamed to the empty car and floored the vehicle until she knew she was driving so fast she couldn't control it. She'd driven mopeds and motorbikes, driven Mr. Franklin's truck sometimes. But not often. And not for very long.

She slowed down to a pace that wouldn't kill her when she turned onto the gravel road by Kara's. Gates was ahead of her, and he was less than two miles from her house now.

Dinah tore down the road between her house and Kara's. No trucks parked by her house yet. The place looked empty.

It wasn't.

She drove right into the yard and behind the house. Jerked the car to a stop and grabbed her gun and knives from the passenger seat. She threw the door open and ran for the house just as the back door opened.

Kwamé.

"He's coming, he's here in under a minute, he knows we're here," she panted.

Kwamé ran inside, yelling into his radio.

"Pull my texter and Cole's off the loop," she shouted as she ran up the back steps. "He has them both. Cole told him we were here."

Everyone scrambled over each other. Johnny threw himself toward her, but he stopped short and gingerly touched the blood on her face. "God," he said. "Are you okay?"

She wrapped her arms around him for one instant. "I'm fine. You have a minute. Seconds. Where's Alan Fry and whoever was with him?"

Kara stood by the crate of stun grenades, staring at Dinah, her lips parted slightly.

"Dead," Rich DeVos, the young married guy from Kansas City, said. "It went . . . badly."

Burns and Mrs. Franklin were shouting directions to her daughter, Chrissa, and Sarah, the other sniper, as they ran out the door with them to the woods.

Her dad came over, looked her in the eye. "I'm so glad you're alright."

She nodded. This could be the last time she'd see him, and no matter what, she had loved him once.

"I knew you'd be okay," he said. "Like before, when I left. I knew you'd take care of them."

She stared at him, unblinking. And then she turned away from him.

"Who was the lookout?" Dinah asked Johnny quietly. "On the road to town. Who was it?"

"Kwamé's brother. Kobe," he said.

"Gates shot him. He's dead," she whispered. She pulled on her belt, slid her knives into her sheaths, holstered her pistol.

Johnny stumbled a step backward.

Burns and Mrs. Franklin ran back in. Slammed and locked the back door.

Kara still hadn't moved.

"Everyone else is coming," Jay Kang said. "I texted the group and Kwamé called everyone he could get over the radio. We have"—she paused to count— "fourteen people here, counting the snipers. How many is he bringing?"

"I couldn't see," Dinah said. "Two or three trucks, at least. He bolted steel panels to them."

"Grab the riot guns. We were hoping for maybe four people with him at the worst," Akosua said. "We don't have the firepower for this."

Jay and Lissa and everyone else scrambled for the capsaicin capsules and the 12-gauge shotguns. Kwamé, Akosua, and Burns took position by the windows and the door.

Kara finally moved. Her eyes were swollen, eyeliner smeared into dark circles. She slowly walked toward her, across the living room. Across the house that had once been Dinah's mother's, now filled with guns and stun grenades.

Her best friend's gaze was spilling over with something Dinah couldn't translate. She had always been able to read this girl so well, knew confusion brought that line between her eyebrows, knew when she was afraid that she shut down and refused to let anyone see. But now Dinah couldn't read her at all.

Kara's warm hand slipped over Dinah's cold palm. "Cielo. You're alive? You're okay?" The girl whispered so quietly Dinah had to read it from her lips.

And then engines shattered the air.

Dinah went rigid with the memory. Warren beside her as cars sped over the grass. Their feet pounding across the yard. Her grasping Warren's small hand in hers as they sprinted over the rocks.

The rumble of the trucks came to a standstill in the yard.

"Might as well give up," Gates yelled.

Dinah tore away from Kara and dropped to her knees by the window. A barricade of three trucks in a semicircle, only fifty feet from the house. Narrow strips of corrugated steel bolted to the sides extended the height of the beds and protected the truck itself.

Maybe gunfire could still pierce the panels, but it would slow the bullet down so much it probably wouldn't be fatal by the time the round penetrated the steel, and it made it impossible to take direct aim. Holes drilled through the steel allowed rifle barrels to stick through like splinters, slits beside each barrel for the gunman to sight.

She counted three rifle barrels nosed through the steel in each truck. Plus a driver each. A minimum of twelve armed men.

"You want to punish me for your own failure?" Gates yelled. "It's not my fault you're poor and don't like it. You've got thirty seconds to come out here and drop your guns."

"No one move," Johnny said. "Fuck him."

"Any sign of Sheriff Anders?" Dinah asked. He could be hiding in the beds, but if he was here, he'd want to bluster about his authority and pretend this was an official arrest.

"Not so far." Johnny touched her back. His hand felt desperate. "I thought we were going to have to do this first and come for you after. Leave you waiting."

Dinah spoke to the windowpane, smeared with oval marks. Warren's fingerprints. "I wasn't waiting."

He hadn't dropped everything to save her. He'd stayed here, he'd trusted her, he'd followed through on what had been worth everything to her.

That was the kind of love she needed.

"We're staying," Kwamé said. "If he thinks we'll surrender, he's gonna rot out there."

Sheriff Anders must not have come—had this finally been too far for him? Or maybe he was too much of a shit to act on his threats. Or maybe he was still coming, and this would turn from a nightmare to something worse. Mitch Harding did not seem to be here, either.

"Five seconds," Shaw yelled, his heavy russet beard a bright target.

"Get away from the windows," Lissa said. "Behind the furniture. Anything that can collect shrapnel."

The others, at least ten others, were coming, but they'd never get here in time.

"Four," Shaw bellowed.

Kara dropped to her knees beside her.

"Three!"

Kara grabbed Dinah's hand and hauled her with Johnny behind the couch.

"Time's up," Gates yelled.

Gunfire ruptured the air. The windows exploded. Glass rained everywhere, splinters of wood flying through the room, rounds slamming into walls.

"Come out," Gates said. "Last chance."

But Rich was on the ground, his leg a red mess. He stared at it, his face pale. Burns knelt down beside him and cut off Rich's pant leg.

"Help me," Burns grunted. "Full of glass and wood. If we put pressure on it, we'll make it worse. Gotta clean it fast."

Her dad and Kwamé helped carry Rich into her mom's bedroom. The motion must have worn through the shock because Rich started screaming.

Mrs. Franklin picked up her radio. "Chrissa. Sarah. Take them out."

Gunfire broke from the woods. Two shots. Two more, carefully timed. Then six. They must be high in the trees, higher than the top of the house. High enough to fire over the steel panels. The windshield on the first truck cracked into a spiderweb and crumbled. Someone started yelling from the trucks.

"I found their frequency," Akosua said.

The voices of the men outside came in over her radio. "Two down," Adwell said quietly, from behind the cover of a truck bed. "Jeremy and Aaron. Headshots." Silence. "Boss? You hear me?"

Nothing.

Still crouched behind the couch in the middle of the living room, Dinah met Akosua's eyes.

Rich's screaming cut off suddenly.

Burns and Kwamé came back from her mom's room, hunched over beneath the windows. "Couldn't get the bullet, but the shrapnel's mostly out and we've got it wrapped. Best we can do. He needs a hospital, fast."

He wasn't going to get one.

"Boss?" Adwell said again, louder. This time they heard his voice coming over the radio and through the shattered windows.

Lissa risked a look. "Gates is on the phone. Yelling. Adwell is sending two guys into the woods. They're running."

"They're going after Chrissa and Sarah," Mrs. Franklin said. She hoarsely whispered a warning into her radio.

Kwamé sprinted for the back of the house and flung the door open. He pulled his rifle to his shoulder, and shots exploded through the house.

Silence again. "Don't know if I got them or not," Kwamé said.

"They're down four right now—two dead, two somewhere in the woods, but maybe alive. And Gates is distracted," Jay said. "This is our chance."

All of them—Burns, Kwamé, Yaw, Lissa and Akosua, Jay Kang, Kara, Mrs. and Mr. Franklin, and Johnny all knelt in the fragments of wood and glass by the windows.

"Flush them out of the trucks. It's all we can do," Mr. Franklin said.

Lissa and Akosua picked up the shotguns. They opened fire with the pepper rounds, aiming low so that the rounds burst on the trucks and sprayed the capsaicin powder into the air. The sound of coughing and hacking rose from outside. "Hopefully that screws up their ability to aim, too," Lissa said. One of the tailgates slammed down and three people jumped out and ran behind the vehicle.

Burns raised his rifle. "Guns up. Here we go."

And then she remembered. "Wait. Cole is with him," Dinah said. "He's out there."

"What?" Johnny demanded.

"He went with Gates. He said he had to. He was going to try to warn you." Sarah and Chrissa already could have hit him.

"After telling that man where we were? Little shit," Burns said.

"We don't have another option," Jay said. "He chose his side."

It wasn't that simple.

"We can't open fire on my twelve-year-old brother." Johnny had gone rigid beside her.

"Do you have any idea which truck he's in?" Lissa said.

No.

Wait. "He'll be with Gates. He was trying to get his texter

back. And Gates has this real control thing about him."

Gates was still on his phone, in the cab of the middle truck, half protected by the steel panels. Yelling.

They couldn't make that shot from here. Not at this angle.

"Avoid the middle truck. Make it count," Lissa said.

"Aim for the tires. And aim for the steel panels anyway—an injured man is better than nothing, and we don't know how many he's got in those truck beds," Burns said.

Dinah pulled the rifle steady into her shoulder. This was going to be deafening. She felt in her pocket and pulled out her earplugs. Johnny shoved in his, and she shoved in hers. She looked out across her yard—the porch where she'd spilled the pears, the worn, brown grass dusted with muddy snow. The bare patch where Warren's chicken shed had stood.

Burns counted them down. Dinah breathed out, and in the space between breaths, they opened fire. Rifles, shotguns, handguns.

Holes punched through steel. Tires went flat. Windows crumbled. Pepper shots followed the bullets into the cabs.

"Again, before they can recover," Kwamé said.

Thunder washed over her a second time. Pounded against the bits of foam in her ears. Eleven shots. Twenty-two. Thirty-three. Forty-four.

The steel panels looked like a sieve.

Kwamé jerked back to reload. "Some of us are half-empty. Count off, one shot from each down the line, every three seconds. After you fire, stop to reload. You'll have less than thirty seconds to your turn again." His voice was muted by the earplugs, but she could still make it out.

Kara fired. Three seconds. Then Mrs. Franklin fired. Then Mr. Franklin. Then Jay. Then Yaw.

Gates threw the door of his truck open, coughing. One hand held his gun, the other hand gripped Cole by the collar of his coat. He forced Cole down to his knees and stood behind him. "Go ahead and shoot me now, if you'll risk hitting the kid."

Everyone held their fire. Johnny's hands trembled on his Glock. Dinah touched his knee. On the other side of him, Kara touched his shoulder. Dinah risked a glance at her, but she was staring out the window at the boy on the ground.

Johnny didn't seem to be able to feel either of them.

"No? No one's going to take the shot?" Gates shouted, eyes red and swollen from the capsaicin. "Fine. Surrender now, or he dies." Gates touched the barrel of the gun to Cole's head.

Cole was utterly motionless. His head hung down, brown hair hanging in front of his eyes.

How had she thought she could save lives? She'd let this boy stay in the crosshairs, even when she'd known what would come for him.

"We have to do what he wants," Johnny said, his voice barely audible.

"We can't, Johnny boy," Burns said. "We surrender, and the kid dies anyway. We all do."

No. Because they had planned for innocent people in the firing range. They'd planned to minimize loss of life. It just wasn't supposed to be right now.

Johnny turned to her. His eyes were shocked with pain and a fear she knew. Fear so deep there wasn't any piece of you left—just someone crouching over Warren, forehead on his chest, screaming until she spit blood. Someone watching dirt fall over a sunshine-yellow quilt, sprinkle into her mother's hair.

"He's my brother," Johnny said. "He's twelve."

Gates's voice invaded her home again. "Dinah Caldwell is in there right now, isn't she? I got this call, you see, and they told me she was gone. All you did was trade your life for his, honey. Heroic escapes have a cost."

She might be inadequate to save lives, but she was goddamned adequate enough to cost lives.

Dinah stood up slowly. Cole had said if Gates found her, he'd make her an example.

Then let him fucking do it. He'd find out what kind of example she made.

The crate of stun grenades sat behind the tipped-over table. She glanced at it.

"Dinah," Kara said. Her voice cracked.

"Don't," Johnny said.

"If I surrender, he'll let Cole go," Dinah said.

"No way." Burns shook his head, his mane of bushy white hair moving with him. "You go out there, you're dead."

"You promised me." Johnny stood up next to her. "Last night. You promised you wouldn't do this. If you go out there, this will be it. He will kill both of you."

A shot cracked in the woods. A woman's scream followed it, then a burst of gunfire that ended abruptly.

Mrs. Franklin screamed into her hands. Her husband shook where he knelt and started saying his daughter's name like a prayer.

Johnny was utterly frozen, staring out the window toward his brother, so Dinah took Kara's hand and pulled the girl toward her.

She wouldn't break her promise to either of them. But she would not be his puppet.

It was blasphemy to violate someone this way, to dig into their family and pry out a piece. To dig into a body and sever their soul.

If she was to be a sister, to be a daughter, to be as strong and kind and brave as her mom had believed she was—if she was going to be the terror this man could not understand, then she had to do this.

Dinah traced her thumb over Kara's cheekbone. "Don't let today control your life."

"I love you." Eyes full of desperation, Kara yanked Dinah into a hug.

"I love you too," Dinah whispered into her hair.

Dinah pulled back a little, but Kara didn't. Kara leaned her forehead on Dinah's, her breathing harsh. Kara's eyes opened, and Dinah felt it—her asking. Kara's breath was on Dinah's lips, and Kara was waiting, so she let herself do what she'd wanted to for six years.

It was okay, even though she was all in for Johnny and he was right here. This was good-bye. Dinah touched her lips to Kara's and kissed her. Just for an instant. Just long enough to turn herself inside out. It felt like something she'd done a hundred times before and it was too much to believe that this would be the last time, too.

Dinah pulled back before Kara could. She hugged her tight. "Make sure Johnny's okay?" she whispered.

Kara nodded, slowly. Her hand went up, touched her own lips with a finger.

Johnny was still staring out the window at Cole.

Dinah touched his shoulder, turned him gently toward her. "Trust me," she said. "I'm doing this so we can live. Have the grenades ready." She tapped her ear. "I've still got these. Watch my hands. I'll count to three."

"I'm coming with you. He's more likely to trade Cole for both of us."

Dinah shook her head. "I need you here. You're the one I trust to do this. Please."

Johnny didn't say anything. He hugged her too tight, his hands curling over her ribs like he could weave her to him. When he let her go, his gaze traced over her face, but his eyes were steady. He nodded.

If it was blasphemy for Gabriel Gates to kill her mother, kill Warren, Kobe, Chrissa and Sarah, maybe Rich now too, and for him to hold Cole's life at the end of his gun—then it was blasphemy for her to kill him, too.

For these people, she'd accept that condemnation.

"He won't let you live," Kwamé said.

Lissa shook her head. "Dinah, please, it won't help."

She didn't have time to explain. Gates wouldn't wait much longer. "Be ready," she said. "Johnny, tell them what to do."

Dinah opened the door. Cold air breathed across her skin, sneaking through the gaps around the buttons of her shirt. The gray sky hung heavy, promising rain. But like whoever might still be on the way, it wouldn't be here in time. She walked across her own porch, the planks sounding hollow under her boots.

She raised her hands. "Me for Cole," she said.

# TWENTY-ONE

COLE RAISED HIS HEAD. WHEN HIS EYES MET HERS, THEY were so full of shame and fear that she wanted to say *it will be okay,* but she couldn't. She wouldn't put it past this man, the moment the words left her lips, to pull the trigger and kill the boy, just to prove her a liar.

Gates kept the gun to Cole's head. Shaw and Adwell came up beside him, covering her with their rifles. But her hands were in the air and she'd left her gun inside. They'd only take it from her, anyway.

"Step off the porch, where we can see you," Adwell said. "Lace your fingers over your head." She'd been right to think of him as a snake, his face quick and mean.

Dinah walked down the steps to the yard. She laced her fingers together, hands resting on her head. Cole was only forty feet away now.

"Drop to your knees," Adwell said.

Her knees smacked the ground. This dirt was hers. Her knees pressed into the soil that covered the bodies of her family. The rain-heavy sky overhead was the gray of her brother's eyes.

"Why would I bother trading Cole for you? Neither of you matters," Gates said.

All they were was leverage. And wasn't that exactly what he'd said in the bunkhouse? None of this was personal to him—they were all just leverage. Pieces he could move around when he needed, prey for a predator.

"I'll confess to attempted murder." Cold seeped through the knees of her jeans. "That would mean a public trial. Sentencing."

The gun eased back from Cole's head a fraction—he'd relaxed his arm a little. She could see him thinking. Judge Harding would convict her. His term was almost up, but Gates had funded his campaign, so he'd do it.

Convicting her of attempted first-degree murder would give Gates a public threat to hang over everyone. Look at this rebellious girl, in prison for life. This is what happens when you revolt.

Gates pulled his gun away from Cole. "You also confess to assaulting Alan Fry. And two counts of attempted murder—you tried to knife me in your kitchen, and you set up this ambush. And now I have four men dead in the bed of my truck and two more injured. You're responsible for that."

He wanted to paint her as the violent one. Point to her as the problem and the source of disruption.

Those men were dead because he'd brought them here with guns and fired on the house.

A spit of rain struck her neck. "Fine. I'll confess to all of that. And I did try to kill you. I dreamed about it. I practiced for the moment I could put a bullet between your eyes."

Gates motioned to Adwell. "Tie the kid."

The man took zip-ties from his pocket and pulled Cole's hands together. Cole yanked his hands away. "It's my fault. I'm not going."

Adwell pinned his wrists and jerked the tie.

"Hold still or I kill you right here. I don't have enough men to control two hostages right now," Gates said.

Adwell yanked Cole to his feet and snaked a tie around each foot, then linked a third through them both, tight enough he could barely shuffle.

"Go to the house," Gates said.

"No." That stubborn look surfaced on Cole's face. "I won't let you trade me for her."

"Do it, Cole," Dinah said.

If she lost today, this man would use it against the entire county.

Adwell pushed him forward. Cole had to stumble a step toward her or he'd fall. He shuffled a few steps to regain his balance. He stared into her eyes, terror seeping from every piece of him.

"Go to Johnny," she said.

He took another step. Slowly started across the fifty feet to the house. Completely helpless and on his own. No one could leave the house, and she couldn't do a thing to help him right now.

Cole kept walking. He was halfway to her when Gates twitched his gun.

God damn it, no.

The man met her eyes and flicked the barrel up toward Cole.

Dinah couldn't help the jerk of her body. But Cole saw it and tried to look behind him. His feet were tied so tight that he fell.

Gates laughed. "Can't take a joke, huh?"

Cole had to roll over in order to sit up. It took him a minute of twisting and pulling his feet under him to struggle to a stand again.

He shuffled past Dinah. "I'm sorry," he whispered.

"It's okay," she said. "Just go inside."

She couldn't turn to look, but after a minute she heard the uncoordinated clunk of feet on the low steps. The door opened and boots sounded on the wood. Someone had come out. Then the door closed.

Quiet.

He'd actually gone through with it—Gates had let her trade herself for Cole.

"Stand up," Gates said.

Dinah got to her feet, hands still on top of her head. She held them as still as possible. If Johnny misunderstood, she would die.

"Walk toward me."

Shaw kept his gun leveled on her. Adwell had his trained on the house.

She stepped forward. After all this time imagining this moment, it was surreal to stare at his face. At his body. He was wearing jeans, and it made her angry that he would wear something so normal, pretend to be so normal.

He was, though, wasn't he?

"Stop there. Adwell, search her."

The man, this stranger, started with her hair and searched every wrinkle and pocket of her clothing. He found the knife in the boot sheath. She'd hoped leaving them something to find might satisfy them.

"Take her boots off," Gates said.

Adwell made her raise one foot at a time while he yanked them off.

She stood in her yard in her socks, shivering. The breeze was cold, but it wasn't the wind. It was nerves, the percussion of her blood.

Gates crooked a finger at her. "Come here."

He was enjoying making her do things. Saying the word, making her obey.

Dinah walked toward him. She stopped a foot away. The cold ground touched her through her socks. She dug her toes into the dirt of her home.

"Hands on your head again. Kneel." His jaw was set, his wrinkled face and his angry, normal eyes and normal nose marking the center of a person who could not see her.

Dinah put her hands behind her head and laced her fingers together. She waited for Gates to make her move her hands to the top of her head instead, but he didn't.

She sank down to her knees in front of him. Johnny would not take his eyes off her. He wouldn't.

"Adwell," Gates said. "The house. Do it."

Adwell flicked a lighter and threw something to the roof.

Shingles parched from the drought crackled to life like dry sticks. Tar and wood burst into flame.

Gates just watched her while it happened. Her whole body clenched.

Maybe she could will it to rain. Force the sky to crack open and save her home and the people inside it.

Gabriel Gates would never see them, but she saw the shard of eternity in him. The thing he'd denied so often it had soured.

His belief that he was somehow better, his belief that he'd earned all this—all his anger and bitterness had curdled together, and that made it nothing for him to take a life. It had dehumanized him, and that was why he'd dehumanized them.

Hands laced together behind her head, she raised one finger.

Johnny would be watching her. Even with the house on fire. He had stayed here to do what needed done, even when she'd been kidnapped. He would follow through.

Dinah raised a second finger. She stared up into the eyes of the man at whose feet she knelt.

If this was her last moment on earth, she would have lived fully. She would have done what only she could do and spent every piece of herself to protect and to build what she loved.

Dinah raised a third finger.

She clamped her hands over her ears and shoved the earplugs in as far as she could. *Come on, Johnny.*

Gates lunged for her.

The entire world exploded in a flash of light. She could see the burn even around the arm she'd thrown in front of her eyes. Bodies lurched into her. Distantly, someone was screaming.

A second explosion slammed into her. A third, a few feet farther away.

She uncovered her face and rolled to her knees. The motion made her want to puke. But she had to be faster. Five seconds, Johnny had said.

Shaw was on his stomach in the dirt, vomiting into his red beard. Men climbed out of the truck beds like they were drunk. Smoke clouded the air and blurred everyone into smudges.

Dinah jerked her shirt open. Slid her finger into the slice in her bra and popped the stitches.

Gabriel Gates lay on his stomach. He was trying to roll to his side.

This man was not her god, he was not her law, he was not a system she couldn't change. He was nothing but a man. And men could bleed out.

Dinah pulled the razor blade out of her bra.

The wind snapped up and whirls of rain struck her skin. Sheets of water fell from the sky.

Swallowed in rain and smoke, Gates pulled his knees under him. She threw herself at him, feeling for his throat. He grabbed her shoulders and threw her to her back on the ground. She clenched the tiny razor blade so hard to keep from dropping it that the blade slit her palm open. He pinned her arms to her sides as he weaved dizzily over top of her on his hands and knees.

Gates heaved in air, and she took that second to move the blade to a grip between her thumb and forefinger. She stabbed upward into his groin and ripped.

His scream was inhuman. He fumbled for her hands but could barely hold himself up. Someone behind him lurched toward her, a gun in their hand.

She grabbed his jaw with her left hand, forced his head upward. His hands scrambled for hers. She raised her right hand with the razor blade and slashed his jugular vein deep.

Blood spurted over her. It fell like the rain in a veil to drench her. He collapsed on top of her, his throat working, hands digging into the ground beside her.

The body with the gun pulled Gabriel Gates off her.

Clasped her hand and helped her sit up.

It was Kara.

Dinah only knew she'd been screaming once she stopped. She dropped the razor blade into the mud made by blood and dirt.

Kara turned her back to Dinah. Kept her gun up.

So many people were screaming. Engines were revving. Gunshots cracked like popcorn. Her eyes burned with the powdery fog of the capsaicin powder, tears streaming down her face.

Her gaze pulled down to Gabriel Gates. He was facedown in

the yard, his throat split like a bloody pocket.

His eyes stared endlessly.

A gun pressed into her hands. The gun she'd set down inside. "Come on," Kara said. "You can do this. Get up."

Blood covered her like oil. It left handprints on the gun in her lap.

Kara's voice broke. "We don't have any cover. Please, Dinah."

The yard was a roiling mass of bodies. Everyone had been forced out of the house. Her home was fully on fire, backlighting the bodies and drowning everyone in smoke. The flames ate the rain as quickly as it fell.

Two men, hired rovers she didn't recognize, ran toward the woods, coughing and clutching their faces. Kwamé, perched in the bed of the truck at the end, watched them down the sights of his rifle but let them go.

Dinah stumbled to her feet. Gates and four others down. At least two had just run off. They had to outnumber the rest of them now.

Adwell lurched out of the fog, shrouded in smoke. His pistol was pointed right at her.

Kara screamed and fired at him, but her shot missed. Adwell's eyes were swollen almost completely shut, but he swung toward Kara. "Drop your guns. Both of you, get in the truck," he said.

Johnny appeared from nowhere and shot him in the head at point-blank range.

"Johnny," Cole screamed, so loud it rose over everything else. Johnny dropped to the ground and rolled to the side, and a rifle shot pounded into the truck behind them. By the time Dinah realized Johnny hadn't been hurt, that he dropped to get out of the line of sight, he was gone.

Dinah put her back to Kara's and raised her gun. "Help me clear a path to that truck," Kara said.

Shaw was huddled in the bed of the vehicle first in line, protected by the steel panel on one side as he fired toward the house. But the tailgate was open to her. Dinah took aim and breathed out. Pulled the trigger. The shot missed him and shattered the rear windshield.

Kara fired, but Dinah didn't look to see why. They quickly moved forward, back to back, Kara watching their front while Dinah scanned their back. Shaw was turning toward her, so she fired again. Again, as he leaped over the far side of the truck and disappeared.

"Inside," Dinah said. They ran for the driver's door.

The windshield and the windows had all been shattered. Dinah pulled her hand inside her sleeve and swiped crumbled glass off the seat as they both climbed in through the driver's door. Her eyes burned and watered. The rain was washing it away outside, but inside the truck, the pepper fog still lingered.

Johnny and Kwamé ran across the yard with one of the modified shotguns, cranking round after round of capsaicin capsules after three fleeing men. The men piled into the truck at the end of the line and peeled out of the yard.

The keys were still in the ignition. Kara cranked the truck to life. "You're the better shot," Kara said. "Let's go."

Dinah wiped her eyes on the inside of her shirt and could barely make out that the person ahead was Johnny. He'd found Cole and was heading for her with his brother, but Shaw was right behind him. He didn't know, he didn't see the man's arm coming up. Dinah threw herself toward the door, leaning out the broken window with her pistol. But Shaw suddenly dropped like a rock.

Burns. Burns and Kwamé had now taken over the bed of the remaining truck, rifles threaded through the gun ports in the steel panel.

But their backs were open, and a man she didn't even recognize stood in the road and fired. Burns fell. Kwamé whipped around toward Burns.

"Go!" Dinah yelled.

Kara gunned the engine toward the man in the road. Dinah slid on the seat as the truck jerked onto the gravel. The man swung his gun toward them, but Kara drove the truck right into him. His body hit the grill and flew up over the cab. It landed with a slap on the road behind them. The truck careened to the side as Kara spun them around. The body didn't move.

Kara drove back into the yard and jerked to a stop by Johnny and Cole. The boys leaped into the bed.

"There," Dinah yelled. "Lissa and Akosua." Over by the new pump house, the two women were using the building for cover, firing toward the house.

Kara drove behind the building and Akosua's gun came up before she saw who they were.

"Get in!" Dinah said. The women jumped in with Johnny and Cole.

They rounded the side of the house to see a truck and a van coming from the Franklins' house. "My parents," Kara said. The Hernándezes, Mr. and Mrs. Franklin's twin boys, Alice and her siblings.

The last two men who had come with Gates were sprinting into the trees at the end of the road.

Kara stopped the truck by the porch. Johnny and Dinah jumped out, Akosua and Lissa covering them from the bed.

The yard was all but empty, punctuated by horror. Kwamé and Yaw scrambled over Burns in the other truck. Mr. Franklin carried Rich, limp and unmoving, out of the burning house. Mrs. Franklin was working on her dad's arm—he must have been shot? Or stabbed? He was sagging against the porch.

Across the yard, Chrissa stumbled from the woods. Her parents left what they were doing and ran for her. Dinah could hear them crying and yelling her name all the way across the yard.

A man she didn't even know lay dead in the road. Shaw had folded over double, unmoving. Adwell had collapsed where Johnny had shot him. Water ran off their bodies as the sky poured itself over them.

Gabriel Gates was dead in the dirt.

The neighbors parked beside her and piled out of the vehicles. Akosua and Lissa directed everyone to the pump house, and Dinah followed. They rolled out a huge hose Gates had installed, and water poured onto the roof of her house.

Was anyone inside? She couldn't count everyone; she couldn't remember who had been inside to start with.

No. Mr. and Mrs. Franklin had brought Rich out. They wouldn't have left anyone else inside.

The rain had kept the whole house from burning. The most stubborn flames were at the back corner, her bedroom, where the fire had taken hold before the rain had started.

All this water, pouring over her house and sinking into the ground.

There was nothing left she could do to save her home. Eight people were already helping with the one hose.

Dinah walked over to Gates's body. She squeezed her cut hand so it would hurt again. The pain rode down the adrenaline as she stared into his unseeing face. Rain drizzled off his hands and washed his bloody neck clean.

It had rained because she'd willed it to. It wasn't an answered prayer; it was her actions and her breath. Those were her prayers. The force of her body and her soul and the eternity inside her, spinning the atmosphere around her fingers and bringing the rain when she called for it. She'd made the sky crack open.

When she'd buried her family, she'd known there was no God in that sky. Her God was here. In the mud smeared onto her skin, in the earth she was formed out of, in the blood that ran through her organs. She had deity inside her, she was life and death, she was the beginning and end, and so were Warren and her mother and Kara and Johnny and Lissa and Kwamé and Akosua and Burns. Fragments of divinity, every piece endless.

She had killed Gabriel Gates, but his damage wasn't done. She'd seen the look on Cole's face when that man had hauled him out of the truck and forced him to his knees. Alice was right now weeping over her husband's body. The low, gut-wrenching sobs of someone whose life had just been pulled apart.

Kwamé, Akosua, and Yaw were slowly lifting Kobe's body from Mr. Franklin's truck. That was why they'd been late. They'd stopped for Kobe.

Johnny was sitting motionless beside Burns, like he was magnetized to him.

Lissa held her crying wife when Akosua set her brother's body down.

Mr. and Mrs. Hernández brought Sarah's body out of the woods—Chrissa had lived, but the other woman had not. They set her beside Rich, her young husband. He'd died of shock. At least neither of them had known about the other.

Dinah was on her knees and she wasn't sure how she'd gotten there.

She touched Gabriel Gates's cold hand, and suddenly she was crying, hunched over her knees.

She gripped his dead hand and wept into the noise and rain around them. The more she cried, the harder she cried, until she couldn't stop.

Johnny knelt beside her, and she only knew it was him because he touched her neck. No one else would do that. He pulled her back against his chest, away from Gates.

She buried her face in his chest and cried.

He was bloody. He was alive.

So was she.

She took a breath.

"It's over." He looked at her like she was some kind of miracle.

An engine sounded on the road. All over the yard, guns came up.

Johnny jumped to his feet and pulled her up with him. "Stop! That's my parents."

The little van parked in the driveway.

Cole froze in the middle of the yard. His dads opened the van doors and stepped out into the rain. A man about Johnny's height—who looked so much like him—and a taller, slighter blond man who must be Adam.

Johnny took a step toward them. "I thought you'd left already."

Their shocked faces took in the ruined vehicles, the bodies, the last embers burning on the flooded house.

"We couldn't leave without Cole," Adam said.

Cole still didn't move. His face was a page of guilt and anger. Anger at himself. And it would be so much work for him to find a way past it.

The men waved Cole over, but he was motionless.

Johnny waved him over. Cole hesitated, then took a step forward. And then he kept going. His dads pulled him into their arms, and she could see from here that Cole's knees buckled. Muffled sobs rose over the rain.

The man who looked so much like Johnny pulled his other son in, too.

Dinah turned away. This wasn't for her.

Where was her family?

She had Johnny, and she had Kara, and she had her neighbors. But where was her family? This was done, but what could ever be next?

She walked behind the house, because she couldn't stand for anyone else to see her, to have to deal with her grief when they already had their own, condensed into bodies that they would have to bury in the ground.

She turned the corner and almost walked right into Kara.

Her best friend was leaning against the back of the house. Her hair and clothes were soaked. "The fire's out," Kara said.

Steam still rose from the roof into the sky, but the smoke was clearing. The far back corner was charred to ash. Part of the roof had fallen in.

"Thank you." Dinah turned away from the fire damage to find Kara pinning her with the same incomprehensible gaze she'd had when Kara had realized she'd escaped and was safe.

Rain trickled down Kara's warm brown skin. Down her neck and across her collarbone, into her shirt. "You kissed me," Kara said.

She'd thought—Kara had seemed to want it, too. "I'm sorry," Dinah said.

Kara's gaze fastened on Dinah's socked feet. She swallowed

hard. "Do you really not . . . feel that way about me anymore?"

Dinah touched her hand. "You said——"

Kara shook her head, too hard. "I'm asking about *you*. Do you want him now, instead of me?"

There was no instead. "I chose being your friend." Her chest felt so heavy right now. Why was Kara making her do this?

"You're the one person I thought I'd always have." Kara stepped toward her.

Dinah backed up. Kara kept going, until Dinah hit the wall of her house.

"You gave me your last razor," Kara said. "When I was too embarrassed to go to the Christmas dance without shaving. I never understood why you wouldn't play your guitar for me, and it made me so upset. I think I never dated anyone because I had you. I didn't want anyone else."

Dinah was holding her breath, but she had no idea why. She only knew that if she breathed, this would be over.

Kara closed the miniscule space between them, so close their legs and stomachs were touching. "Please be honest with me. More honest than you've ever been. I thought you were going to die. Do you still have feelings for me?"

Good-bye. She'd said good-bye to this already.

Her wet curls brushed Dinah's arm. The blood on her own skin was washing away, and she was splitting into eager, heartbroken pieces.

Kara was in her DNA. Scarring her skin, cutting her bangs, running muscle into her legs and lifting buckets of fruit and pumping barrels of water until her arms burned. This girl was marked on her body. "I still want you," she said, because it was the truth.

Kara, fear and something else in her eyes, leaned in, then hesitated. Dinah held completely still. Waiting.

Kara leaned all the way in and kissed her. She grabbed the collar of Dinah's shirt and pulled her closer. It was still unbuttoned, hanging open. Kara's wet shirt was cold on her skin. Goose bumps streamed down her back like water.

Dinah clutched Kara's curls. This girl tasted like ash and rain and every hope Dinah had ever had. She pulled on her curls gently, the way she'd wanted to since she first wondered what it would feel like to have these curls wind around delicate fingertips.

Kara's hands slipped down to Dinah's bare stomach, traced around behind her back, and suddenly Dinah wasn't cold anymore.

Dinah touched Kara's collarbone, felt the ridge and the softness of the skin, and hoped it was okay. Kara's tongue brushed hers, so it must have been.

This was nothing like kissing a best friend. It was like reading her favorite book again and discovering something she'd never seen before. Like playing a song for the hundredth time but hearing the lyrics just a little differently, and they suddenly made sense.

Kara eased back. "Since you told me—and then your text. And now today."

Dinah wound one of Kara's curls around her finger.

"We have to talk," Kara said, a little breathlessly.

"Yeah. But—" Dinah glanced to the front yard, as if she could see it through the house. Johnny, though, was already walking toward them. His eyes found her.

She couldn't split herself in two.

"Hey now. Don't look like that. I saw his face when you walked out to Gates. I saw you with him, when he pulled you away from that man's body. He was the one who was there during the worst weeks of your life." Kara turned Dinah's face back toward her, until their eyes met. "I am not asking you to leave anyone."

One heartbeat. Two.

Three.

"What do you mean?" Dinah whispered.

"I only asked you about me," Kara said.

She could hear the question. "Yes," Dinah said. "Are you sure?"

For her, Johnny was a simple fact. Kara was a deep truth.

Kara slid her fingers through Dinah's belt loops. Pulled her away from the wall and up against her own body. "Twice today, I thought I would lose you. So I have to see if we're right about this."

Johnny stopped a few steps away, in her peripheral vision. He glanced from girl to girl. His face was hesitant, shaken. "I—Dinah, I . . . will you come meet my parents? They need to leave soon."

Dinah squeezed Kara's hand. "Give me a minute?" She walked over to Johnny. His eyes seemed like they couldn't look anywhere but at her. She touched his wrist.

He took her hand and they walked toward the front yard and his parents.

He stopped suddenly. "You kissed her. Are you picking between us?"

Dinah gripped his hand hard. "Johnny, no. I wouldn't leave you. You know that, right? I could never leave either of you."

His shoulders relaxed. "No. I know."

How could she choose between water and air? This boy was hers. He belonged with her.

Dinah turned to look over her shoulder and Kara was watching them both, hands in her back pockets.

She would spend everything she had, give herself endlessly, to be home to them.

Johnny stopped by his parents. Cole was sitting quietly in their van, his face masked by the tint on the windows.

"Dinah, these are my dads, Adam and David."

David shook her hand. It felt so strange, almost inappropriate, to be shaking hands and introducing herself to her boyfriend's parents when her hands and feet were covered in blood and the air everyone breathed was pierced with grief.

"We don't want to leave, now, not after this," David said. Johnny's eyes looked back at her from a face that was thirty years older.

"But we have to," Adam cut in. He seemed strong, steady, and his hands were careful and warm when he shook Dinah's. "David needs this treatment, or we wouldn't go. But we'll stay in touch. We plan to get to know you, Dinah. And to take care of our sons, even though they're almost too old for it."

"No, they aren't," Dinah said.

Adam's shoulders slumped a little. "I hope not."

"I'm glad he has you," David said.

Johnny shifted his weight from one foot to the other, scuffed the toe of his boot against the ground. The wind tugged his bloody shirt against his chest.

"He's given me a lot more than I've given him," Dinah said.

"Untrue," Johnny said softly.

Adam smiled and reached out to hug her, a little awkwardly. "We'll see you again." And then he hugged his son. Whispered something to him that made Johnny hug him tighter.

The men headed for the old van, Adam's hand resting lightly on David's lower back.

Johnny waved, but Cole didn't lift his head as they drove away.

"He's going to stay with them for a few days," Johnny said. "Then Cole will—" He paused. "He'll come live with me. My dads think he needs more stability and attention than they have while Dad's in this trial. And they don't want him alone in St. Louis, so I insisted he stay with me. Maybe I should have discussed it with you first?"

"Of course not. He's your brother."

Johnny slid an arm around her waist. They walked back toward the smoldering house, the steam still rising hot into the slowing rain and the dimming sky.

Everyone stood near the covered bodies, the yard flooded with shock and grief.

Gabriel Gates was dead on the ground behind her, and it wasn't him she cared about.

# TWENTY-TWO

EVERYONE STAYED AWAKE ALL NIGHT AT KWAMÉ'S. NO ONE seemed to know how to go to sleep, just washed the blood off themselves and sat around in blankets on the floor, holding mugs of hot tea but never really drinking it. Even the Franklins with Chrissa and the twin boys came, and Kara and her parents, along with Hannah and little Matías. No one wanted to risk being alone, and no one was quite sure what would happen next or what Sheriff Anders would do.

The plan had been for Burns to take a group into town with an official petition signed by everyone for him to resign. They'd demand his resignation and install Jay Kang as the acting sheriff until an election could be held. But now Burns was dead, and Kwamé was shut in his room with Yaw and Akosua and Lissa and Mr. Adu.

Her dad was lying on the couch, pale and looking worn through. The gunshot to his arm had broken the bone, but the traveling doctor Johnny knew had finally come six hours ago and had said he would be fine. The man had checked everyone over, even the ones who insisted they were fine. He'd found the cut from the razor blade on Dinah's hand, which she kept forgetting about until she tried to reach for anything or pick anything up or even touch someone. He'd treated it and wrapped it in gauze before he left.

Now they were alone in the living room, sleeping in shifts through the morning and afternoon once they could no longer stay awake.

Kara had curled up on the floor next to her, and Dinah couldn't stop herself from running her fingers through her hair.

To have one love was a lifelong gift. How could she claim two? But Kara was as much her family as Johnny was. She could not turn her back on her town or her neighbors and she couldn't, wouldn't turn away from this, either.

She leaned on Johnny's shoulder where he sat slouched against the wall, sleeping.

"I'll earn your trust back," someone whispered.

Her father, watching her from the couch.

"I appreciate that you want to." Dinah found Johnny's hand with hers. "But there's no way to make up for what you did. You can't earn back anything."

He met her eyes, a little of that stubbornness of hers looking back at her. But he didn't say a word.

Cole was a child, and he thought he'd been alone. The adults who had fled the fight, the neighbors and relatives whose lives they'd worked to avoid taking—she hadn't wanted to cost their lives, but she had not forgiven them yet and there might be life-long breaches in their families. That would be up to them to settle.

Even though he was asleep, Dinah gripped Johnny's hand. "Whatever I decide to give you is a gift." She'd have time to decide what that would be. She could give him that.

He nodded.

Dinah looked away from him. Johnny's thumb stroked her hand. He was awake, and she didn't know for how long. He pulled her down against his chest so she could sleep. She could hear his heart, and she held his wrist where she could feel his pulse. So she wouldn't forget.

People were simply bodies and blood. But her body and her blood were so much more than she had ever thought.

It only took two days of everyone working to tear out the portion of the roof and the wall that had been damaged by the fire. The Franklins and Kwamé and Lissa and everyone else fitted new shingles, boarded up the windows with plywood and insulation for the time being until they could afford to replace the glass, hauled out the burned furniture from the bedroom and scrubbed the smoke and char out of the house. David and Adam even came to help for the day, and Dinah had Cole help her rake the ash and charred shingles out of the yard.

He alternated between raking the ground way too hard and looking like he was going to cry, but she let him just work it out as she talked. "Akosua and Lissa are going to take over the goat farm. You never met the McCaffreys, but they fled in the middle of the night. Just left forty goats and three dairy cows there. Akosua and Lissa apparently always wanted a little farm, so they're going to move in there. Alice might stay with them for a while. It's closer to her siblings."

Cole nodded.

"Johnny says you're good with animals."

He shrugged.

"They'll probably need a hired hand. Especially because they're going to keep distilling. So there will be a lot of work."

Cole's motion with the rake slowed a little. "I wouldn't mind that."

"I can ask them, if you want."

"Thank you," he whispered.

He knew what he'd done couldn't be taken away. But it was what it was, and he saw that, and he was trying.

She squeezed his shoulder.

He nodded, brown hair flopping in his face.

Hooves sounded on the road. Kara, with Maisy pulling the cart. It was loaded down with a huge lunch Mr. and Mrs. Hernández had made for everyone—red beans and rice, Mrs. Hernández's potato salad with chicken sausage, and the sancocho Mr. Hernández made, even though every time he served it, he insisted it wasn't as good as it should be, since he couldn't find auyama, yuca, or plantains in the Ozarks.

Kara handed one of the huge pots of sancocho to Dinah. "Oh, I forgot. Set that down. I have something else for you first."

Dinah handed the bowl off to Lissa, who was helping unload. Every time she'd seen Kara in the last two days, she kept expecting Kara to have changed her mind. To have somehow forgotten the way she'd kissed Dinah. But every time, Kara's eyes had found hers first, and every time Kara smiled at her just like she was doing now, and it always turned Dinah into a helpless, ridiculous fool.

Kara pulled a guitar in a hard case out of the cart. "This was my dad's. He doesn't use it anymore, and I think you should have it."

Dinah ran her hand slowly over the case. "But—I can't take this."

"Papi said it was okay. You need to have a guitar."

Dinah tried to say something, but her throat was too tight. So she just nodded. After a second of hesitation, she leaned in just far enough to kiss Kara's cheek.

Kara blushed so hard her brown skin flushed. "Just promise me something? Play for me sometime. Doesn't have to be soon. Just sometime."

She could do that. She would love to do that.

Questions had plagued her for two days, what this meant with Kara and with Johnny, and what it would mean for all of them— what they would be to each other. But she had no answers yet, and there had been no space for her to bring it up.

Mr. and Mrs. Hernández came a bit later with the kids, and Kwamé had set up a big sawhorse table in the yard for everyone.

Kwamé and Akosua had gotten over two hundred signatures on the petition to recall Sheriff Anders, but it turned out no one needed to demand the man's badge and gun, because he and his deputies were gone. The sheriff's office was empty, completely cleaned out, and everything down to the coffee pot had gone with him. Mitch Harding was gone, too. Moved to the city, supposedly, to launch a new branch of his company.

The election wasn't far off, and Kwamé, Jay, and someone from town she'd never heard of were all running for sheriff.

Other places had to have their own Gabriel Gates and Sheriff Anders. Maybe Ward County would hear about what had happened here, and they'd recall their sheriff. So many people had come back here to help. Maybe the places they were from would eventually need the help of the community they were building here.

On the third day, everyone quit working on the house for the funeral. They had a joint service outside for Burns Holloway, Rich and Sarah DeVos, Kobe Adu, and Ellen and Warren Caldwell. It was cold and windy standing out in the big field, but Dinah was glad of it.

Over a hundred people came, all grouped loosely together in the pasture grass. They started with Kobe, and his sister spoke about his love for playing piano and his keen sense of justice and the time he'd tied Yaw and Kwamé's feet together while they were asleep and then couldn't get the knots undone and they had to stay like that until their parents came home. Then Alice's sister and Johnny spoke for Burns.

During the end of the service, when her dad and Kara and Mrs. Hernández got up to talk about Warren and her mom, Dinah slipped toward the back of the crowd. She wasn't ready to hear that, and this service wasn't for her anyway, really.

The walk home took her over an hour, but her feet moving along with her mind helped, laying a piece of herself into the gravel every time her foot met the ground.

The road took her past Kara's house with the big orchard and Maisy watching her from underneath a pear tree, ears pricked. Down the hill and to the ravine with the little bridge across it. To the woods behind her house with the fallen tree that Warren had turned into his log.

The mossy log looked like nothing had happened. Dinah sank down beside it and touched the bark. This dead tree lying here in the woods, the point of life for all this moss and the little ants scurrying along the grooves and her brother's imagination. She reached into the end and pulled out a handful of small stones he'd liked enough to save here. She tipped them back and forth in her hand, trying to see what he'd seen in them. Rough edges smoothed over, bits of blue and black and pink and quartz. She set the stones back in the log and pulled out the little bird he'd carved out of a piece of wood. Feathers marked with careful, life-like lines. She folded it into her hand and pressed her forehead to the mossy log like it was some kind of altar.

"I'm gonna get more chickens," she said. "You'll like that. The Hernándezes are gonna help us till up a potato patch like Mom wanted. It's a good idea. And the well is really deep now. We tried to run it dry to see how much it held by filling the McCaffreys' cattle tank and everyone's house tanks. The water pressure slowed a bit but that was it. The rain is helping Kara's orchard, too."

Her thumb stroked over the bird's wing. "When we went to the lumberyard to fix the roof, I found a piece of birch you'd like. Has this really pretty knot with swirling colors in it. I'm gonna save it for you."

Warren would want to know these things. He loved to know things, and he loved to create things. He was a lot like Johnny that way. Warren would have loved Johnny, and they would have built a lot of things together.

Dinah stayed there on her knees, forehead pressed to the log, just breathing, long past when her bruised knees stiffened.

She'd have to build things for him now, but she could do that. He built things because he loved most people and most things, and he'd loved what his hands and his mind and his body could do.

His whole life, he'd been showing her how to love, and that would be her memorial to him. She'd love stronger, she would love the way he had.

Her knees hurt when she stood up. She walked toward the house, but she stopped at the graves first. At the stone with her and Warren's names and ages. "I love you," she whispered. She'd so often seen her mother as over-worrying, as pretending, as too pragmatic for her own good. But her mother had never given up, had never stayed down, had always kept going. One day, she hoped she'd have that kind of strength.

Her mother had woven roots here to protect her family, and it had kept their home together. It would still.

"Dinah?" someone called.

Kara stood on the porch. The lights in the house were on, glowing warm in the twilight.

Dinah walked toward the house as Johnny came outside, too. "We thought we'd wait here for you. Are you okay?" he asked.

She was not okay, not really. But she was home.

People lived heartbroken. That was what she was learning. Heartbreak could kill you, but you could also let it into your day and talk with it and sit down to breakfast with it and share the weight of it with someone who loved you.

"I'm okay," she said.

"Do you want some tea?" Johnny asked.

She almost laughed. "Yes."

They walked inside, and Dinah closed the door. "Where's Cole?"

Johnny tipped his head toward her old bedroom. "He got really quiet. Wanted to be by himself. He lay down on one of the beds in there."

Kara twisted a dish towel around her hands. "Mom and Papá went home but said to let them know if we needed anything. I wanted to stay. I hope that's okay."

"That's always okay." She slid off her boots so she didn't track dirt across the floor.

Maybe one day, she'd be able to talk about Warren and her mom with her father. He'd lost them, too. But right now, it felt too much like he'd been part of why she'd lost them. And she needed time to figure out if that was true.

Johnny pulled three mugs from the cupboard while the water heated. When he poured the tea, he handed the third mug to Kara.

Dinah watched it happen and couldn't tear her gaze away from him. From either of them. Johnny set his mug on the table and walked around it to her.

He hugged her to him and whispered into her hair. "I don't know how to handle this. But you loved her long before you met me, and you loved me anyway. So she hasn't taken anything from me. I want you to be happy. If she's part of that, then that is important to me."

This was guilt. This had to be him feeling like he had to give her this or he'd lose her. "But—"

"Trust me to know my own self," he said. "I've spent the last three days thinking about it. It makes no difference to me. What does make a difference is you."

Dinah hugged him hard to her, forehead on his chest.

She'd love a little stronger, she'd told Warren.

"You two barely know each other," Dinah said. She turned to Kara. "What about that?"

Kara shrugged. She met Johnny's eyes over Dinah's head. "We'll be friends?"

Johnny nodded, face a bit flushed. "We'll figure it out. It's . . . There's time. We'll figure out what will work."

"And if there's a problem, we can talk about it." Kara narrowed her eyes at Johnny, but Dinah could see the tease in them. "If she likes you this much, there must be something good about you."

Johnny's eyebrows went up.

"Well," Dinah said. "The tea's getting cold."

She could sit here and drink tea with Johnny and Kara. It was just tea. Just for now. They were young, and they still had the rest of their lives.

Dinah motioned to Kara and the three of them went over to the couch, steaming mugs in hand. Dinah took the middle seat and tucked her feet up under her. Kara sat sideways, her socks touching Dinah's thigh. Johnny was slouched back, his long legs spread out in front of him.

Kara took a breath. "Dinah's told me about your cave. I'd like to see it sometime."

Johnny nodded. "Sure."

Dinah held the hot mug between her palms even though it stung her skin. Johnny was going to keep living in his cave. Take Cole on some trips up there. Keep distilling. He needed to get another batch of moonshine running, but he'd refused to go tonight. He was staying for a day or two, so she wouldn't be alone. She wanted to be at home—she couldn't leave this place empty.

He would go in a few days, and Cole would go with him. They needed time together, without her. Dinah turned toward him on the couch. "Are you *sure* you don't want to go home tonight? I'll be fine."

Johnny set his tea down. "Nah. I figure you'll fall apart if you don't have access to me every second."

Kara laughed so hard she snorted.

Dinah glared at them both. And then she nudged him with her toe. "Play something for me."

"Really?" he asked. "Right now?"

"Please." This first night home, here with these people who were her family now, there was too much to be said and too much to think about.

Johnny reached down beside the couch and lifted his dulcimer onto his lap. Dinah moved down to the floor, between his knees, to give him more room to play on the small couch. His hands slid over the strings with the noter and the pick, and music rippled through the room.

Cole's door creaked open. Rubbing his eyes, he came out and sat in her mother's rocker, listening. Maybe he would need to go live with his dads in a few months. Maybe Johnny would, too. Or maybe Adam and David would come back.

Dinah leaned her head back against Johnny's knee. "What are you playing?" The song wasn't one she'd heard before. But it was beautiful, both bright and haunting.

"Just something I'm working on. Doesn't have a name yet," he said.

She tipped her head up to see his face, his thick eyebrows hiding light eyes. "You wrote this?"

He ducked his head. "It still needs work."

"I like it." She leaned back against his legs and closed her eyes to listen.

Something shifted on the couch and Kara sat down beside her on the floor. On her mother's rug, singed by sparks and embers from the fire. Kara leaned her head on Dinah's shoulder.

Dinah took Kara's hand in hers. "I don't want to keep you here."

Kara brushed her socked foot against Dinah's ankle. "You won't. If I'm here, it's because I want to be. Maybe I'll leave someday. But this is home, you know? The school still needs me.

My family needs me. This is where I matter right now." She ran her thumb over the back of Dinah's hand. "But I might save up and one day take some university classes, online."

They all listened while Johnny played his song.

There was room for each of them to have their lives, and maybe that was how all of this would work. They would each bring all of who they were, and they would be there for each other, and they would be the version of themselves only they could be. And it would be hard but it would be good, and together they would be more than they were apart.

Kara reached over and lifted her dad's guitar out of its case. She handed it to Dinah. "You should play, too. If you want."

Dinah lifted the guitar into her lap. Touched the fretboard and ran her hand along the body.

Johnny kept playing, but she could feel him watching her.

Dinah played a few notes to hear the sound. Warm and bassy, not muddy. She adjusted the tuning pegs a little and then played alongside Johnny. Kara had her eyes closed, listening. So did Cole.

It felt like something she'd forgotten, to play music like this. To have strings under her fingers.

She'd once thought she was sound but not meaning—like the notes she was playing now, but with no song to hold them together. Maybe she'd been wrong then, or maybe she was different now because here, like this, she was whole.

## ACKNOWLEDGMENTS

I'd be nowhere without the support and encouragement and brilliance of a few wonderful people. Kat Ellis, Nikki Urang, Alex Yuschik, Bethany Robison, Kiersi Burkhart, Blair Thornburgh, Tonya Kuper, Tosca Lee, Lydia Kang, Pintip Dunn, Darcy Woods, and Jen Malone have been my support for years, and it's made all the difference. Thank you eternally, to each of you, for your notes on this book especially, and for your belief, encouragement, care packages, writing sprints, writing retreats, and the many ways you have each made this possible. I could not have done this without you, and I love you all so much.

My publishing team at Page Street Publishing has been so wonderful to work with. Thank you, always, to Ashley Hearn, who saw what I wanted to do with this book and helped me make that real. Thank you to Tamara Grasty, whose insightful edits, guidance, and unending support made all the difference. To Mary Beth Garhart, my copy editor Heather Taylor, Hayley Gundlach,

Lauren Knowles, Lizzy Mason, Molly Young, Ashley Tenn, and the entire Page Street team, and to Rosie Stewart for the brilliant cover design. Thank you for such an incredible job with this book and for believing in the story. Thank you as well to the sensitivity readers who worked on this book and contributed their time, effort, and knowledge. I'm so grateful.

To my agent, Bridget Smith—thank you for seeing something in this book and in me. I am so lucky to have you on my team and I'm so thankful for your insight, skill, dedication, and all the ways you help me reach my goals. Thank you to the entire JABberwocky team for their wonderful support.

I wanted to write a book about family, the kind we're born with and the kind we create. My own siblings, my mother, Londa and Paul Revis, Sam Revis, Loren and Kitty Wagner, Lynn Edwards, Harley Hightower, Jesse Brauning—you are each woven into this book and into my life in irreplaceable ways. Thank you for being my reasons.

Jesse, thank you for your boundless, true-to-the-end support and love. You've read this book so many times I've lost count. Matt, thank you for helping me build the agriculture and future of this world—your knowledge, investment, and integrity amaze me. Lydia and Lynn—thank you for being my constant support and for always being there when I need you for ass-kickings, real talk, hard things, celebrating good things, and every other shade of friendship. Harley, you've made this book so much better with your knowledge of and passion for motorcycles, and how much you love what you love is just one reason I'm so glad you're in my life. Mom, I know you'll probably not read this book, but you will give it to everyone you know, painstakingly keep track of all my career updates, and encourage me to write what I love, no matter what. I love you all endlessly.

# ABOUT THE AUTHOR

Kate Brauning is an author of young adult thrillers with a twist of the unusual, including *How We Fall*, *The Ballad of Dinah Caldwell*, and the short story "Godzilla Girls." As a child, she spent a lot of time in her local library, wandering the shelves and discovering all kinds of stories about all kinds of people. At fifteen, she decided she wanted someone to find her own books by searching through the shelves of a library, and she's been writing ever since.

Kate lives in Austin, Texas, with her family and her Siberian husky, Willow. She loves traveling, snorkeling, equality, pie, and talking about books. Visit her at www.katebrauning.com or on Twitter at @KateBrauning.